DAN-63 DANTES SUBJECT STANDARDIZED TESTS (DSST)

*This is your
PASSBOOK for...*

War and Peace in the Nuclear Age

*Test Preparation Study Guide
Questions & Answers*

COPYRIGHT NOTICE

This book is SOLELY intended for, is sold ONLY to, and its use is RESTRICTED to individual, bona fide applicants or candidates who qualify by virtue of having seriously filed applications for appropriate license, certificate, professional and/or promotional advancement, higher school matriculation, scholarship, or other legitimate requirements of education and/or governmental authorities.

This book is NOT intended for use, class instruction, tutoring, training, duplication, copying, reprinting, excerption, or adaptation, etc., by:

1) Other publishers
2) Proprietors and/or Instructors of "Coaching" and/or Preparatory Courses
3) Personnel and/or Training Divisions of commercial, industrial, and governmental organizations
4) Schools, colleges, or universities and/or their departments and staffs, including teachers and other personnel
5) Testing Agencies or Bureaus
6) Study groups which seek by the purchase of a single volume to copy and/or duplicate and/or adapt this material for use by the group as a whole without having purchased individual volumes for each of the members of the group
7) Et al.

Such persons would be in violation of appropriate Federal and State statutes.

PROVISION OF LICENSING AGREEMENTS – Recognized educational, commercial, industrial, and governmental institutions and organizations, and others legitimately engaged in educational pursuits, including training, testing, and measurement activities, may address request for a licensing agreement to the copyright owners, who will determine whether, and under what conditions, including fees and charges, the materials in this book may be used them. In other words, a licensing facility exists for the legitimate use of the material in this book on other than an individual basis. However, it is asseverated and affirmed here that the material in this book CANNOT be used without the receipt of the express permission of such a licensing agreement from the Publishers. Inquiries re licensing should be addressed to the company, attention rights and permissions department.

All rights reserved, including the right of reproduction in whole or in part, in any form or by any means, electronic or mechanical, including photocopying, recording, or by any information storage and retrieval system, without permission in writing from the Publisher.

Copyright © 2024 by
National Learning Corporation

212 Michael Drive, Syosset, NY 11791
(516) 921-8888 • www.passbooks.com
E-mail: info@passbooks.com

PUBLISHED IN THE UNITED STATES OF AMERICA

PASSBOOK® SERIES

THE *PASSBOOK® SERIES* has been created to prepare applicants and candidates for the ultimate academic battlefield – the examination room.

At some time in our lives, each and every one of us may be required to take an examination – for validation, matriculation, admission, qualification, registration, certification, or licensure.

Based on the assumption that every applicant or candidate has met the basic formal educational standards, has taken the required number of courses, and read the necessary texts, the *PASSBOOK® SERIES* furnishes the one special preparation which may assure passing with confidence, instead of failing with insecurity. Examination questions – together with answers – are furnished as the basic vehicle for study so that the mysteries of the examination and its compounding difficulties may be eliminated or diminished by a sure method.

This book is meant to help you pass your examination provided that you qualify and are serious in your objective.

The entire field is reviewed through the huge store of content information which is succinctly presented through a provocative and challenging approach – the question-and-answer method.

A climate of success is established by furnishing the correct answers at the end of each test.

You soon learn to recognize types of questions, forms of questions, and patterns of questioning. You may even begin to anticipate expected outcomes.

You perceive that many questions are repeated or adapted so that you can gain acute insights, which may enable you to score many sure points.

You learn how to confront new questions, or types of questions, and to attack them confidently and work out the correct answers.

You note objectives and emphases, and recognize pitfalls and dangers, so that you may make positive educational adjustments.

Moreover, you are kept fully informed in relation to new concepts, methods, practices, and directions in the field.

You discover that you are actually taking the examination all the time: you are preparing for the examination by "taking" an examination, not by reading extraneous and/or supererogatory textbooks.

In short, this PASSBOOK®, used directedly, should be an important factor in helping you to pass your test.

NONTRADITIONAL EDUCATION

Students returning to school as adults bring more varied experience to their studies than do the teenagers who begin college shortly after graduating from high school. As a result, there are numerous programs for students with nontraditional learning curves. Hundreds of colleges and universities grant degrees to people who cannot attend classes at a regular campus or have already learned what the college is supposed to teach.

You can earn nontraditional education credits in many ways:
- Passing standardized exams
- Demonstrating knowledge gained through experience
- Completing campus-based coursework, and
- Taking courses off campus

Some methods of assessing learning for credit are objective, such as standardized tests. Others are more subjective, such as a review of life experiences.

With some help from four hypothetical characters – Alice, Vin, Lynette, and Jorge – this article describes nontraditional ways of earning educational credit. It begins by describing programs in which you can earn a high school diploma without spending 4 years in a classroom. The college picture is more complicated, so it is presented in two parts: one on gaining credit for what you know through course work or experience, and a second on college degree programs. The final section lists resources for locating more information.

Earning High School Credit

People who were prevented from finishing high school as teenagers have several options if they want to do so as adults. Some major cities have back-to-school programs that allow adults to attend high school classes with current students. But the more practical alternatives for most adults are to take the General Educational Development (GED) tests or to earn a high school diploma by demonstrating their skills or taking correspondence classes.

Of course, these options do not match the experience of staying in high school and graduating with one's friends. But they are viable alternatives for adult learners committed to meeting and, often, continuing their educational goals.

GED Program

Alice quit high school her sophomore year and took a job to help support herself, her younger brother, and their newly widowed mother. Now an adult, she wants to earn her high school diploma – and then go on to college. Because her job as head cook and her family responsibilities keep her busy during the day, she plans to get a high school equivalency diploma. She will study for, and take, the GED tests. Every year, about half a million adults earn their high school credentials this way. A GED diploma is accepted in lieu of a high school one by more than 90 percent of employers, colleges, and universities, so it is a good choice for someone like Alice.

The GED testing program is sponsored by the American Council on Education and State and local education departments. It consists of examinations in five subject areas: Writing, science, mathematics, social studies, and literature and the arts. The tests also measure skills such as analytical ability, problem solving, reading comprehension, and ability to understand and apply information. Most of the questions are multiple choice; the writing test includes an essay section on a topic of general interest.

Eligibility rules for taking the exams vary, but some states require that you must be at least 18. Tests are given in English, Spanish, and French. In addition to standard print, versions in large print, Braille, and audiocassette are also available. Total time allotted for the tests is 7 1/2 hours.

The GED tests are not easy. About one-fourth of those who complete the exams every year do not pass. Passing scores are established by administering the tests to a sample of graduating high school seniors. The minimum standard score is set so that about one-third of graduating seniors would not pass the tests if they took them.

Because of the difficulty of the tests, people need to prepare themselves to take them. Often, they start by taking the Official GED Practice Tests, usually available through a local adult education center. Centers are listed in your phone book's blue pages under "Adult Education," "Continuing Education," or "GED." Adult education centers also have information about GED preparation classes and self-study materials. Classes are generally arranged to accommodate adults' work schedules. National Learning Corporation publishes several study guides that aim to thoroughly prepare test-takers for the GED.

School districts, colleges, adult education centers, and community organizations have information about GED testing schedules and practice tests. For more information, contact them, your nearest GED testing center, or:

GED Testing Service
One Dupont Circle, NW, Suite 250
Washington, DC 20036-1163
1(800) 62-MY GED (626-9433)
(202) 939-9490

Skills Demonstration

Adults who have acquired high school level skills through experience might be eligible for the National External Diploma Program. This alternative to the GED does not involve any direct instruction. Instead, adults seeking a high school diploma must demonstrate mastery of 65 competencies in 8 general areas: Communication; computation; occupational preparedness; and self, social, consumer, scientific, and technological awareness.

Mastery is shown through the completion of the tasks. For example, a participant could prove competency in computation by measuring a room for carpeting, figuring out the amount of carpet needed, and computing the cost.

Before being accepted for the program, adults undergo an evaluation. Tests taken at one of the program's offices measure reading, writing, and mathematics abilities. A take-home segment includes a self-assessment of current skills, an individual skill evaluation, and an occupational interest and aptitude test.

Adults accepted for the program have weekly meetings with an assessor. At the meeting, the assessor reviews the participant's work from the previous week. If the task has not been completed properly, the assessor explains the mistake. Participants continue to correct their errors until they master each competency. A high school diploma is awarded upon proven mastery of all 65 competencies.

Fourteen States and the District of Columbia now offer the External Diploma Program. For more information, contact:

External Diploma Program
One Dupont Circle, NW, Suite 250
Washington, DC 20036-1193
(202) 939-9475

Correspondence and Distance Study

Vin dropped out of high school during his junior year because his family's frequent moves made it difficult for him to continue his studies. He promised himself at the time he dropped out that he would someday finish the courses needed for his diploma. For people like Vin, who prefer to earn a traditional diploma in a nontraditional way, there are about a dozen accredited courses of study for earning a high school diploma by correspondence, or distance study. The programs are either privately run, affiliated with a university, or administered by a State education department.

Distance study diploma programs have no residency requirements, allowing students to continue their studies from almost any location. Depending on the course of study, students need not be enrolled full time and usually have more flexible schedules for finishing their work. Selection of courses ranges from vo-tech to college prep, and some programs place different emphasis on the types of diplomas offered. University affiliated schools, for example, allow qualified students to take college courses along with their high school ones. Students can then apply the college credits toward a degree at that university or transfer them to another institution.

Taking courses by distance study is often more challenging and time consuming than attending classes, especially for adults who have other obligations. Success depends on each student's motivation. Students usually do reading assignments on their own. Written exercises, which they complete and send to an instructor for grading, supplement their reading material.

A list of some accredited high schools that offer diplomas by distance study is available free from the Distance Education and Training Council, formerly known as the National Home Study Council. Request the "DETC Directory of Accredited Institutions" from:

The Distance Education and Training Council
1601 18th Street, NW.
Washington, DC 20009-2529
(202) 234-5100

Some publications profiling nontraditional college programs include addresses and descriptions of several high school correspondence ones. See the Resources section at the end of this article for more information.

Getting College Credit For What You Know

Adults can receive college credit for prior coursework, by passing examinations, and documenting experiential learning. With help from a college advisor, nontraditional students should assess their skills, establish their educational goals, and determine the number of college credits they might be eligible for.

Even before you meet with a college advisor, you should collect all your school and training records. Then, make a list of all knowledge and abilities acquired through experience, no matter how irrelevant they seem to your chosen field. Next, determine your educational goals: What specific field do you wish to study? What kind of a degree do you want? Finally, determine how your past work fits into the field of study. Later on, you will evaluate educational programs to find one that's right for you.

People who have complex educational or experiential learning histories might want to have their learning evaluated by the Regents Credit Bank. The Credit Bank, operated by Regents College of the University of the State of New York, allows people to consolidate credits earned through college, experience, or other methods. Special assessments are available for Regents College enrollees whose knowledge in a specific field cannot be adequately evaluated by standardized exams. For more information, contact the Regents Credit Bank at:

Regents College
7 Columbia Circle
Albany, NY 12203-5159
(518) 464-8500

Credit For Prior College Coursework

When Lynette was in college during the 1970s, she attended several different schools and took a variety of courses. She did well in some classes and poorly in others. Now that she is a successful business owner and has more focus, Lynette thinks she should forget about her previous coursework and start from scratch. Instead, she should start from where she is.

Lynette should have all her transcripts sent to the colleges or universities of her choice and let an admissions officer determine which classes are applicable toward a degree. A few credits here and there may not seem like much, but they add up. Even if the subjects do not seem relevant to any major, they might be counted as elective credits toward a degree. And comparing the cost of transcripts with the cost of college courses, it makes sense to spend a few dollars per transcript for a chance to save hundreds, and perhaps thousands, of dollars in books and tuition.

Rules for transferring credits apply to all prior coursework at accredited colleges and universities, whether done on campus or off. Courses completed off campus, often called extended learning, include those available to students through independent study and correspondence. Many schools have extended learning programs; Brigham Young University, for example, offers more than 300 courses through its Department of Independent Study. One type of extended learning is distance learning, a form of correspondence study by technological means such as television, video and audio, CD-ROM, electronic mail, and computer tutorials. See the Resources section at the end of this article for more information about publications available from the National University Continuing Education Association.

Any previously earned college credits should be considered for transfer, no matter what the subject or the grade received. Many schools do not accept the transfer of courses graded below a C or ones taken more than a designated number of years ago. Some colleges and universities also have limits on the number of credits that can be transferred and applied toward a degree. But not all do. For example, Thomas Edison State College, New Jersey's State college for adults, accepts the transfer of all 120 hours of credit required for a baccalaureate degree – provided all the credits are transferred from regionally accredited schools, no more than 80 are at the junior college level, and the student's grades overall and in the field of study average out to C.

To assign credit for prior coursework, most schools require original transcripts. This means you must complete a form or send a written, signed request to have your transcripts released directly to a college or university. Once you have chosen the schools you want to apply to, contact the schools you attended before. Find out how much each transcript costs, and ask them to send your transcripts to the ones you are applying to. Write a letter that includes your name (and names used during attendance, if different) and dates of attendance, along with the names and addresses of the schools to which your transcripts should be sent. Include payment and mail to the registrar at the schools you have attended. The registrar's office will process your request and send an official transcript of your coursework to the colleges or universities you have designated.

Credit For Noncollege Courses

Colleges and universities are not the only ones that offer classes. Volunteer organizations and employers often provide formal training worth college credit. The American Council on Education has two programs that assess thousands of specific courses and make recommendations on the amount of college credit they are worth. Colleges and universities accept the recommendations or use them as guidelines.

One program evaluates educational courses sponsored by government agencies, business and industry, labor unions, and professional and voluntary organizations. It is the Program on Noncollegiate Sponsored Instruction (PONSI). Some of the training seminars Alice has participated in covered topics such as food preparation, kitchen safety, and nutrition. Although she has not yet earned her GED, Alice can earn college credit because of her completion of these formal job-training seminars. The number of credits each seminar is worth does not hinge on Alice's current eligibility for college enrollment.

The other program evaluates courses offered by the Army, Navy, Air Force, Marines, Coast Guard, and Department of Defense. It is the Military Evaluations Program. Jorge has never attended college, but the engineering technology classes he completed as part of his military training are worth college credit. And as an Army veteran, Jorge is eligible for a service that takes the evaluations one step further. The Army/American Council on Education Registry Transcript System (AARTS) will provide Jorge with an individualized transcript of American Council on Education credit recommendations for all courses he completed, the military occupational specialties (MOS's) he held, and examinations he passed while in the Army. All Army and National Guard enlisted personnel and veterans who enlisted after October 1981 are eligible for the transcript. Similar services are being considered by the Navy and Marine Corps.

To obtain a free transcript, see your Army Education Center for a 5454R transcript request form. Include your name, Social Security number, basic active service date, and complete address where you want the transcript sent. Mail your request to:
AARTS Operations Center
415 McPherson Ave.
Fort Leavenworth, KS 66027-1373

Recommendations for PONSI are published in *The National Guide to Educational Credit for Training Programs;* military program recommendations are in *The Guide to the Evaluation of Educational Experiences in the Armed Forces.* See the Resources section at the end of this article for more information about these publications.

Former military personnel who took a foreign language course through the Defense Language Institute may request course transcripts by sending their name, Social Security number, course title, duration of the course, and graduation date to:

Commandant, Defense Language Institute
Attn: ATFL-DAA-AR
Transcripts
Presidio of Monterey
Monterey, CA 93944-5006

Not all of Jorge's and Alice's courses have been assessed by the American Council on Education. Training courses that have no Council credit recommendation should still be assessed by an advisor at the schools they want to attend. Course descriptions, class notes, test scores, and other documentation may be helpful for comparing training courses to their college equivalents. An oral examination or other demonstration of competency might also be required.

There is no guarantee you will receive all the credits you are seeking – but you certainly won't if you make no attempt.

Credit By Examination

Standardized tests are the best-known method of receiving college credit without taking courses. These exams are often taken by high school students seeking advanced placement for college, but they are also available to adult learners. Testing programs and colleges and universities offer exams in a number of subjects. Two U.S. Government institutes have foreign language exams for employees that also may be worth college credit.

It is important to understand that receiving a passing score on these exams does not mean you get college credit automatically. Each school determines which test results it will accept, minimum scores required, how scores are converted for credit, and the amount of credit, if any, to be assigned. Most colleges and universities accept the American Council on Education credit recommendations, published every other year in the 250-page *Guide to Educational Credit by Examination*. For more information, contact:

The American Council on Education
Credit by Examination Program
One Dupont Circle, Suite 250
Washington, DC 20036-1193
(202) 939-9434

Testing programs:

You might know some of the five national testing programs by their acronyms or initials: CLEP, ACT PEP: RCE, DANTES, AP, and NOCTI. (The meanings of these initialisms are explained below.) There is some overlap among programs; for example, four of them have introductory accounting exams. Since you will not be awarded credit more than once for a specific subject, you should carefully evaluate each program for the subject exams you wish to take. And before taking an exam, make sure you will be awarded credit by the college or university you plan to attend.

CLEP (College-Level Examination Program), administered by the College Board, is the most widely accepted of the national testing programs; more than 2,800 accredited schools award credit for passing exam scores. Each test covers material taught in basic undergraduate courses. There are five general exams – English composition, humanities, college mathematics, natural sciences, and social sciences and history – and many subject exams. Most exams are entirely multiple-choice, but English composition exams may include an essay section. For more information, contact:

    CLEP
    P.O. Box 6600
    Princeton, NJ 08541-6600
    (609) 771-7865

ACT PEP: RCE (American College Testing Proficiency Exam Program: Regents College Examinations) tests are given in 38 subjects within arts and sciences, business, education, and nursing. Each exam is recommended for either lower- or upper-level credit. Exams contain either objective or extended response questions, and are graded according to a standard score, letter grade, or pass/fail. Fees vary, depending on the subject and type of exam. For more information or to request free study guides, contact:

    ACT PEP: Regents College Examinations
    P.O. Box 4014
    Iowa City, IA 52243
    (319) 337-1387
    (New York State residents must contact Regents College directly.)

DANTES (Defense Activity for Nontraditional Education Support) standardized tests are developed by the Educational Testing Service for the Department of Defense. Originally administered only to military personnel, the exams have been available to the public since 1983. About 50 subject tests cover business, mathematics, social science, physical science, humanities, foreign languages, and applied technology. Most of the tests consist entirely of multiple-choice questions. Schools determine their own administering fees and testing schedules. For more information or to request free study sheets, contact:

    DANTES Program Office
    Mail Stop 31-X
    Educational Testing Service
    Princeton, NJ 08541
    1(800) 257-9484

The AP (Advanced Placement) Program is a cooperative effort between secondary schools and colleges and universities. AP exams are developed each year by committees of college and high school faculty appointed by the College Board and assisted by consultants from the Educational Testing Service. Subjects include arts and languages, natural sciences, computer science, social sciences, history, and mathematics. Most tests are 2 or 3 hours long and include both multiple-choice and essay questions. AP courses are available to help students prepare for exams, which are offered in the spring. For more information about the Advanced Placement Program, contact:

    Advanced Placement Services
    P.O. Box 6671
    Princeton, NJ 08541-6671
    (609) 771-7300

NOCTI (National Occupational Competency Testing Institute) assessments are designed for people like Alice, who have vocational-technical skills that cannot be evaluated by other tests. NOCTI assesses competency at two levels: Student/job ready and teacher/experienced worker. Standardized evaluations are available for occupations such as auto-body repair, electronics, mechanical drafting, quantity food preparation, and upholstering. The tests consist of multiple-choice questions and a performance component. Other services include workshops, customized assessments, and pre-testing. For more information, contact:

NOCTI
500 N. Bronson Ave.
Ferris State University
Big Rapids, MI 49307
(616) 796-4699

Colleges and universities:

Many colleges and universities have credit-by-exam programs, through which students earn credit by passing a comprehensive exam for a course offered by the institution. Among the most widely recognized are the programs at Ohio University, the University of North Carolina, Thomas Edison State College, and New York University.

Ohio University offers about 150 examinations for credit. In addition, you may sometimes arrange to take special examinations in non-laboratory courses offered at Ohio University. To take a test for credit, you must enroll in the course. If you plan to transfer the credit earned, you also need written permission from an official at your school. Books and study materials are available, for a cost, through the university. Exams must be taken within 6 months of the enrollment date; most last 3 hours. You may arrange to take the exam off campus if you do not live near the university.

Ohio University is on the quarter-hour system; most courses are worth 4 quarter hours, the equivalent of 3 semester hours. For more information, contact:

Independent Study
Tupper Hall 302
Ohio University
Athens, OH 45701-2979
1(800) 444-2910
(614) 593-2910

The University of North Carolina offers a credit-by-examination option for 140 independent study (correspondence) courses in foreign languages, humanities, social sciences, mathematics, business administration, education, electrical and computer engineering, health administration, and natural sciences. To take an exam, you must request and receive approval from both the course instructor and the independent studies department. Exams must be taken within six months of enrollment, and you may register for no more than two at a time. If you are not near the University's Chapel Hill campus, you may take your exam under supervision at an accredited college, university, community college, or technical institute. For more information, contact:

Independent Studies
CB #1020, The Friday Center
UNC-Chapel Hill
Chapel Hill, NC 27599-1020
1(800) 862-5669 / (919) 962-1134

The Thomas Edison College Examination Program offers more than 50 exams in liberal arts, business, and professional areas. Thomas Edison State College administers tests twice a month in Trenton, New Jersey; however, students may arrange to take their tests with a proctor at any accredited American college or university or U.S. military base. Most of the tests are multiple choice; some also include short answer or essay questions. Time limits range from 90 minutes to 4 hours, depending on the exam. For more information, contact:

Thomas Edison State College
TECEP, Office of Testing and Assessment
101 W. State Street
Trenton, NJ 08608-1176
(609) 633-2844

New York University's Foreign Language Program offers proficiency exams in more than 40 languages, from Albanian to Yiddish. Two exams are available in each language: The 12-point test is equivalent to 4 undergraduate semesters, and the 16-point exam may lead to upper level credit. The tests are given at the university's Foreign Language Department throughout the year.

Proof of foreign language proficiency does not guarantee college credit. Some colleges and universities accept transcripts only for languages commonly taught, such as French and Spanish. Nontraditional programs are more likely than traditional ones to grant credit for proficiency in other languages.

For an informational brochure and registration form for NYU's foreign language proficiency exams, contact:

New York University
Foreign Language Department
48 Cooper Square, Room 107
New York, NY 10003
(212) 998-7030

Government institutes:
The Defense Language Institute and Foreign Service Institute administer foreign language proficiency exams for personnel stationed abroad. Usually, the tests are given at the end of intensive language courses or upon completion of service overseas. But some people – like Jorge, who knows Spanish – speak another language fluently and may be allowed to take a proficiency exam in that language before completing their tour of duty. Contact one of the offices listed below to obtain transcripts of those scores. Proof of proficiency does not guarantee college credit, however, as discussed above.

To request score reports from the Defense Language Institute for Defense Language Proficiency Tests, send your name, Social Security number, language for which you were tested, and, most importantly, when and where you took the exam to:

Commandant, Defense Language Institute
Attn: ATFL-ES-T
DLPT Score Report Request
Presidio of Monterey
Monterey, CA 93944-5006

To request transcripts of scores for Foreign Service Institute exams, send your name, Social Security number, language for which you were tested, and dates or year of exams to:

Foreign Service Institute
Arlington Hall
4020 Arlington Boulevard
Rosslyn, VA 22204-1500
Attn: Testing Office (Send your request to the attention of the testing office of the foreign language in which you were tested)

Credit For Experience

Experiential learning credit may be given for knowledge gained through job responsibilities, personal hobbies, volunteer opportunities, homemaking, and other experiences. Colleges and universities base credit awards on the knowledge you have attained, not for the experience alone. In addition, the knowledge must be college level; not just any learning will do. Throwing horseshoes as a hobby is not likely to be worth college credit. But if you've done research on how and where the sport originated, visited blacksmiths, organized tournaments, and written a column for a trade journal – well, that's a horseshoe of a different color.

Adults attempting to get credit for their experience should be forewarned: Having your experience evaluated for college credit is time-consuming, tedious work – not an easy shortcut for people who want quick-fix college credits. And not all experience, no matter how valuable, is the equivalent of college courses.

Requesting college credit for your experiential learning can be tricky. You should get assistance from a credit evaluations officer at the school you plan to attend, but you should also have a general idea of what your knowledge is worth. A common method for converting knowledge into credit is to use a college catalog. Find course titles and descriptions that match what you have learned through experience, and request the number of credits offered for those courses.

Once you know what credit to ask for, you must usually present your case in writing to officials at the college you plan to attend. The most common form of presenting experiential learning for credit is the portfolio. A portfolio is a written record of your knowledge along with a request for equivalent college credit. It includes an identification and description of the knowledge for which you are requesting credit, an explanatory essay of how the knowledge was gained and how it fits into your educational plans, documentation that you have acquired such knowledge, and a request for college credit. Required elements of a portfolio vary by schools but generally follow those guidelines.

In identifying knowledge you have gained, be specific about exactly what you have learned. For example, it is not enough for Lynette to say she runs a business. She must identify the knowledge she has gained from running it, such as personnel management, tax law, marketing strategy, and inventory review. She must also include brief descriptions about her knowledge of each to support her claims of having those skills.

The essay gives you a chance to relay something about who you are. It should address your educational goals, include relevant autobiographical details, and be well organized, neat, and convey confidence. In his essay, Jorge might first state his goal of becoming an engineer. Then he would explain why he joined the Army, where he got hands-on training and experience in developing and servicing electronic equipment.

This, he would say, led to his hobby of creating remote-controlled model cars, of which he has built 20. His conclusion would highlight his accomplishments and tie them to his desire to become an electronic engineer.

Documentation is evidence that you've learned what you claim to have learned. You can show proof of knowledge in a variety of ways, including audio or video recordings, letters from current or former employers describing your specific duties and job performance, blueprints, photographs or artwork, and transcripts of certifying exams for professional licenses and certification – such as Alice's certification from the American Culinary Federation. Although documentation can take many forms, written proof alone is not always enough. If it is impossible to document your knowledge in writing, find out if your experiential learning can be assessed through supplemental oral exams by a faculty expert.

Earning a College Degree

Nontraditional students often have work, family, and financial obligations that prevent them from quitting their jobs to attend school full time. Can they still meet their educational goals? Yes.

More than 150 accredited colleges and universities have nontraditional bachelor's degree programs that require students to spend little or no time on campus; over 300 others have nontraditional campus-based degree programs. Some of those schools, as well as most junior and community colleges, offer associate's degrees nontraditionally. Each school with a nontraditional course of study determines its own rules for awarding credit for prior coursework, exams, or experience, as discussed previously. Most have charges on top of tuition for providing these special services.

Several publications profile nontraditional degree programs; see the Resources section at the end of this article for more information. To determine which school best fits your academic profile and educational goals, first list your criteria. Then, evaluate nontraditional programs based on their accreditation, features, residency requirements, and expenses. Once you have chosen several schools to explore further, write to them for more information. Detailed explanations of school policies should help you decide which ones you want to apply to.

Get beyond the printed word – especially the glowing words each school writes about itself. Check out the schools you are considering with higher education authorities, alumni, employers, family members, and friends. If possible, visit the campus to talk to students and instructors and sit in on a few classes, even if you will be completing most or all of your work off campus. Ask school officials questions about such things as enrollment numbers, graduation rate, faculty qualifications, and confusing details about the application process or academic policies. After you have thoroughly investigated each prospective college or university, you can make an informed decision about which is right for you.

Accreditation

Accreditation is a process colleges and universities submit to voluntarily for getting their credentials. An accredited school has been investigated and visited by teams of observers and has periodic inspections by a private accrediting agency. The initial review can take two years or more.

Regional agencies accredit entire schools, and professional agencies accredit either specialized schools or departments within schools. Although there are no national accrediting standards, not just any accreditation will do. Countless "accreditation associations" have been invented by schools, many of which have no academic programs and sell phony degrees, to accredit themselves. But 6 regional and about 80 professional accrediting associations in the United States are recognized by the U.S. Department of Education or the Commission on Recognition of Postsecondary Accreditation. When checking accreditation, these are the names to look for. For more information about accreditation and accrediting agencies, contact:

> Institutional Participation Oversight Service Accreditation and State Liaison Division
> U.S. Department of Education
> ROB 3, Room 3915
> 600 Independence Ave., SW
> Washington, DC 20202-5244
> (202) 708-7417

Because accreditation is not mandatory, lack of accreditation does not necessarily mean a school or program is bad. Some schools choose not to apply for accreditation, are in the process of applying, or have educational methods too unconventional for an accrediting association's standards. For the nontraditional student, however, earning a degree from a college or university with recognized accreditation is an especially important consideration. Although nontraditional education is becoming more widely accepted, it is not yet mainstream. Employers skeptical of a degree earned in a nontraditional manner are likely to be even less accepting of one from an unaccredited school.

Program Features

Because nontraditional students have diverse educational objectives, nontraditional schools are diverse in what they offer. Some programs are geared toward helping students organize their scattered educational credits to get a degree as quickly as possible. Others cater to those who may have specific credits or experience but need assistance in completing requirements. Whatever your educational profile, you should look for a program that works with you in obtaining your educational goals.

A few nontraditional programs have special admissions policies for adult learners like Alice, who plan to earn their GEDs but want to enroll in college in the meantime. Other features of nontraditional programs include individualized learning agreements, intensive academic counseling, cooperative learning and internship placement, and waiver of some prerequisites or other requirements – as well as college credit for prior coursework, examinations, and experiential learning, all discussed previously.

Lynette, whose primary goal is to finish her degree, wants to earn maximum credits for her business experience. She will look for programs that do not limit the number of credits awarded for equivalency exams and experiential learning. And since well-documented proof of knowledge is essential for earning experiential learning credits, Lynette should make sure the program she chooses provides assistance to students submitting a portfolio.

Jorge, on the other hand, has more credits than he needs in certain areas and is willing to forego some. To become an engineer, he must have a bachelor's degree; but because he is accustomed to hands-on learning, Jorge is interested in getting experience as he gains more technical skills. He will concentrate on finding schools with strong cooperative education, supervised fieldwork, or internship programs.

Residency Requirements

Programs are sometimes deemed nontraditional because of their residency requirements. Many people think of residency for colleges and universities in terms of tuition, with in-state students paying less than out-of-state ones. Residency also may refer to where a student lives, either on or off campus, while attending school.

But in nontraditional education, residency usually refers to how much time students must spend on campus, regardless of whether they attend classes there. In some nontraditional programs, students need not ever step foot on campus. Others require only a very short residency, such as one day or a few weeks. Many schools have standard residency requirements of several semesters but schedule classes for evenings or weekends to accommodate working adults.

Lynette, who previously took courses by independent study, prefers to earn credits by distance study. She will focus on schools that have no residency requirement. Several colleges and universities have nonresident degree completion programs for adults with some college credit. Under the direction of a faculty advisor, students devise a plan for earning their remaining credits. Methods for earning credits include independent study, distance learning, seminars, supervised fieldwork, and group study at arranged sites. Students may have to earn a certain number of credits through the degree-granting institution. But many programs allow students to take courses at accredited schools of their choice for transfer toward their degree.

Alice wants to attend lectures but has an unpredictable schedule. Her best course of action will be to seek out short residency programs that require students to attend seminars once or twice a semester. She can take courses that are televised and videotape them to watch when her schedule permits, with the seminars helping to ensure that she properly completes her coursework. Many colleges and universities with short residency requirements also permit students to earn some credits elsewhere, by whatever means the student chooses.

Some fields of study require classroom instruction. As Jorge will discover, few colleges and universities allow students to earn a bachelor's degree in engineering entirely through independent study. Nontraditional residency programs are designed to accommodate adults' daytime work schedules. Jorge should look for programs offering evening, weekend, summer, and accelerated courses.

Tuition and Other Expenses

The final decisions about which schools Alice, Jorge, and Lynette attend may hinge in large part on a single issue: Cost. And rising tuition is only part of the equation. Beginning with application fees and continuing through graduation fees, college expenses add up.

Traditional and nontraditional students have some expenses in common, such as the cost of books and other materials. Tuition might even be the same for some courses, especially for colleges and universities offering standard ones at unusual times. But for nontraditional programs, students may also pay fees for services such as credit or transcript review, evaluation, advisement, and portfolio assessment.

Students are also responsible for postage and handling or setup expenses for independent study courses, as well as for all examination and transcript fees for transferring credits. Usually, the more nontraditional the program, the more detailed the fees. Some schools charge a yearly enrollment fee rather than tuition for degree completion candidates who want their files to remain active.

Although tuition and fees might seem expensive, most educators tell you not to let money come between you and your educational goals. Talk to someone in the financial aid department of the school you plan to attend or check your library for publications about financial aid sources. The U.S. Department of Education publishes a guide to Federal aid programs such as Pell Grants, student loans, and work-study. To order the free 74-page booklet, *The Student Guide: Financial Aid from the U.S. Department of Education,* contact:

> Federal Student Aid Information Center
> P.O. Box 84
> Washington, DC 20044
> 1 (800) 4FED-AID (433-3243)

Resources

Information on how to earn a high school diploma or college degree without following the usual routes is available from several organizations and in numerous publications. Information on nontraditional graduate degree programs, available for master's through doctoral level, though not discussed in this article, can usually be obtained from the same resources that detail bachelor's degree programs.

National Learning Corporation publishes study guides for all of these exams, for both general examinations and tests in specific subject areas. To order study guides, or to browse their catalog featuring more than 5,000 titles, visit NLC online at www.passbooks.com, or contact them by phone at (800) 632-8888.

Organizations

Adult learners should always contact their local school system, community college, or university to learn about programs that are readily available. The following national organizations can also supply information:

> American Council on Education
> One Dupont Circle
> Washington, DC 20036-1193
> (202) 939-9300

Within the American Council on Education, the Center for Adult Learning and Educational Credentials administers the National External Diploma Program, the GED Program, the Program on Noncollegiate Sponsored Instruction, the Credit by Examination Program, and the Military Evaluations Program.

DANTES Subject Standardized Tests

INTRODUCTION

The DANTES (Defense Activity for Non-Traditional Education Support) subject standardized tests are comprehensive college and graduate level examinations given by the Armed Forces, colleges and graduate schools as end-of-subject course evaluation final examinations or to obtain college equivalency credits in the various subject areas tested.

The DANTES Examination Program enables students to obtain college credit for what they have learned on the job, through self-study, personal interest, correspondence courses or by any other means. It is used by colleges and universities to award college credit to students who demonstrate that they know as much as students completing an equivalent college course. It is a cost-efficient, time-saving way for students to use their knowledge to accomplish their educational goals.

Most schools accept the American Council on Education (ACE) recommendations for the minimum score required and the amount of credit awarded, but not all schools do. Be sure to check the policy regarding the score level required for credit and the number of credits to be awarded.

Not all tests are accepted by all institutions. Even when a test is accepted by an institution, it may not be acceptable for every program at that institution. Before considering testing, ascertain the acceptability of a specific test for a particular course.

Colleges and universities that administer DANTES tests may administer them to any applicant – or they may administer the tests only to students registered at their institution. Decisions about who will be allowed to test are made by the school. Students should contact the test center to determine current policies and schedules for DANTES testing.

Colleges and universities authorized to administer DANTES tests usually do so throughout the calendar year. Each school sets its own fee for test administration and establishes its own testing schedule. Contact the representative at the administering school directly to make arrangements for testing.

Checklist
For Students

✓ Visit **www.getcollegecredit.com** to obtain a list of tests, fact sheets, test preparation materials, participating colleges and universities, and much more.

✓ Contact your school advisor to confirm that the DSST you selected will fit into your curriculum.

✓ Consult the ***DSST Candidate Information Bulletin*** for answers to specific questions.

✓ Contact the test site to schedule your test.

✓ Prepare for your examination by using the fact sheet as a guide.

✓ Take the test.

If you would like a score report sent to your college or university, it is a good idea to bring the four-digit code with you. You must write the DSST Test Center Code for that institution on your answer sheet at the time of testing. DSST Test Center Codes are noted in the DSST Participating Colleges and Universities listing on the Web site.

If you prefer to send a score report to an institution at a later date, there is a transcript fee of $20 for each transcript ordered.

Thomson Prometric
DSST Program
2000 Lenox Drive, Third Floor
Lawrenceville, NJ 08648

Toll-free: 877-471-9860
609-895-5011

E-mail: pnj-dsst@thomson.com

MAKING A COLLEGE DEGREE WITHIN YOUR REACH

Today, there are many educational alternatives to the classroom—you can learn from your job, your reading, your independent study, and special interests you pursue. You may already have learned the subject matter covered by some college-level courses.

The DSST Program is a nationally recognized testing program that gives you the opportunity to receive college credit for learning acquired outside the traditional college classroom. Colleges and universities throughout the United States administer the program, developed by Thomson Prometric, year-round. Annually, over 90,000 DSSTs are administered to individuals who are interested in continuing their education. Take advantage of the DSST testing program; it speeds the educational process and provides the flexibility adults need, making earning a degree more feasible.

Since requirements differ from college to college, please check with the credit-awarding institution before taking a DSST. More than 1,800 colleges and universities currently award credit for DSSTs, and the number is growing every day. You can choose from 37 test titles in the areas of Social Science, Business, Mathematics, Applied Technology, Humanities, and Physical Science. A brief description of each examination is found on the pages that follow.

Reach Your Career Goals Through DSSTs

Use DSSTs to help you earn your degree, get a promotion, or simply demonstrate that you have college-level knowledge in subjects relevant to your work.

Save Time...

You don't have to sit through classes when you have previously acquired the knowledge or experience for most of what is being taught and can learn the rest yourself. You might be able to bypass introductory-level courses in subject areas you already know.

Save Money...

DSSTs save you money because the classes you bypass by earning credit through the DSST Program are classes you won't have to pay for on your way to earning your degree. You can use the money instead to take more advanced courses that can be more challenging and rewarding.

Improve Your Chances for Admission to College

Each college has its own admission policies; however, having passing scores for DSSTs on your transcript can provide strong evidence of how well you can perform at the college level.

Gain Confidence Performing at a College Level

Many adults returning to college find that lack of confidence is often the greatest hurdle to overcome. Passing a DSST demonstrates your ability to perform on a college level.

Make Up for Courses You May Have Missed

You may be ready to graduate from college and find that you are a few credits short of earning your degree. By using semester breaks, vacation time, or leisure time to study independently, you can prepare to take one or more DSSTs, fulfill your academic requirements, and graduate on time.

If You Cannot Attend Regularly Scheduled Classes...

If your lifestyle or responsibilities prevent you from attending regularly scheduled classes, you can earn your college degree from a college offering an external degree program. The DSST Program allows you to earn your degree by study and experience outside the traditional classroom.

Many colleges and universities offer external degree or distance learning programs. For additional information, contact the college you plan to attend or:

Center for Lifelong Learning
American Council on Education
One DuPont Circle NW, Suite 250
Washington, DC 20036
202-939-9475
www.acenet.edu
(Select "Center for Lifelong Learning" under "Programs & Services"
for more information)

Fact Sheets

For each test, there is a Fact Sheet that outlines the topics covered by each test and includes a list of sample questions, a list of recommended references of books that would be useful for review, and the number of credits awarded for a passing score as recommended by the American Council on Education (ACE). *Please note that some schools require scores that are higher than the minimum ACE-recommended passing score.* It is suggested that you check with your college or university to determine what score they require in order to earn credit. You can obtain Fact Sheets by:
- Downloading them from www.getcollegecredit.com
- E-mailing a request to pnj-dsst@thomson.com
- Completing a Candidate Publications Order Form

DSST Online Practice Tests

DSST online practice tests contain items that reflect a *partial range of difficulty* identified in the Content Outline section on each Fact Sheet. There is an online DSST Practice Test in the following categories:
- Mathematics
- Social Science
- Business
- Physical Science
- Applied Technology
- Humanities

Although the online DSST Practice Test questions do not indicate the full range of difficulty you would find in an actual DSST test, they will help you assess your knowledge level. Each online DSST Practice Test can be purchased by visiting www.getcollegecredit.com and clicking on DSST Practice Exams.

TAKING DSST EXAMINATIONS

Earning College Credit for DSST Examinations

To find out if the college of your choice awards credit for passing DSST scores, contact the admissions office or counseling and testing office. The college can also provide information on the scores required for awarding credit, the number of credit hours awarded, and any courses that can be bypassed with satisfactory scores.

It is important that you contact the institution of your choice as early as possible since credit-awarding policies differ among colleges and universities.

Where to Take DSSTs

DSSTs are administered at colleges and universities nationwide. Each location determines the frequency and scheduling of test administrations. To obtain the most current list of participating DSST colleges and universities:

- Visit and download the information from www.getcollegecredit.com
- E-mail pnj-dsst@thomson.com

Scheduling Your Examination

Please be aware that some colleges and universities provide DSST testing services to enrolled students only. After you have selected a college or university that administers DSSTs, you will need to contact them to schedule your test date.

The fee to take a DSST is $60 per test. This fee entitles you to two score reports after the test is scored. One will be sent directly to you and the other will be sent to the college or university that you designate on your answer sheet. You may pay the test fee with a certified check or U.S. money order made payable to Thomson Prometric or you may charge the test fee to your Visa, MasterCard or American Express credit card. Note: The credit card statement will reflect a charge from Thomson Prometric for all DSST examinations. *(Declined credit card charges will be assessed an additional $25 processing fee.)*

In addition, the test site may also require a test administration fee for each examination, to be paid directly to the institution. Contact the test site to determine its administration fee and payment policy.

Other Testing Arrangements

If you are unable to find a participating DSST college or university in your area, you may want to contact the testing office of a local accredited college or university to determine whether a representative from that office will agree to administer the test(s) for you.

The school's representative should then contact the DSST Program at 866-794-3497 to arrange for this administration. If you are unable to locate a test site, contact Thomson Prometric for assistance at pnj-dsst@thomson.com or 866-794-3497.

Testing Accommodations for Students with Disabilities

Thomson Prometric is committed to serving test takers with disabilities by providing services and reasonable testing accommodations as set forth in the provisions of the *Americans with Disabilities Act* (ADA). If you have a disability, as prescribed by the ADA, and require special testing services or arrangements, please contact the test administrator at the test site. You will be asked to submit to the test administrator documentation of your disability and your request for special accommodations. The test administrator will then forward your documentation along with your request for testing accommodations to Thomson Prometric for approval.

Please submit your request as far in advance of your test date as possible so that the necessary accommodations can be made. Only test takers with documented disabilities are eligible for special accommodations.

On the Day of the Examination

It is important to review this information and to have the correct identification present on the day of the examination:

- Arrive on time as a courtesy to the test administrator.
- Bring a valid form of government-issued identification that includes a current photo and your signature (acceptable documents include a driver's license, passport, state-issued identification card or military identification). *Anyone who fails to present valid identification will not be allowed to test.*
- Bring several No. 2 (soft-lead) sharpened pencils with good erasers, a watch, and a black pen if you will be writing an essay.
- Do not bring books or papers.
- Do not bring an alarm watch that beeps, a telephone, or a phone beeper into the testing room.
- The use of nonprogrammable calculators, slide rules, scratch paper and/or other materials is permitted for some of the tests.

DSST SCORING POLICIES

Your DSST examination scores are reported only to you, unless you request that they be sent elsewhere. If you want your scores sent to your college, you must provide the correct DSST code number of the school on your answer sheet at the time you take the test. See the *DSST Directory of Colleges and Universities* on the Web site www.getcollegecredit.com.

If your institution is not listed, contact Thomson Prometric at 866-794-3497 to establish a code number. (Some schools may require a student to be enrolled prior to receiving a score report.)

Receiving Your Score Report

Allow approximately four weeks after testing to receive your score report.

Calling DSST Customer Service before the required four-week score processing time has elapsed will not expedite the processing of your scores. Due to privacy and security requirements, scores will not be reported to students over the telephone under any circumstance.

Scoring of Principles of Public Speaking Speeches

The speech portion of the *Principles of Public Speaking* examination will be sent to speech raters who are faculty members at accredited colleges that currently teach or have previously taught the course. Scores for the *Principles of Public Speaking* examination are available six to eight weeks from receipt by Thomson Prometric. If you take the *Principles of Public Speaking* examination and fail (either the objective, speech portion, or both), you must follow the retesting policy waiting period of six months (180 days) before retaking the entire exam.

Essays

The essays for *Ethics in America* and *Technical Writing* are <u>optional</u> and thus are not scored by raters. The essays are forwarded to the college or university that you designate, along with your score report, for their use in determining the award of credit. <u>Before taking the *Ethics in America* or *Technical Writing* examinations, check with your college or university to determine whether the essay is required.</u>

NOTE: *Principles of Public Speaking* speech topic cassette tapes and essays are kept on file at Thomson Prometric for one year from the date of administration.

How to Get Transcripts

There is a $20 fee for each transcript you request. Payment must be in the form of a certified check, U.S. money order payable to Thomson Prometric, or credit card. Personal checks and debit cards are NOT an acceptable method of payment. One transcript may include scores for one or more examinations taken. To request a transcript, download the Transcript Order Form from www.getcollegecredit.com.

DESCRIPTION OF THE DSST EXAMINATIONS

Mathematics

- **Fundamentals of College Algebra** covers mathematical concepts such as fundamental algebraic operations; linear, absolute value; quadratic equations, inequalities, radials, exponents and logarithms, factoring polynomials and graphing. The use of a nonprogrammable, handheld calculator is permitted.

- **Principles of Statistics** tests the understanding of the various topics of statistics, both qualitatively and quantitatively, and the ability to apply statistical methods to solve a variety of problems. The topics included in this test are descriptive statistics; correlation and regression; probability; chance models and sampling and tests of significance. The use of a nonprogrammable, handheld calculator is permitted.

Social Science

- **Art of the Western World** deals with the history of art during the following periods: classical; Romanesque and Gothic; early Renaissance; high Renaissance, Baroque; rococo; neoclassicism and romanticism; realism, impressionism and post-impressionism; early twentieth century; and post-World War II.

- **Western Europe Since 1945** tests the knowledge of basic facts and terms and the understanding of concepts and principles related to the areas of the historical background of the aftermath of the Second World War and rebuilding of Europe; national political systems; issues and policies in Western European societies; European institutions and processes; and Europe's relations with the rest of the world.

- **An Introduction to the Modern Middle East** emphasizes core knowledge (including geography, Judaism, Christianity, Islam, ethnicity); nineteenth-century European impact; twentieth-century Western influences; World Wars I and II; new nations; social and cultural changes (1900-1960) and the Middle East from 1960 to present.

- **Human/Cultural Geography** includes the Earth and basic facts (coordinate systems, maps, physiography, atmosphere, soils and vegetation, water); culture and environment, spatial processes (social processes, modern economic systems, settlement patterns, political geography); and regional geography.

- **Rise and Fall of the Soviet Union** covers Russia under the Old Regime; the Revolutionary Period; New Economic Policy; Pre-war Stalinism; The Second World War; Post-war Stalinism; The Khrushchev Years; The Brezhnev Era; and reform and collapse.

- **A History of the Vietnam War** covers the history of the roots of the Vietnam War; the First Vietnam War (1946-1954); pre-war developments (1954-1963); American involvement in the Vietnam War; Tet (1968); Vietnamizing the War (1968-1973); Cambodia and Laos; peace; legacies and lessons.

- **The Civil War and Reconstruction** covers the Civil War from presecession (1861) through Reconstruction. It includes causes of the war; secession; Fort Sumter; the war in the east and in the west; major battles; the political situation; assassination of Lincoln; end of the Confederacy; and Reconstruction.

- **Foundations of Education** includes topics such as contemporary issues in education; past and current influences on education (philosophies, democratic ideals, social/economic influences); and the interrelationships between contemporary issues and influences.

- **Life-span Developmental Psychology** covers models and theories; methods of study; ethical issues; biological development; perception, learning and memory; cognition and language; social, emotional, and personality development; social behaviors, family life cycle, extrafamilial settings; singlehood and cohabitation; occupational development and retirement; adjustment to life stresses; and bereavement and loss.

- **Drug and Alcohol Abuse** includes such topics as drug use in society; classification of drugs; pharmacological principles; alcohol (types, effects of, alcoholism); general principles and use of sedative hypnotics, narcotic analgesics, stimulants, and hallucinogens; other drugs (inhalants, steroids); and prevention/treatment.

- **General Anthropology** deals with anthropology as a discipline; theoretical perspectives; physical anthropology; archaeology; social organization; economic organization; political organization; religion; and modernization and application of anthropology.

- **Introduction to Law Enforcement** includes topics such as history and professional movement of law enforcement; overview of the U.S. criminal justice system; police systems in the U.S.; police organization, management, and issues; and U.S. law and precedents.

- **Criminal Justice** deals with criminal behavior (crime in the U.S., theories of crime, types of crime); the criminal justice system (historical origins, legal foundations, due process); police; the court system (history and organization, adult court system, juvenile court, pre-trial and post-trial processes); and corrections.

- **Fundamentals of Counseling** covers historical development (significant influences and people); counselor roles and functions; the counseling relationship; and theoretical approaches to counseling.

Business
- **Principles of Finance** deals with financial statements and planning; time value of money; working capital management; valuation and characteristics; capital budgeting; cost of capital; risk and return; and international financial management. The use of a nonprogrammable, handheld calculator is permitted.

- **Principles of Financial Accounting** includes topics such as general concepts and principles, accounting cycle and classification; transaction analysis; accruals and deferrals; cash and internal control; current accounts; long- and short-term liabilities; capital stock; and financial statements. The use of a nonprogrammable, handheld calculator is permitted.

- **Human Resource Management** covers general employment issues; job analysis; training and development; performance appraisals; compensation issues; security issues; personnel legislation and regulation; labor relations and current issues; an overview of the Human Resource Management Field; Human Resource Planning; Staffing; training and development; compensation issues; safety and health; employee rights and discipline; employment law; labor relations and current issues and trends.

- **Organizational Behavior** deals with the study of organizational behavior (scientific approaches, research designs, data collection methods); individual processes and characteristics; interpersonal and group processes and characteristics; organizational processes and characteristics; and change and development processes.

- **Principles of Supervision** deals with the roles and responsibilities of the supervisor; management functions (planning, organization and staffing, directing at the supervisory level); and other topics (legal issues, stress management, union environments, quality concerns).

- **Business Law II** covers topics such as sales of goods; debtor and creditor relations; business organizations; property; and commercial paper.

- **Introduction to Computing** includes topics such as history and technological generations; hardware/software; applications to information technology; program development; data management; communications and connectivity; and computing and society. The use of a nonprogrammable, handheld calculator is permitted.

- **Management Information Systems** covers systems theory, analysis and design of systems, hardware and software; database management; telecommunications; management of the MIS functional area and informational support.

- **Introduction to Business** deals with economic issues affecting business; international business; government and business; forms of business ownership; small business, entrepreneurship and franchise; management process; human resource management; production and operations; marketing management; financial management; risk management and insurance; and management and information systems.

- **Money and Banking** covers the role and kinds of money; commercial banks and other financial intermediaries; central banking and the Federal Reserve system; money and macroeconomics activity; monetary policy in the U.S.; and the international monetary system.

- **Personal Finance** includes topics such as financial goals and values; budgeting; credit and debt; major purchases; taxes; insurance; investments; and retirement and estate planning. The use of auxiliary materials, such as calculators and slide rules, is NOT permitted.

- **Business Mathematics** deals with basic operations with integers, fractions, and decimals; round numbers; ratios; averages; business graphs; simple interest; compound interest and annuities; net pay and deductions; discounts and markups; depreciation and net worth; corporate securities; distribution of ownership; and stock and asset turnover.

Physical Science
- **Astronomy** covers the history of astronomy, celestial mechanics; celestial systems; astronomical instruments; the solar system; nature and evolution; the galaxy; the universe; determining astronomical distances; and life in the universe.

- **Here's to Your Health** covers mental health and behavior; human development and relationships; substance abuse; fitness and nutrition; risk factors, disease, and disease prevention; and safety, consumer awareness, and environmental concerns.

- **Environment and Humanity** deals with topics such as ecological concepts (ecosystems, global ecology, food chains and webs); environmental impacts; environmental management and conservation; and political processes and the future.

- **Principles of Physical Science I** includes physics: Newton's Laws of Motion; energy and momentum; thermodynamics; wave and optics; electricity and magnetism; chemistry: properties of matter; atomic theory and structure; and chemical reactions.

- **Physical Geology** covers Earth materials; igneous, sedimentary, and metamorphic rocks; surface processes (weathering, groundwater, glaciers, oceanic systems, deserts and winds, hydrologic cycle); internal Earth processes; and applications (mineral and energy resources, environmental geology).

Applied Technology
- **Technical Writing** covers topics such as theory and practice of technical writing; purpose, content, and organizational patterns of common types of technical documents; elements of various technical reports; and technical editing. Students have the option to write a short essay on one of the technical topics provided. Thomson Prometric will not score the essay; however, for determining the award of credit, a copy of the essay will be forwarded to the college or university you've designated along with the score report or transcript.

Humanities
- **Ethics in America** deals with ethical traditions (Greek views, Biblical traditions, moral law, consequential ethics, feminist ethics); ethical analysis of issues arising in interpersonal and personal-societal relationships and in professional and occupational roles; and relationships between ethical traditions and the ethical analysis of situations. Students have the option to write an essay to analyze a morally problematic situation in terms of issues relevant to a decision and arguments for alternative positions. Thomson Prometric will not score the essay; however, for determining the award of credit, a copy of the essay will be forwarded to the college or university you've designated along with the score report or transcript.

- **Introduction to World Religions** covers topics such as dimensions and approaches to religion; primal religions; Hinduism; Buddhism; Confucianism; Taoism; Judaism; Christianity; and Islam.

- **Principles of Public Speaking** consists of two parts: Part One consists of multiple-choice questions covering considerations of Principles of Public Speaking; audience analysis; purposes of speeches; structure/organization; content/supporting materials; research; language and style; delivery; communication apprehension; listening and feedback; and criticism and evaluation. Part Two requires the student to record an impromptu persuasive speech that will be scored.

FREQUENTLY ASKED QUESTIONS ABOUT DSSTs

In order to pass the test, must I study from one of the recommended references?

The recommended references are a listing of books that were being used as textbooks in college courses of the same or similar title at the time the test was developed. Appropriate textbooks for study are not limited to those listed in the fact sheet. If you wish to obtain study resources to prepare for the examination, you may reference either the current edition of the listed titles or textbooks currently used at a local college or university for the same class title. It is recommended that you reference more than one textbook on the topics outlined in the fact sheet. You should begin by checking textbook content against the content outline included on the front page of the DSST fact sheet before selecting textbooks that cover the text content from which to study. Textbooks may be found at the campus bookstore of a local college or university offering a course on the subject.

Is there a penalty for guessing on the tests?

There is no penalty for guessing on DSSTs, so you should mark an answer for each question.

How much time will I have to complete the test?

Many DSSTs can be completed within 90 minutes; however, additional time can be allowed if necessary.

What should I do if I find a test question irregularity?

Continue testing and then report the irregularity to the test administrator after the test. This may be done by asking that the test administrator note the irregularity on the Supervisor's Irregularity Report or you can write to Thomson Prometric, DSST Program, 2000 Lenox Drive, Third Floor, Lawrenceville, NJ 08648, and indicate the form and question number(s) or circumstances as well as your name and address.

When will I receive my score report?

Allow approximately four weeks from the date of testing to receive your score report. Allow six to eight weeks to receive a score report for the *Principles of Public Speaking* examination.

Will my test scores be released without my permission?

Your test score will not be released to anyone other than the school you designate on your answer sheet unless you write to us and ask us to send a transcript elsewhere. Instructions about how to do this can be found on your score report. Your scores may be used for research purposes, but individual scores are never made public nor are individuals identified if research findings are made public.

If I do not achieve a passing score on the test, how long must I wait until I can take the test again?

If you do not receive a score on the test that will enable you to obtain credit for the course, you may take the test again after six months (180 days). Please do not attempt to take the test before six months (180 days) have passed because you will receive a score report marked *invalid* and your test fee will not be refunded.

Can my test scores be canceled?

The test administrator is required to report any irregularities to Thomson Prometric. <u>The consequence of bringing unauthorized materials into the testing room, or giving or receiving help, will be the forfeiture of your test fee and the invalidation of test scores.</u> The DSST Program reserves the right to cancel scores and not issue score reports in such situations.

What can I do if I feel that my test scores were not accurately reported?

Thomson Prometric recognizes the extreme importance of test results to candidates and has a multi-step quality-control procedure to help ensure that reported scores are accurate. If you have reason to believe that your score(s) were not accurately reported, you may request to have your answer sheet reviewed and hand scored.

The fees for this service are:
- $20 fee if requested within six months of the test date
- $30 fee if requested more than six months from the test date
- $30 fee if a re-evaluation of the *Principles of Public Speaking* speech is requested

The fee for this service can be paid by credit card or by certified check or U.S. money order payable to Thomson Prometric. Submit your request for score verification along with the appropriate fee or credit card information (credit card number and expiration date) to Thomson Prometric, DSST Program, 2000 Lenox Drive, Third Floor, Lawrenceville, NJ 08648. Include your full name, the test title, the date you took the test, and your Social Security number. Candidates will be notified if a scoring discrepancy is discovered within four weeks of receipt of the request.

What does ACE recommendation mean?

The ACE recommendation is the minimum passing score recommended by the American Council on Education for any given test. It is equivalent to the average score of students in the DSST norming sample who received a grade of C for the course. Some schools require a score higher than the ACE recommendation.

Who is NLC?

National Learning Corporation (NLC) has been successfully preparing candidates for 40 years for over 5,000 exams. NLC publishes Passbook® study guides to help candidates prepare for all DANTES and CLEP exams and almost every other type of exam from high school through adult career.

Go to our website — www.passbooks.com — or call (800) 632-8888 for information about ordering our Passbooks.

To get detailed information on the DSST program and DSST preparation materials, visit www.getcollegecredit.com.

If you are interested in taking the DSST exams, call 877-471-9860 or e-mail pnj-dsst@thomson.com.

HOW TO TAKE A TEST

You have studied long, hard and conscientiously.

With your official admission card in hand, and your heart pounding, you have been admitted to the examination room.

You note that there are several hundred other applicants in the examination room waiting to take the same test.

They all appear to be equally well prepared.

You know that nothing but your best effort will suffice. The "moment of truth" is at hand: you now have to demonstrate objectively, in writing, your knowledge of content and your understanding of subject matter.

You are fighting the most important battle of your life—to pass and/or score high on an examination which will determine your career and provide the economic basis for your livelihood.

What extra, special things should you know and should you do in taking the examination?

I. YOU MUST PASS AN EXAMINATION

A. WHAT EVERY CANDIDATE SHOULD KNOW
Examination applicants often ask us for help in preparing for the written test. What can I study in advance? What kinds of questions will be asked? How will the test be given? How will the papers be graded?

B. HOW ARE EXAMS DEVELOPED?
Examinations are carefully written by trained technicians who are specialists in the field known as "psychological measurement," in consultation with recognized authorities in the field of work that the test will cover. These experts recommend the subject matter areas or skills to be tested; only those knowledges or skills important to your success on the job are included. The most reliable books and source materials available are used as references. Together, the experts and technicians judge the difficulty level of the questions.
Test technicians know how to phrase questions so that the problem is clearly stated. Their ethics do not permit "trick" or "catch" questions. Questions may have been tried out on sample groups, or subjected to statistical analysis, to determine their usefulness.
Written tests are often used in combination with performance tests, ratings of training and experience, and oral interviews. All of these measures combine to form the best-known means of finding the right person for the right job.

II. HOW TO PASS THE WRITTEN TEST

A. BASIC STEPS

1) Study the announcement

How, then, can you know what subjects to study? Our best answer is: "Learn as much as possible about the class of positions for which you've applied." The exam will test the knowledge, skills and abilities needed to do the work.

Your most valuable source of information about the position you want is the official exam announcement. This announcement lists the training and experience qualifications. Check these standards and apply only if you come reasonably close to meeting them. Many jurisdictions preview the written test in the exam announcement by including a section called "Knowledge and Abilities Required," "Scope of the Examination," or some similar heading. Here you will find out specifically what fields will be tested.

2) Choose appropriate study materials

If the position for which you are applying is technical or advanced, you will read more advanced, specialized material. If you are already familiar with the basic principles of your field, elementary textbooks would waste your time. Concentrate on advanced textbooks and technical periodicals. Think through the concepts and review difficult problems in your field.

These are all general sources. You can get more ideas on your own initiative, following these leads. For example, training manuals and publications of the government agency which employs workers in your field can be useful, particularly for technical and professional positions. A letter or visit to the government department involved may result in more specific study suggestions, and certainly will provide you with a more definite idea of the exact nature of the position you are seeking.

3) Study this book!

III. KINDS OF TESTS

Tests are used for purposes other than measuring knowledge and ability to perform specified duties. For some positions, it is equally important to test ability to make adjustments to new situations or to profit from training. In others, basic mental abilities not dependent on information are essential. Questions which test these things may not appear as pertinent to the duties of the position as those which test for knowledge and information. Yet they are often highly important parts of a fair examination. For very general questions, it is almost impossible to help you direct your study efforts. What we can do is to point out some of the more common of these general abilities needed in public service positions and describe some typical questions.

1) General information

Broad, general information has been found useful for predicting job success in some kinds of work. This is tested in a variety of ways, from vocabulary lists to questions about current events. Basic background in some field of work, such as sociology or economics, may be sampled in a group of questions. Often these are principles which have become familiar to most persons through exposure rather than through formal training. It is difficult to advise you how to study for these questions; being alert to the world around you is our best suggestion.

2) Verbal ability

An example of an ability needed in many positions is verbal or language ability. Verbal ability is, in brief, the ability to use and understand words. Vocabulary and grammar tests are typical measures of this ability. Reading comprehension or paragraph interpretation questions are common in many kinds of civil service tests. You are given a paragraph of written material and asked to find its central meaning.

IV. KINDS OF QUESTIONS

1. Multiple-choice Questions

Most popular of the short-answer questions is the "multiple choice" or "best answer" question. It can be used, for example, to test for factual knowledge, ability to solve problems or judgment in meeting situations found at work.

A multiple-choice question is normally one of three types:
- It can begin with an incomplete statement followed by several possible endings. You are to find the one ending which best completes the statement, although some of the others may not be entirely wrong.
- It can also be a complete statement in the form of a question which is answered by choosing one of the statements listed.
- It can be in the form of a problem – again you select the best answer.

Here is an example of a multiple-choice question with a discussion which should give you some clues as to the method for choosing the right answer:

When an employee has a complaint about his assignment, the action which will best help him overcome his difficulty is to
    A. discuss his difficulty with his coworkers
    B. take the problem to the head of the organization
    C. take the problem to the person who gave him the assignment
    D. say nothing to anyone about his complaint

In answering this question, you should study each of the choices to find which is best. Consider choice "A" – Certainly an employee may discuss his complaint with fellow employees, but no change or improvement can result, and the complaint remains unresolved. Choice "B" is a poor choice since the head of the organization probably does not know what assignment you have been given, and taking your problem to him is known as "going over the head" of the supervisor. The supervisor, or person who made the assignment, is the person who can clarify it or correct any injustice. Choice "C" is, therefore, correct. To say nothing, as in choice "D," is unwise. Supervisors have and interest in knowing the problems employees are facing, and the employee is seeking a solution to his problem.

2. True/False

3. Matching Questions

Matching an answer from a column of choices within another column.

V. RECORDING YOUR ANSWERS

Computer terminals are used more and more today for many different kinds of exams.

For an examination with very few applicants, you may be told to record your answers in the test booklet itself. Separate answer sheets are much more common. If this separate answer sheet is to be scored by machine – and this is often the case – it is highly important that you mark your answers correctly in order to get credit.

VI. BEFORE THE TEST

YOUR PHYSICAL CONDITION IS IMPORTANT

If you are not well, you can't do your best work on tests. If you are half asleep, you can't do your best either. Here are some tips:

1) Get about the same amount of sleep you usually get. Don't stay up all night before the test, either partying or worrying—DON'T DO IT!
2) If you wear glasses, be sure to wear them when you go to take the test. This goes for hearing aids, too.
3) If you have any physical problems that may keep you from doing your best, be sure to tell the person giving the test. If you are sick or in poor health, you relay cannot do your best on any test. You can always come back and take the test some other time.

Common sense will help you find procedures to follow to get ready for an examination. Too many of us, however, overlook these sensible measures. Indeed, nervousness and fatigue have been found to be the most serious reasons why applicants fail to do their best on civil service tests. Here is a list of reminders:

- Begin your preparation early – Don't wait until the last minute to go scurrying around for books and materials or to find out what the position is all about.
- Prepare continuously – An hour a night for a week is better than an all-night cram session. This has been definitely established. What is more, a night a week for a month will return better dividends than crowding your study into a shorter period of time.
- Locate the place of the exam – You have been sent a notice telling you when and where to report for the examination. If the location is in a different town or otherwise unfamiliar to you, it would be well to inquire the best route and learn something about the building.
- Relax the night before the test – Allow your mind to rest. Do not study at all that night. Plan some mild recreation or diversion; then go to bed early and get a good night's sleep.
- Get up early enough to make a leisurely trip to the place for the test – This way unforeseen events, traffic snarls, unfamiliar buildings, etc. will not upset you.
- Dress comfortably – A written test is not a fashion show. You will be known by number and not by name, so wear something comfortable.
- Leave excess paraphernalia at home – Shopping bags and odd bundles will get in your way. You need bring only the items mentioned in the official notice you received; usually everything you need is provided. Do not bring reference books to the exam. They will only confuse those last minutes and be taken away from you when in the test room.

- Arrive somewhat ahead of time – If because of transportation schedules you must get there very early, bring a newspaper or magazine to take your mind off yourself while waiting.
- Locate the examination room – When you have found the proper room, you will be directed to the seat or part of the room where you will sit. Sometimes you are given a sheet of instructions to read while you are waiting. Do not fill out any forms until you are told to do so; just read them and be prepared.
- Relax and prepare to listen to the instructions
- If you have any physical problem that may keep you from doing your best, be sure to tell the test administrator. If you are sick or in poor health, you really cannot do your best on the exam. You can come back and take the test some other time.

VII. AT THE TEST

The day of the test is here and you have the test booklet in your hand. The temptation to get going is very strong. Caution! There is more to success than knowing the right answers. You must know how to identify your papers and understand variations in the type of short-answer question used in this particular examination. Follow these suggestions for maximum results from your efforts:

1) Cooperate with the monitor

The test administrator has a duty to create a situation in which you can be as much at ease as possible. He will give instructions, tell you when to begin, check to see that you are marking your answer sheet correctly, and so on. He is not there to guard you, although he will see that your competitors do not take unfair advantage. He wants to help you do your best.

2) Listen to all instructions

Don't jump the gun! Wait until you understand all directions. In most civil service tests you get more time than you need to answer the questions. So don't be in a hurry. Read each word of instructions until you clearly understand the meaning. Study the examples, listen to all announcements and follow directions. Ask questions if you do not understand what to do.

3) Identify your papers

Civil service exams are usually identified by number only. You will be assigned a number; you must not put your name on your test papers. Be sure to copy your number correctly. Since more than one exam may be given, copy your exact examination title.

4) Plan your time

Unless you are told that a test is a "speed" or "rate of work" test, speed itself is usually not important. Time enough to answer all the questions will be provided, but this does not mean that you have all day. An overall time limit has been set. Divide the total time (in minutes) by the number of questions to determine the approximate time you have for each question.

5) Do not linger over difficult questions

If you come across a difficult question, mark it with a paper clip (useful to have along) and come back to it when you have been through the booklet. One caution if you do this – be sure to skip a number on your answer sheet as well. Check often to be sure that you have not lost your place and that you are marking in the row numbered the same as the question you are answering.

6) Read the questions

Be sure you know what the question asks! Many capable people are unsuccessful because they failed to read the questions correctly.

7) Answer all questions

Unless you have been instructed that a penalty will be deducted for incorrect answers, it is better to guess than to omit a question.

8) Speed tests

It is often better NOT to guess on speed tests. It has been found that on timed tests people are tempted to spend the last few seconds before time is called in marking answers at random – without even reading them – in the hope of picking up a few extra points. To discourage this practice, the instructions may warn you that your score will be "corrected" for guessing. That is, a penalty will be applied. The incorrect answers will be deducted from the correct ones, or some other penalty formula will be used.

9) Review your answers

If you finish before time is called, go back to the questions you guessed or omitted to give them further thought. Review other answers if you have time.

10) Return your test materials

If you are ready to leave before others have finished or time is called, take ALL your materials to the monitor and leave quietly. Never take any test material with you. The monitor can discover whose papers are not complete, and taking a test booklet may be grounds for disqualification.

VIII. EXAMINATION TECHNIQUES

1) Read the general instructions carefully. These are usually printed on the first page of the exam booklet. As a rule, these instructions refer to the timing of the examination; the fact that you should not start work until the signal and must stop work at a signal, etc. If there are any special instructions, such as a choice of questions to be answered, make sure that you note this instruction carefully.

2) When you are ready to start work on the examination, that is as soon as the signal has been given, read the instructions to each question booklet, underline any key words or phrases, such as least, best, outline, describe and the like. In this way you will tend to answer as requested rather than discover on reviewing your paper that you listed without describing, that you selected the worst choice rather than the best choice, etc.

3) If the examination is of the objective or multiple-choice type – that is, each question will also give a series of possible answers: A, B, C or D, and you are called upon to select the best answer and write the letter next to that answer on your answer paper – it is advisable to start answering each question in turn. There may be anywhere from 50 to 100 such questions in the three or four hours allotted and you can see how much time would be taken if you read through all the questions before beginning to answer any. Furthermore, if you

come across a question or group of questions which you know would be difficult to answer, it would undoubtedly affect your handling of all the other questions.

4) If the examination is of the essay type and contains but a few questions, it is a moot point as to whether you should read all the questions before starting to answer any one. Of course, if you are given a choice – say five out of seven and the like – then it is essential to read all the questions so you can eliminate the two that are most difficult. If, however, you are asked to answer all the questions, there may be danger in trying to answer the easiest one first because you may find that you will spend too much time on it. The best technique is to answer the first question, then proceed to the second, etc.

5) Time your answers. Before the exam begins, write down the time it started, then add the time allowed for the examination and write down the time it must be completed, then divide the time available somewhat as follows:
    - If 3-1/2 hours are allowed, that would be 210 minutes. If you have 80 objective-type questions, that would be an average of 2-1/2 minutes per question. Allow yourself no more than 2 minutes per question, or a total of 160 minutes, which will permit about 50 minutes to review.
    - If for the time allotment of 210 minutes there are 7 essay questions to answer, that would average about 30 minutes a question. Give yourself only 25 minutes per question so that you have about 35 minutes to review.

6) The most important instruction is to read each question and make sure you know what is wanted. The second most important instruction is to time yourself properly so that you answer every question. The third most important instruction is to answer every question. Guess if you have to but include something for each question. Remember that you will receive no credit for a blank and will probably receive some credit if you write something in answer to an essay question. If you guess a letter – say "B" for a multiple-choice question – you may have guessed right. If you leave a blank as an answer to a multiple-choice question, the examiners may respect your feelings but it will not add a point to your score. Some exams may penalize you for wrong answers, so in such cases only, you may not want to guess unless you have some basis for your answer.

7) Suggestions
    a. Objective-type questions
        1. Examine the question booklet for proper sequence of pages and questions
        2. Read all instructions carefully
        3. Skip any question which seems too difficult; return to it after all other questions have been answered
        4. Apportion your time properly; do not spend too much time on any single question or group of questions
        5. Note and underline key words – all, most, fewest, least, best, worst, same, opposite, etc.
        6. Pay particular attention to negatives
        7. Note unusual option, e.g., unduly long, short, complex, different or similar in content to the body of the question
        8. Observe the use of "hedging" words – probably, may, most likely, etc.

9. Make sure that your answer is put next to the same number as the question
10. Do not second-guess unless you have good reason to believe the second answer is definitely more correct
11. Cross out original answer if you decide another answer is more accurate; do not erase until you are ready to hand your paper in
12. Answer all questions; guess unless instructed otherwise
13. Leave time for review

b. Essay questions
   1. Read each question carefully
   2. Determine exactly what is wanted. Underline key words or phrases.
   3. Decide on outline or paragraph answer
   4. Include many different points and elements unless asked to develop any one or two points or elements
   5. Show impartiality by giving pros and cons unless directed to select one side only
   6. Make and write down any assumptions you find necessary to answer the questions
   7. Watch your English, grammar, punctuation and choice of words
   8. Time your answers; don't crowd material

8) Answering the essay question

Most essay questions can be answered by framing the specific response around several key words or ideas. Here are a few such key words or ideas:

M's: manpower, materials, methods, money, management
P's: purpose, program, policy, plan, procedure, practice, problems, pitfalls, personnel, public relations

a. Six basic steps in handling problems:
   1. Preliminary plan and background development
   2. Collect information, data and facts
   3. Analyze and interpret information, data and facts
   4. Analyze and develop solutions as well as make recommendations
   5. Prepare report and sell recommendations
   6. Install recommendations and follow up effectiveness

b. Pitfalls to avoid
   1. Taking things for granted – A statement of the situation does not necessarily imply that each of the elements is necessarily true; for example, a complaint may be invalid and biased so that all that can be taken for granted is that a complaint has been registered
   2. Considering only one side of a situation – Wherever possible, indicate several alternatives and then point out the reasons you selected the best one
   3. Failing to indicate follow up – Whenever your answer indicates action on your part, make certain that you will take proper follow-up action to see how successful your recommendations, procedures or actions turn out to be
   4. Taking too long in answering any single question – Remember to time your answers properly

EXAMINATION SECTION

EXAMINATION SECTION
TEST 1

DIRECTIONS: Each question or incomplete statement is followed by several suggested answers or completions. Select the one that BEST answers the question or completes the statement. *PRINT THE LETTER OF THE CORRECT ANSWER IN THE SPACE AT THE RIGHT.*

1. While many Americans had never heard of Al-Qaeda until 9/11, members of the Clinton administration had linked them to previous terrorist attacks. Which of the following attacks did the Clinton administration believe Al-Qaeda was responsible for?
   A. The bombings of two embassies in Kenya and Tanzania
   B. Assassination of Russian citizens in a Moscow theater
   C. 9/11 was the first time the Clinton administration had heard of Al-Qaeda
   D. An assault on U.S. troops in Somalia

   1.____

2. Most of the hijackers involved with September 11, 2001, were from which country?
   A. Iran
   B. Saudi Arabia
   C. Somalia
   D. Pakistan

   2.____

3. The troops pictured above are the same ones who helped take control of Kabul in November 2001. Where are they from?
   A. The Taliban
   B. The Northern Alliance
   C. Al Qaeda
   D. U.S. and British forces

   3.____

4. Many terrorist groups are funded by all of the following EXCEPT   4._____
   A. criminal activities
   B. governments
   C. public businesses
   D. private supporters

5. Many experts theorize that 21st century conflict will differ from 20th century conflict in what way?   5._____
   A. Countries will fight battles on a large scale
   B. Most battles will be fought on the digital frontier
   C. Many countries will only sanction special forces with limited operations
   D. Both B and C

6. While "proxy wars" fought during the Cold War era saw a greater number of people killed, wars fought in the 21st century, like Somalia or Syria, have seen   6._____
   A. more damage to buildings
   B. direct involvement by First World countries
   C. extreme brutality toward civilians
   D. less attacks on government officials

7. Many government officials want to try terrorists as criminals in a domestic courts while others would prefer terrorists be   7._____
   A. executed for treason
   B. put into hidden jails and never tried in court
   C. tried as unlawful combatants under laws of war
   D. none of the above

8. The Crimean crisis involves which of the following countries?   8._____
   A. Somalia and Kenya
   B. North Korea and South Korea
   C. Croatia and Slovenia
   D. Russia and Ukraine

9. What major difference has primarily caused Chad's civil war?   9._____
   A. Tribal politics
   B. Racial differences
   C. Different religions
   D. Living standards between the rich and poor

10. Most experts theorize that the majority of terrorists are 10._____
    A. on anti-psychotic medication
    B. diagnosed with antisocial disorders
    C. leaders of a movement or cause
    D. followers of a movement or cause

11. From World War II through today, which of the following Latin American 11._____
    groups have proven the most resistant to social and economic changes?
    A. Coalition leaders
    B. Lower-class farmers
    C. Middle class
    D. Military

12. Since the beginning of the 21st century, what have many Latin American 12._____
    countries seen happen?
    A. An increase in popularly elected leaders
    B. The successful implementation of communist regimes
    C. A greater dependence on Cuba for financial support
    D. A call to return to their former status as colonies

13. Due to political instability and infighting, what major economic problems still 13._____
    plague Latin American countries today?
    A. A great decline in birth rate
    B. No capital for developing their industries
    C. Larger acceptance of communism as a way of life
    D. Lack of labor for factories

14. The U.S. decided that Syrian officials "crossed the line" when they 14._____
    A. engaged in chemical warfare against their own people
    B. killed more than 100,000 innocents due to bombs and errant shooting
    C. purchased their weapons from al-Qaeda
    D. asked for Russian troop support to quell the rebellion

15. Large-scale issues of unbalanced economic growth, pollution of ecosystems 15._____
    and global hunger all reflect the need for
    A. more spending on military operations by all nations
    B. returning to policies of economic nationalism
    C. increased international cooperation
    D. reducing foreign aid provided by First World countries

16. 9/11 and the Iraqi War have intensified global feelings that the Middle East is incredibly vital because it   16._____
    A. has demonstrated how to become equal both economically and politically
    B. is still a major source of the world's uranium
    C. lets European countries to keep their spheres of influence
    D. provides a large amount of the petroleum used by industrialized nations

17. Which of the factors listed below have made the Middle East significant to the rest of the world?   17._____
    I. Technological innovations
    II. Production of nuclear power
    III. Religious and ethnic conflict
    A. I
    B. II
    C. III
    D. I and II

18. The interwoven feelings of national pride and religious fervor in India and Pakistan see conflicts between which two religious groups?   18._____
    A. Muslims and Christians
    B. Christians and Buddhists
    C. Buddhists and Hindus
    D. Hindus and Muslims

19. Which of the following headlines best exemplifies human rights violations?   19._____
    A. "America Hands Down Economic Sanctions Against Russia"
    B. "North Korean Protesters Arrested After Demonstration"
    C. "Sunnis Targeted in Hate Crimes"
    D. All of the above

20. In the last decade, most of the violations of human rights have been in countries in which   20._____
    A. leaders have absolute power
    B. there is strong freedom of press
    C. government is limited by law
    D. protests are outlawed

21. Which of the following events made citizens of Kiev believe war was inevitable during the 2014 Crimean crisis?   21._____
    A. A border town was attacked with nerve gas, which killed soldiers and civilians
    B. Crimea voted to secede and join the attacking nation
    C. The U.S. sent troops over to help fight the battle
    D. There were reports of the enemy troops advancing on the capital

22. This leader is seen as the main culprit behind why the Crimean crisis has reached such a critical stage.   22._____
    A. President Barack Obama
    B. President Elect Viktor Yanukovych
    C. President Vladimir Putin
    D. Secretary of State Hilary Clinton

A person grows up in the 21st century seeing others in the world around them raised with proper resources (food and water) as well as technology and money. When they are in their early 20s, they get sick and tired of everyone who has grown up in comfort and never known what it is like to be hungry or poor. This person decides they want to do something about it, and when they join a group with a history of bombing buildings, they are labeled a terrorist.

23. Which of the following causes of terrorism does this scenario BEST illustrate?   23._____
    A. Psychological
    B. Political
    C. Socio-Economic
    D. Religious

24. Which of the following terms describes a hacker's software that allows them to remotely take control of a government computer, attempting to steal state secrets, without being detected?   24._____
    A. Rootkit
    B. Linus
    C. DDos
    D. Botnet

25. Which of the following is an example of cyber warfare? 25._____
   A. In 2007, a number of computers brought down government, business and media websites across the country. The attack supposedly originated in Russia.
   B. In 2013, Edward Snowden leaked classified documents to the New York Times
   C. In 2009, Sudanese pirates hacked a ship's computer system to kill the ship's engine and make them easier to catch
   D. Both A and B

KEY (CORRECT ANSWERS)

1. A	11. D	21. B
2. B	12. A	22. C
3. B	13. B	23. C
4. C	14. A	24. A
5. D	15. C	25. A
6. C	16. D	
7. C	17. C	
8. D	18. D	
9. C	19. D	
10. D	20. A	

TEST 2

DIRECTIONS: Each question or incomplete statement is followed by several suggested answers or completions. Select the one that BEST answers the question or completes the statement. *PRINT THE LETTER OF THE CORRECT ANSWER IN THE SPACE AT THE RIGHT.*

1. Which of the following is TRUE concerning the country of Israel?   1.____
    A. It has an abundance of oil
    B. The country boasts a democratically elected government
    C. It has fought against countries that hold Islam as the official religion
    D. Israel has friendly ties to Jordan

2. People who subscribe to this type of terrorism believe one should try to kill as many "infidels" as possible.   2.____
    A. Modern
    B. State-sanctioned
    C. Non-religious
    D. Radical

3. Osama bin Laden is originally from   3.____
    A. Afghanistan
    B. Turkey
    C. Saudi Arabia
    D. the United States

4. Which main city of Syria saw 1,400 of its inhabitants die due to sarin, a nerve agent?   4.____
    A. Homs
    B. Ghouta
    C. Damascus
    D. Dara'a

5. Terrorism in the Middle East continues to be a major issue in large part because of which major factor listed below?   5.____
    A. Lowering of oil prices on the global market
    B. The U.N.'s forces being present in Lebanon
    C. Global refusal to use violence to end conflicts
    D. The Palestinian effort to create and hold their own homeland

2 (#2)

6. Despite the terrorism and violence prevalent in Middle East conflicts, the actions of the majority of Islamic fundamentalists show they are in favor of
    A. women's equality
    B. traditional Muslim teachings focused on the Quran
    C. a new and approved attempt to become modern
    D. none of the above

6._____

7. Attempts to peacefully resolve the Arab-Israeli conflict frequently get caught up on which issue?
    A. Who should own and operate the Suez Canal
    B. The land and civil rights for Palestinian Arabs
    C. The control of the Arabian Peninsula
    D. How Arabs of Palestine and Israelis will be represented

7._____

8. Since the beginning of the Syrian Civil War, approximately _____ people have been killed.
    A. more than 100,000
    B. 15,000
    C. 35,000
    D. 50,000

8._____

9. Which of the following would be considered a structural cause for conflict?
    A. Human rights abuses
    B. Assassination of a key leader
    C. Lack of equal economic and social opportunities
    D. None of the above

9._____

10. Conflict has continued for decades in Sudan, primarily because of
    A. hatred and greed
    B. cultural and political differences
    C. political and religious differences
    D. religious and cultural differences

10._____

11. Partially as a result of the conflict in south Sudan, what happens to many of the children of this region?
    A. They must work on communal farms
    B. They cannot attend school even if they want to
    C. Most will die before reaching the age of 5
    D. Many of the children are taken from their families by the army

11._____

12. Sudan split into two countries in 2011. The primary reason for this change was
    A. there was a democratic vote and the people wanted to separate
    B. the government decided it was the only way to maintain peace in the region
    C. South Sudan declared itself an independent and sovereign state
    D. the northern territory of Sudan became occupied by a general turned dictator

13. Western politics revolve around which of the following classical Athens concepts?
    A. Personal appreciation obstructs public progress
    B. Individuals should not be afraid to oppose nature and society to become great
    C. People by themselves are inconsequential when it comes to shaping ideas, society and the government
    D. Personal achievement and self worth are of immense value

14. Country X in Africa has just become an independent state. It is currently creating its own constitution in which the branches of government are to be independent of each other. Country X is holding to which constitutional principle?
    A. Separation of powers
    B. Federalism
    C. Indirect egalitarianism
    D. Popular sovereignty

15. There are many similarities between the current conflict in Syria and the one that took place in 1982 with current Syrian President Bashar al-Assad's father, Hafez al-Assad. How did the Syrian conflict of 1982 end?
    A. President al-Assad had laws put into place to reallocate power, which allowed Sunni Muslims better rights
    B. President al-Assad decreed that the price of food, chiefly bread, should be lowered so that the Muslim Brotherhood would support his rule
    C. President al-Assad called for the military to put down the opposition in the city of Hama to bring a violent end to the conflict
    D. None of the above

16. Which of the following publications wrote an article praising Bashar al-Assad and his wife, Asma, a month before the start of the Syrian Civil War?
    A. Esquire
    B. The New York Times
    C. Vogue
    D. The Atlantic

17. As the United States got further involved in Operation Enduring Freedom, people began to see the enemy use martyrdom tactics. What is the best way to describe this method of attack?   17._____
    A. It is the sacrifice of one's life for a cause
    B. It is an attack on government assets
    C. It is a way to infiltrate an enemy's border
    D. It is an attack on a community because of their religious beliefs

18. Leading up to September 11, 2001, this Afghanistan group allowed bin Laden and Al-Qaeda to train their "troops" in Afghanistan.   18._____
    A. Sleeper Agents from Saudi Arabia
    B. Jabhat al-Nusra
    C. Hezbollah
    D. Taliban

19. You are in Syria listening to a speech in the town square. Which of the following things should you do while the speech is going on?   19._____
    A. Throw vegetables any time Iran is mentioned
    B. Hold a moment of silence whenever Hefez Al-Assad's name is spoken
    C. Clap and cheer if the speaker says the name "Bashar Al-Assad"
    D. Recite the Syrian National Anthem whenever the speaker pauses

20. Which U.N. country repeatedly blocks the U.N. from imposing sanctions on the Syrian government, thus prolonging the Syrian conflict?   20._____
    A. Russia
    B. Saudi Arabia
    C. Afghanistan
    D. China

21. Which of the following is a modern political trend seen in Latin American countries?   21._____
    A. Many of the countries are turning into military police states
    B. Democratically elected officials are replacing autocrats
    C. Communism is spreading throughout the area
    D. Theocracy is becoming more widespread

22. There are a number of operations to maintain peace in the world's "trouble spots." The Charter, a plan put together by this organization, states that these peacekeepers have the authority to intervene and use force if necessary.   22._____
    A. OAS (Organization of American States)
    B. European Union
    C. World Court
    D. United Nations

"What harms the victim most is not the cruelty of the oppressor, but the silence of the bystander."

23. This quote from Elie Wiesel suggests that   23._____
    A. despotic states are usually in favor of civil rights
    B. other nations always need to denounce violation of human rights whenever they happen
    C. genocide is not something the United Nations should concern itself with
    D. protests against human rights violations are a waste of time

24. Many people have suggested that one major cause of the Syrian conflict is the fact   24._____
    that most Syrians are Sunni Muslims while many members of the government
    belong to which religious group?
    A. Alawite Muslim
    B. Christian
    C. Sunni Muslim
    D. Druze

25. If you were someone who believe in the "Just War Theory," which of the following   25._____
    would be a good reason for going to war?
    A. War profiteering
    B. Avenging your fallen soldiers
    C. Self-defense against an attack
    D. Conversion of infidels

KEY (CORRECT ANSWERS)

1. B	11. A	21. C
2. C	12. C	22. A
3. D	13. A	23. C
4. C	14. C	24. C
5. C	15. D	25. B
6. D	16. A	
7. A	17. A	
8. D	18. B	
9. C	19. A	
10. D	20. A	

TEST 3

DIRECTIONS: Each question or incomplete statement is followed by several suggested answers or completions. Select the one that BEST answers the question or completes the statement. *PRINT THE LETTER OF THE CORRECT ANSWER IN THE SPACE AT THE RIGHT.*

1. Which of the following countries was not allowed to send charitable organizations and aid to Syria?
    A. Iran
    B. Canada
    C. India
    D. Turkey

    1._____

2. Which anti-government movement was chosen to represent the Syrian opposition in Geneva for the peace talks?
    A. The Muslim Brotherhood
    B. The Syrian National Coalition
    C. The Syrian Islamic Front
    D. The Kurdish Supreme Committee

    2._____

3. Which of the following groups was first rumored and then later confirmed to be an Al Qaeda group operating in Syria?
    A. Jabhat al-Nusra
    B. Syria Martyrs' Brigade
    C. Kurdish Supreme Committee
    D. Syrian National Council

    3._____

4. Which of the following prominent Syrian politicians denounced his own government and went over to the opposition in August 2012, just as violence started to intensify.
    A. General Maher al-Assad, brother to President Bashar Al-Assad
    B. Riyad Hijab, Prime Minister
    C. Mohamed Gillati, Secretary of the Treasury
    D. Asma al-Assad, wife of President Bashar Al-Assad

    4._____

5. In the United States, Pearl Harbor is to World War II as 9/11 is to the
    A. Iraqi War
    B. War On Terror
    C. Afghanistan Conflict
    D. Egyptian uprising

    5._____

6. When the United Nations sent its final resolution to Saddam Hussein, giving him one final chance to comply to their sanctions, what did it name the resolution?
    A. Resolution Final Chance
    B. Resolution Final
    C. Resolution 54
    D. Resolution 1441

6._____

7. From start to finish, it took the United States armed forces _____ to gain control over Baghdad?
    A. 1 year   B. 10 weeks   C. 3 months   D. 3 weeks

7._____

8. In the minds of most people, the "War on Terror" and the "War on Drugs" are linked because terrorists and drug traffickers work with each other for a number of reasons. With that said, which of the following is not true of these two groups?
    A. Terrorist groups will sometimes offer training and weapons to drug lords in exchange for cash or capital to fund their efforts
    B. Each group learns the others' skills and methods
    C. Drug traffickers can learn about explosives, bombing and weapons from terrorists
    D. Terrorists and drug traffickers combine their skills to become counterfeiters

8._____

9. Which of the following principles adheres to the idea that war is morally permissible under stipulated conditions?
    A. Just Cause theory
    B. Just War theory
    C. Realistic pacifism
    D. Jus ad bellum

9._____

10. When the United States was exploring options for a disciplinary military strike against Syria, which country decided not to help the U.S. in this endeavor against Syrian president Bashar Al-Assad?
    A. Israel
    B. France
    C. Britain
    D. Canada

10._____

11. This term, used frequently in conflict analysis, is best described as a single key event that can set off or escalate a violent conflict.
    A. Structural cause
    B. Proximate cause
    C. Trigger
    D. Actor Caused event

11._____

12. Unconventional warfare is best illustrated in which of the following examples? 12._____
    A. Armed Force X meets Armed Force Y on a neutral site where no civilians can be hurt during fighting
    B. Country X manipulates economic power of Country Y resulting in hundreds of thousands of deaths in Country Y
    C. While occupying Country Y, Country X engages in conflict with rebels in Country Y's capital city
    D. All of the above are examples of conventional warfare

13. How did Bashar al-Assad become President of Syria? 13._____
    A. In an election where no one else was allowed to run
    B. In a coup he fought against his own father
    C. In the first democratic vote to take place in Syria
    D. In an election which saw him lose but the winner declined his bid to presidency

14. Of the following scenarios, which one would Al-Qaeda operatives be LEAST likely to adhere to? 14._____
    A. Long-range planning of several years prior to attack
    B. Conduct multiple attacks at the same time
    C. Frequent use of WMDs
    D. Flexibility, with a command structure not located in one country or city

15. Many terrorist groups that have been created and thrived in the 21st century can operate on three different levels at any one time. Which one of these is not a level that terrorists will operate at? 15._____
    A. Global level
    B. City level
    C. Regional level
    D. State level

16. During the Afghanistan conflict, this type of violence was preferred by enemy troops because it had the potential for a high death toll and extensive damage to properties. 16._____
    A. Bombing
    B. Kidnapping
    C. Direct Assault
    D. Air raids

17. According to the Commission for 9/11, the attacks cost approximately   17._____
    A. $450,000
    B. $1.25 million
    C. $150,000
    D. $25,000

18. In 2002, _____ became the appointed leader in Afghanistan.   18._____
    A. Osama bin Laden
    B. Lt. General John C. McColl
    C. Abdullah Abdullah
    D. Hamid Karzai

19. There have been five separate conflicts in this country's civil war, which is better   19._____
    known as the Balochistan conflict.
    A. India
    B. Mexico
    C. Egypt
    D. Pakistan

20. In April of 2009, which of the following "Balochistan conflict" events led to a   20._____
    surge in violent riots, work strikes and resistance from civilians?
    A. The government granted the Balochs their own autonomous state separate from the rest of the country
    B. The government was blamed for the capture and killing of Baloch National Movement President Ghulam Mohammed Baloch
    C. U.S. troops were responsible for a military strike that killed innocent civilians in the Balochistan region
    D. Government troops occupied the capital city in the Baloch province and civilians resented the occupation

21. Postmodern or nouveau terrorists differ from their earlier counterparts because they   21._____
    A. have no political agenda
    B. are atheists and therefore not politically motivated
    C. hold new-age and apocalyptic ideologies with system-level goals
    D. both "a" and "c"

22. This term is used to describe a group of terrorists that remain hidden and inactive in   22._____
    a country until they are called upon to carry out their mission.
    A. Undercover terrorism
    B. Sleeper cell
    C. Black Ops
    D. Latent cell

23. Following the attacks on the World Trade Center, the _____ granted federal agencies broader authority and power to fight against terrorists local and foreign. 23.____
    A. CIA
    B. FBI Act
    C. Department of Homeland Security
    D. The Patriot Act

24. Which of the following countries has seen the Balochistan conflict spill over its own borders? 24.____
    A. Iran
    B. Afghanistan
    C. Yemen
    D. Iraq

25. As of the beginning of 2014, approximately _____ Syrians had been displaced and turned into refugees? 25.____
    A. 22,500
    B. 800,000
    C. 2.5 million
    D. 1 million

KEY (CORRECT ANSWERS)

1. D	11. C	21. C
2. B	12. B	22. B
3. A	13. A	23. D
4. B	14. C	24. A
5. B	15. D	25. C
6. C	16. A	
7. D	17. A	
8. D	18. D	
9. A	19. D	
10. C	20. B	

TEST 4

DIRECTIONS: Each question or incomplete statement is followed by several suggested answers or completions. Select the one that BEST answers the question or completes the statement. *PRINT THE LETTER OF THE CORRECT ANSWER IN THE SPACE AT THE RIGHT.*

1. The government of which country is responsible for trying to overthrow the Chadian government in December 2005?
    A. Sudan
    B. Niger
    C. Cameroon
    D. Egypt

    1._____

2. If Country A never involves itself in warfare of any kind because its government and people believe war is never morally justified, that country believes strongly in which of the following theories?
    A. Negativism
    B. Theory of the Coward's War
    C. Just War
    D. Pacifism

    2._____

3. Since 1999, the Ivory Coast has seen how many civil wars fought within its borders?
    A. Four
    B. Zero
    C. Two
    D. Three

    3._____

4. Which country sent troops into Chad after rebel groups attempted to overthrow the Chadian government in February 2008?
    A. United States
    B. France
    C. Portugal
    D. Egypt

    4._____

5. During the Syrian Civil War, this opposition-held city was starved of medicine, food and water by the Syrian army in an attempt to root the rebels out?
    A. Tartus
    B. Qardaha
    C. Damascus
    D. Jableh

    5._____

2 (#4)

6. The Sudanese military has been accused of perpetrating genocide in which of its regions?
   A. Kurdufan
   B. Nuba
   C. South Sudan
   D. Darfur

6.____

7. The violence in Sudan's southern regions, which sparked a civil war, is thought to have started because of which of the following events?
   A. The Sudanese capital, Khartoum, was bombed by military officials
   B. A group of rebel Sudanese attacked government targets
   C. Civilians protested a new law that made army desertion a capital offense
   D. The Sudanese army accidentally killed 10 innocent civilians in a raid on a rebel stronghold

7.____

8. In the early part of 2011, presidents of _____ and _____ resigned because of protests and mounting social pressure.
   A. Egypt; Tunisia
   B. Iran; Syria
   C. Yemen; Saudi Arabia
   D. Sudan; Angola

8.____

9. The protesters that forced the presidents to resign in the above-mentioned countries claimed that all of the following needed to change EXCEPT
   A. greater civil rights
   B. cheaper taxes
   C. better fiscal opportunities
   D. an end to totalitarian governments

9.____

10. Which of the following is largely credited for the overall success of the protests held in the above-mentioned countries?
    A. Men and women set up extensive phone trees
    B. The protesters set up secret morse codes to organize when and where they would protest next
    C. Many of the demonstrators used the Internet and social media to bring awareness to the oppressive regimes in their respective countries
    D. There was no clear organization, which is why it was hard for the government to put a stop to the movement

10.____

11. Which of the following country's rebellion was later referred to as the "Jasmine revolution"?   11._____
    A. Egypt
    B. Yemen
    C. Bahrain
    D. Tunisia

12. How have governments in the Middle East and North Africa reacted to the Arab Spring?   12._____
    A. Improving government procedures
    B. Forcing leaders from power
    C. Viciously repressing activists
    D. All of the above

13. The Middle Eastern and North African political atmosphere prior to the Arab Spring BEST fits which of the following descriptions?   13._____
    A. A total absence of political parties; everyone could speak his or her own mind
    B. Illegal to belong to most political parties particularly those that countered governmental views
    C. Groups with various ideological backgrounds were filling the void left by normal political parties because of a lack of organization
    D. Countries usually had a two party system, much like the United States

14. Later known as the "Duékoué massacre," assailants were reported to have killed over 1,000 civilians in the town of Duékoué, during which of the following country's civil war?   14._____
    A. Cote D'Ivoire
    B. Ghana
    C. Liberia
    D. Senegal

15. Country A and Country B both feature moderate and open-minded democratic states. Despite this, they are arguing over land, which could lead to fighting and violence. Country A and Country B find a way to resolve the dispute without any blood being shed. This scenario helps prove which of the following democratic theories?   15._____
    A. Moderate democracies are peaceful by nature
    B. The system of balance of power works with moderate democracies
    C. Border countries almost never engage in warfare with one another
    D. Open-minded and liberal democracies do not engage in conflict with other countries of a similar mindset.

16. Of the following choices, which one is NOT an example of terrorism?
    A. Exposing civilians to harmful gases because they did not comply with government rules and regulations
    B. Manufacture of facts against a non-guilty party in order to imply blame on the individual
    C. Making threats against citizens so they will act according to the government's wishes
    D. Giving the "green light" to an assassination of government leaders by rebel groups

16._____

17. Of the following countries, only _____ has never been known to sanction government-sponsored terrorism.
    A. North Korea
    B. Cuba
    C. Lebanon
    D. China

17._____

18. One country wages war on another country because they fear that the other country will attack them. This is referred to as
    A. preventive
    B. secret
    C. imminent
    D. preemptive

18._____

19. In 21st-century conflict, one issue that has been more difficult than ever before is determining
    A. combatants and noncombatants
    B. hostile and non-hostile bombs
    C. where an attack will come from next
    D. none of the above

19._____

20. If a government has a "means-end" approach to warfare, which of the following would be permissible?
    A. Torturing a terrorist for information on his organization's hideout
    B. Bombing a village where suspected terrorists have been located
    C. Ordering a preemptive strike against a country before they can attack you
    D. All of the above

20._____

21. The physical or psychological attack on a person that ends up causing them to suffer, injury or possibly death, is usually referred to as
    A. realism
    B. acceptable violence
    C. violence
    D. torture

    21._____

22. Which of the following theories BEST explains the idea that moral standards cannot be applied to war zones and the war must only be judged on how well it serves the government's interests?
    A. Permissible ethics
    B. Political realism
    C. Pacifism
    D. Preventive warfare

    22._____

23. During bin Laden's famous videos, he gave several reasons for his *jihad* against the United States. Which of the following is NOT one of them?
    A. The United States did not try hard enough to support the Saudi Arabian government
    B. Non-Islamic and unethical Arabs are kept in power by the United States government
    C. The United States will not cease its friendship and support of Israel
    D. The United States' army in Saudi Arabia is offensive and inexcusable being so close to Mecca and Medina

    23._____

24. Political violence is BEST defined as
    A. The action or practice of inflicting severe pain on someone as a punishment or to force them to do or say something
    B. Physical force intended to hurt, damage or kill someone without compassion for misery
    C. Physical force intended to hurt, damage or kill someone that is permitted by law
    D. Physical force intended to hurt, damage or kill someone that is sanctioned by the state including things such as civil war, riots and strikes

    24._____

25. The phrase *Al Qaeda* means "The _____."
    A. Chosen Ones
    B. Masters
    C. Base
    D. True Believers

    25._____

KEY (CORRECT ANSWERS)

1. A	11. D	21. C
2. D	12. D	22. B
3. C	13. B	23. A
4. B	14. A	24. D
5. C	15. D	25. C
6. D	16. B	
7. B	17. D	
8. A	18. A	
9. B	19. A	
10. C	20. D	

EXAMINATION SECTION
TEST 1

DIRECTIONS: Each question or incomplete statement is followed by several suggested answers or completions. Select the one that BEST answers the question or completes the statement. *PRINT THE LETTER OF THE CORRECT ANSWER IN THE SPACE AT THE RIGHT*

1. The 2006 Israel-Hezbollah conflict began when
    A. Hezbollah fired rockets and mortars at Israeli military positions and border villages while another Hezbollah unit crossed the border and kidnapped two Israeli soldiers and killed three
    B. Hezbollah ground units launched a ground invasion on Israeli border towns and villages
    C. Israel launched massive airstrikes and artillery fire on the Lebanese civilian infrastructure
    D. Israel launched a ground invasion of southern Lebanon

    1._____

2. Which of the following was a member of the coalition forces during the 1991 Persian Gulf War?
    A. Israel   B. Austria   C. Bahrain   D. Iran

    2._____

3. By 2005, this nation was second to Saudi Arabia in the amount of oil reserves it contained.
    A. Kuwait   B. Russia   C. Iran   D. Canada

    3._____

4. In February of 2005, Israeli Prime Minister Ariel Sharon announced that in the summer, Israel would
    A. engage in formal peace negotiations with representatives of the Palestinian Authority
    B. unilaterally evacuate all Israeli civilians and settlements from the Gaza Strip
    C. double the number of Jewish settlements in the West Bank and the Gaza Strip
    D. hold a new round of parliamentary elections

    4._____

5. In an October 2005 speech, the leader of declared _____that Israel was a "disgraceful blot" that should be "wiped off the map."
    A. Syria
    B. Hezbollah
    C. Iran
    D. the Palestinian Authority

    5._____

6. In the year_____ after the collapse of the South Lebanon Army, Israel withdrew entirely from Lebanese territory.
    A. 1985   B. 1990   C. 2000   D. 2006

    6._____

7. In 2005, Israel established a hotline for instant communication with the government of _____, designed to aid in coordinating antiterrorism efforts.
    A. Egypt   B. India   C. Turkey   D. Iraq

    7._____

8. The first Muslim country to recognize Israel, in 1948, was
   A. Turkey
   B. Jordan
   C. Indonesia
   D. Lebanon

9. The primary reason for Mahmoud Abbas's emergence as a candidate for a more visible leadership role among Palestinians was
   A. his widespread popularity among Palestinians
   B. the ancst and imprisonment of his rival, Marwan Barghouti
   C. the refusal of Israel and the United States to negotiate with Yasser Arafat
   D. his role in negotiating the Oslo Accords

10. In 2006, the United States removed the nation of _____ from its list of state sponsors of terrorism, after it had ended support for armed groups and the development of weapons of mass destruction.
    A. Iran
    B. Iraq
    C. Syria
    D. Libya

11. The religious conflicts that have often plagued the Middle East reached a feverish level during the post-World War I "French Mandate" in
    A. Syria
    B. Iraq
    C. Lebanon
    D. Egypt

12. The first week of air conflict in the 1991 Persian Gulf War saw the escape of more than 150 Iraqi Air Force pilots into
    A. the West Bank
    B. Saudi Arabia
    C. Syria
    D. Iran

13. In August of 2006, in reaction to the Israel-Hezbollah conflict, the United Nations Security Council unanimously passed Resolution 1701. The resolution, which was later approved by both the Lebanese and Israeli governments, called for
    I. Israel to withdraw from Lebanese territory
    II. Hezbollah to completely disarm
    III. the deployment of Lebanese soldiers to southern Lebanon
    IV. Israel to release all Hezbollah prisoners

    The CORRECT answer is:
    A. I only
    B. I and II
    C. I, II and III
    D. I, II, III and IV

14. In 1968, the Palestinian Liberation Organization (PLO) launched its first cross-border attacks on Israel from
    A. southern Lebanon
    B. the Gaza Strip
    C. Golan Heights
    D. the West Bank

15. During the Lebanese Civil War of 1975-1990, _____ replaced Beirut as the Middle East's financial capital.
    A. Manama
    B. Doha
    C. Riyadh
    D. Cairo

16. Immediately after the U.S. assassination of Iraq's al-Qaeda leader, Abu Musab al-Zarqawi, world oil market responded with a   16.____
    A. drop in price
    B. rise in price
    C. brief shutdown due to extreme volatility
    D. long period of virtually no change in price

17. The 20th century Middle Eastern leaders Kemal Ataturk, Yasser Arafat, and David Ben-Gurion were similar in their   17.____
    A. desire to establish a Palestinian state
    B. secular forms of government
    C. strong nationalism
    D. statas as democratically elected leaders

18. The Palestinian Authority, the organization which has security and civilian control over urban Palestinian areas and civilian control over rural areas, was created by the   18.____
    A. 1979 Camp David Accords
    B. Madrid Conference of 1991
    C. 1993 Oslo Accords
    D. 1998 Wye River Memorandum

19. After Israel's complete withdrawal from Lebanese territory following the 2006 conflict, Hezbolla   19.____
    A. called for the complete elimination of the Israeli state
    B. withdrew from Southern Lebanon
    C. agreed to disarm according to a recent United Nations resolution
    D. launched retributive attacks against Lebanese villagers whom they accused of supporting Israel

20. The post-World War I conflict in Palestine can be attributed to each of the following, EXCEPT   20.____
    A. Zionism
    B. British imperialism
    C. Arab nationalism
    D. French interference

21. In 1998, Osama bin Laden and _____co-signed the fatwa that effectively declared war on the United States, its allies, and Israel.   21.____
    A. Mullah Mohammed Omar
    B. Ayman al-Zawahiri
    C. Mohammed Atta
    D. Abu Musab al-Zarqawi

22. In 1995, Israeli Prime Minister Yitzhak Rabin was assassinated by a(n)   22.____
    A. Syrian terrorist who had infiltrated a West Bank border crossing
    B. Palestinian suicide bomber
    C. Lebanese Christian militant
    D. Israeli extremist opposed to the concessions of the Oslo Accords

23. The international reaction to Iraq's 1990 invasion of Kuwait is most clearly an illustration of   23.____
    A. the influence of oil on international politics
    B. an increasingly pessimistic view on the part of Western nations about t e Middle East's ability to solve its own problems
    C. a lack of consensus among Western nations about how to deal with the Middle East
    D. the weakened resolve among European nations to deal with humanitarian crises outside of the West

24. September of 1970 is known to Arabs as "Black September" because it was when the   24.____
    PLO and thousands of Palestinians were expelled from the nation of _____ and moved to _____
    A. Syria; Jordan   C. Iraq; Syria
    B. Egypt; Jordan   D. Jordan; Lebanon

25. After Hamas won a majority of parliamentary seats in the 2006 Palestinian elections,   25.____
    Europe announced that future financial aid would be tied to the "Three Principles" outlined by the international community. Which of the following was NOT one of these principles?
    A. The renunciation of violence
    B. The renunciation of the "right of return" policy for Palestinian refugees
    C. The recognition of Israel's right to exist
    D. The expression of clear support for the Middle East peace process

26. Throughout the late 1980s and early 1990s, the stability of Egypt, Algeria, and Morocco   26.____
    was most clearly threatened by
    A. increasingly aggressive posturing by the fading Soviet Union
    B. an increasing income gap between rich and poor
    C. the economic reforms that were overtaking Eastern Europe
    D. a rise in Islamic fundamentalism

27. In 2004, as more details about Osama bin Laden and his al-Qaeda organization were   27.____
    revealed to the U.S. and its allies, it became known that the governments of_____ had provided the organization with financial aid in the mid- to late 1990s, in exchange for assurances that al Qaeda would not attack within their borders.
    A. Syria and Saudi Arabia
    B. Saudi Arabia and Pakistan
    C. Iran and Syria
    D. Pakistan and Iran

28. Between 2000 and 2004, Israeli Defense Forces discovered and destroyed about   28.____
    ninety tunnels between_____ and _____ that were used by Palestinian militants for the smuggling of weapons, ammunition, fugitives, and other materials.
    A. Syria; Golan Heights
    B. Jordan; the West Bank
    C. Syria; Lebanon
    D. Egypt; the Gaza Strip

29. The Arab Cooperation Council, formed in 1989, was effectively ended by   29.____
    A. Saddam Hussein's invasion of Kuwait
    B. the death of King Hussein of Jordan
    C. the first Intifada
    D. the September 11, 2001 terror attacks

30. Which of the following cities did NOT suffer a bombing attack from 2000-2005 that was attributed to the al-Qaeda terrorist organization?   30._____
    A. Istanbul   C. Beirut
    B. Amman   D. Madrid

31. One purpose of the United Nations sanctions that were imposed upon Iraq after the 1991 Persian Gulf War was to   31._____
    A. make conditions so unpleasant within Iraq that civilians would attempt a coup
    B. eradicate the opium crop in the northern mountains
    C. divide the nation into three spheres of Western influence
    D. force Saddam Hussein to destroy chemical weapons

32. The conflict between the Palestinians and Israelis can be said to be largely an after effect of the   32._____
    A. expulsion of Jews from Judea by the Emperor Hadrian in 135
    B. Balfour Declaration of 1917
    C. Sykes-Picot Agreement of 1916
    D. Marshall Plan of 1947

33. In response to the 2006 Israeli-Hezbollah conflict, each of the following nation's publicly asserted Israel's right to self-defense, EXCEPT   33._____
    A. Germany   C. United Kingdom
    B. France   D. Canada

34. Throughout the 1990s in Afghanistan, a series of internal changes occurred that could be most strongly correlated with the   34
    A. resurgence of Marxist ideology
    B. rise of Islamic fundamentalism
    C. increasing economic importance of the opium crop
    D. continuing influence of the Russian occupation

35. When Mahmoud Abbas ran for President of the Palestinian Authority in 2005, his platform contained the policy of   35._____
    I.   refusing to acknowledge terrorist and militant groups
    II.   the right of Palestinian refugees' return to Israel
    III. peaceful negotiation with Israel
    IV.   nonviolent achievement of Palestinian objectives

    The CORRECT answer is:
    A. I only
    B. II and III
    C. II, III and IV
    D. III and IV

36. The proximate cause of Israel's 1978 invasion of southern Lebanon was   36._____
    A. the murder of 37 Israelis following a bus hijacking by Fatah members
    B. cross-border and artillery fire from Hezbollah militants
    C. the death of 8 hostages and three Israeli soldiers during a PLO kidnapping at a Tel Aviv hotel
    D. a cross-border invasion by the South Lebanon Army

37. The 1979 Iranian Revolution established a(n)
    A. western-style democracy
    B. Islamic republic
    C. theocratic monarchy
    D. Islamist dictatorship

37.____

38. In 2004, following a series of bloody al-Qaeda bombing attacks on its own soil, the nation of _____ withdrew its ground forces from participation Operation Iraqi Freedom.
    A. Spain
    B. Italy
    C. France
    D. Japan

38.____

39. Throughout World War I, Habibullah Kahn, King of Afghanistan,
    A. publicly supported the Ottoman Empire but secretly aided the Allies
    B. joined the Allied Powers
    C. joined with the Central Powers
    D. maintained strict neutrality

39.____

40. The leader of Hezbollah during the 2006 Israeli-Hezbollah conflict was
    A. Hassan Nasrallah
    B. Ibrahim al-Amin
    C. Rafik Hariri
    D. Fouad Siniora

40.____

41. Which of the following two Middle Eastern nations have fought a 20th century war that killed more than 1 million people?
    A. Israel and Egypt
    B. Syria and Lebanon
    C. Afghanistan and Pakistan
    D. Iraq and Iran

41.____

42. Shortly after Mahmoud Ahmadinejad's election as President of Iran in July of 2005, allegations were published in the *Washington Times* and elsewhere that he had
    A. played a role in the 1979 occupation of the U.S. embassy in Tehran
    B. attended al-Qaeda training camps in Afghanistan
    C. provided material support to at least two terrorist organizations
    D. engaged in negotiations for the purchase of long-range missiles with at least one of the former Soviet republics

42.____

43. Saddam Hussein primary motivation for his 1980 invasion of Iran was that he
    A. hoped to loosen the Shah's grip on the region
    B. wanted to consolidate control of the Persian Gulf shipping lanes
    C. feared the spread of Iran's revolutionary zeal to Iraqi Shi'ites
    D. wanted to annex the nation's oil reserves

43.____

44. The Arab-Israeli conflicts from 1948 to 1973 could best be characterized as a struggle between
    A. Israeli technocrats and Arab traditionalists
    B. Arab nationalism and Jewish nationalism
    C. Islamic fundamentalism and Orthodox Judaism
    D. pan-Arabism and Arab appeasement

44.____

45. Saladin, the Muslim here of he crusades who was said to have been particularly admired   45._____
    by Osama bin Laden, was an ethnic
    A. Turk
    B. Arab
    C. Kurd
    D. Persian

46. The 1973 Arab-Israeli War led directly to the   46._____
    A. first Arab oil embargo
    B. first peace negotiations between Jordan and Israel
    C. Israeli occupation of the Sinai Peninsula
    D. end of the Egypt-Syria alliance

47. As of 2006, each of the following states or organizations had listed the entire organization   47._____
    of Hezbollah as a "terrorist organization," EXCEPT
    A. Australia
    B. the European Union
    C. Canada
    D. Netherlands

48. By 2006, about _____ percent of the world's daily oil production was carried on tankers that   48._____
    passed through the Strait of Hormuz.
    A. 70
    B. 50
    C. 25
    D. 10

49. The basic difference between Sunni and Shi'ite Islam can be summed up in the Shi'ite   49._____
    doctrine of the
    A. ulema
    B. jihad
    C. imamate
    D. sharia

50. In August of 1998, 257 people were killed and more than 4,000 wounded in simultaneous   50._____
    car bombings, carried out by the al-Qaeda network, at
    U.S. embassies in
    A. Kabul and Islamabad
    B. Khartoum and Cairo
    C. Sana'a and Riyadh
    D. Dar es Salaam and Nairobi

KEY (CORRECT ANSWERS)

1. E	26. D
2. C	27. D
3. D	28. D
4. A	29. A
5. A	30. C
6. E	31. B
7. D	32. B
8. C	33. D
9. D	34. A
10. B	35. C
11. A	36. B
12. D	37. C
13. C	38. D
14. C	39. A
15. C	40. D
16. B	41. D
17. B	42. C
18. D	43. B
19. B	44. B
20. C	45. A
21. C	46. A
22. C	47. D
23. C	48. B
24. B	49. D
25. D	50. A

TEST 2

DIRECTIONS: Each question or incomplete statement is followed by several suggested answers or completions. Select the one that BEST answers the question or completes the statement. *PRINT THE LETTER OF THE CORRECT ANSWER IN THE SPACE AT THE RIGHT*

1. At various times throughout history, racial and religious prejudices have been exploited for the purpose of
    A. expanding cultural diversity
    B. reinforcing nationalistic sentiments
    C. expanding international trade
    D. furthering the growth of fine arts

    1._____

2. The PRINCIPAL defense used by most Nazis tried at Nuremberg after World War II was that they had been
    A. following orders given by their superiors
    B. serving the good of humanity
    C. carrying out universal ethical principles
    D. reflecting the popular will of their society

    2._____

3. *The white man therefore has not only a stake in, and the right to the land which he has made into a modern industrial state from bare plains, empty valleys and isolated mountains, but according to all principles of morality it was his, is his, and must remain his.*
    The author of this statement is MOST likely a supporter of
    A. Socialism
    B. imperialism
    C. free trade zones
    D. cooperative communities

    3._____

4. Which problem has proved historically to be the MAJOR stumbling block to settlement of the Arab-Israeli conflict in the Middle East?
    A. Claims by both sides to the same territory
    B. Interference by outside religious groups
    C. Failure of the United Nations to become involved
    D. Desire of both sides to control the oil resources in the area

    4._____

5. *Despite all changes in the world, one key reality has remained unchanged: United States participation is still the indispensable condition for any stable and harmonious world order.*
    In this statement, President Nixon was advocating the policy of
    A. isolationism
    B. militarism
    C. internationalism
    D. imperialism

    5._____

6. Recognition by both the United States and the Soviet Union of their mutual ability to destroy the world had encouraged both nations at times to
    A. place greater emphasis on the United Nations as a peacemaker
    B. engage in direct combat with each other using conventional weapons
    C. seek ways of controlling the spread of nuclear weapons a
    D. place great emphasis on civil defense programs

    6._____

31

7. Which United States military involvement was a result of a Presidential order rather than a declaration of war by Congress?   7._____
    A. War of 1812
    B. Spanish-American War
    C. World War I
    D. Korean War

8. The Korean and Vietnam conflicts were similar in that both   8._____
    A. represented United States efforts to contain communism
    B. involved unilateral military action on the part of the United States
    C. brought the United States into direct military conflict with China
    D. were military defeats for the United States

9. The Gulf War was supported by all of the following countries EXCEPT   9._____
    A. Egypt
    B. Syria
    C. Jordan
    D. the United Arab Emirates

10. Domestic opposition to U.S. participation in the Gulf War was based primarily on   10._____
    A. sympathy for the Iraqi people
    B. lingering memories of the Vietnam War
    C. suspicions of U.S. motivations for an armed assault
    D. the apparent effectiveness of diplomacy and economic sanctions

11. In 1943, U.S. military leaders wanted to strike at the Axis forces in   11._____
    A. Africa
    B. Eastern Europe
    C. France
    D. Germany

12. During the conflict with the Huerta regime in Mexico, President Wilson used each of the following to bring resolution, EXCEPT   12._____
    A. economic sanctions
    B. refusal to recognize Huerta
    C. military invasion
    D. diplomacy

13. In effect, Nixon's policy of "Vietnamization" meant that   13._____
    A. eventually all U. S. involvement in the war would cease
    B. the U. S. military would focus its effort on South Vietnam and ignore developments in Cambodia and Laos
    C. the administration recognized the eventual fall of Saigon
    D. a South Vietnamese army would fight on the ground with the support of American aerial bombardment

14. Which of the following was NOT a reason for most Americans' support of the Allies over the Central Powers in World War I?   14._____
    A. The Allies' greater respect of U. S. neutrality rights
    B. Existing trade arrangements
    C. Historical and cultural ties to Britain and France
    D. Opinions presented by the American press

15. When England and France declared war on Germany in 1939, national polls indicated that about ___ percent of Americans were in favor of joining in the war effort   15.____
    A. 10
    B. 30
    C. 50
    D. 70

16. Which of the following international conflicts has most often been compared to America's military involvement in Vietnam?   16.____
    A. The Soviet Union's 1979 invasion of Afghanistan
    B. The Falklands War of 1982
    C. The Serbian invasion of Kosovo in 1990
    D. Rwanda's 1994 civil war

17. During his the 1968 campaign for the presidency Richard Nixon told the American electorate that   17.____
    A. his policy of "Vietnamization" would dramatically reduce America's role in the Vietnam War
    B. the Vietnam War was supported by a "great silent majority"
    C. he had a "secret plan" for ending the Vietnam War
    D. the United States must achieve "peace with honor" in Vietnam

18. In the United States, the first clear evidence of the Nazis' campaign to exterminate European Jews emerged in   18.____
    A. 1930
    B. 1940
    C. 1942
    D. 1944

19. Soon after the inauguration of George W. Bush, Jr., it became clear that the most dangerous threat to U. S. national security was   19.____
    A. a secretive global organization of individuals
    B. a resurgent China
    C. the rising powers of the Middle East
    D. unstable states in Eastern Europe and Asia in the wake of the Cold War

20. Once they had learned of German extermination of European Jews in Nazi death camps, the policy of Franklin Roosevelt's administration was that the best way to liberate these concentration camps was to   20.____
    A. selectively bomb the facilities that were used to kill prisoners
    B. achieve a total Allied victory
    C. open a second front so that the Soviet armies could penetrate and liberate from the east
    D. secretly infiltrate the camps and assassinate their leaders

21. Foreign policy successes for the Clinton administration included   21.____
    I.   the intervention in the Haitian crisis
    II. a peace agreement between Israeli and Palestinian leaders
    III. significant strides in the fight against international terrorism
    IV. the relief effort in Somalia

    A. I and II
    B. I, II and III
    C. II and III
    D. I, II, III and IV

22. In 1949, an American review of its Cold War foreign policy was necessitated by the
    I. fall of Chiang Kai-Shek's government to the Chinese Communists
    II. Soviet Union's test of its first atomic weapon
    III. formation of the Warsaw Pact
    IV. release of NSC-68

    A. I and II
    B. I, III and IV
    C. II and III
    D. I, II, III and IV

23. At the Yalta Conference of 1945, leaders of the U. S., Britain and the Soviet Union reached agreement upon
    I. the future government of Poland
    II. the ultimate fate of Germany
    III. a plan for a new international organization, the United Nations
    IV. Russia's entry into the war against Japan

    A. I and II
    B. II and III
    C. III and IV
    D. I, II, III and IV

24. Provisions of the 1978 Camp David accords included each of the following, EXCEPT
    A. future negotiation of Palestinian autonomy in the West Bank and Gaza Strip
    B. Israeli return of the Sinai peninsula to Egypt
    C. Egyptian recognition of Israeli statehood
    D. Israeli return of the Golan Heights to Syria

25. The most likely reason for the failure of the 1945 Potsdam Agreement is
    A. the exclusion of France from the process
    B. its vague wording and tentative provisions
    C. an over-emphasis on agriculture in rebuilding Germany
    D. the hard line it took toward Japan

26. The event most critical in forming the United States policy of "containment" was
    A. The Cuban missile crisis
    B. China's fall to Communism
    C. The Korean War
    D. The discovery of Ho Chi Minh's ties to the Soviet Union

27. Aftereffects of the 1956 Suez Crisis include
    I. the Eisenhower Doctrine
    II. the Six Day War
    III. containment
    IV. brinksmanship

    A. I and II
    B. II only
    C. II, III and IV
    D. I, II, III and IV

28. Franklin Roosevelt's initial response to Japanese aggression in South Asia was
    A. economic sanctions
    B. placing Pacific naval installations on alert
    C. diplomatic censure
    D. moving naval ships to Subic Bay in the Philippines

28._____

29. The first sign that Cold War tensions were relaxing between the USSR and the United States can MOST accurately said to have occurred during the presidency of

    A. Kennedy
    B. Nixon
    C. Carter
    D. Reagan

29._____

30. Throughout the early decades of the Cold War, American leaders tended to believe that
    A. communism everywhere was controlled by the Kremlin
    B. the fact that American communists existed proved that there were breaches in national security
    C. the Soviet Union was acting alone to effect a world revolution
    D. communism was a domestic policy that had nothing to do with foreign policy

30._____

31. The fundamental reason for Iraq's 1990 invasion of Kuwait was that
    A. it was suspected that Kuwait was pumping oil from reserves on Iraqi land
    B. Saddam Hussein needed a cause to divert public criticism away from himself
    C. it could not afford to repay the creditors who had financed its military buildup
    D. Kuwait was perceived as a constant threat to Iraqi sovereignty

31._____

32. The "new look" in American foreign policy under Eisenhower
    A. discarded the doctrine of containment
    B. endorsed a greater degree of isolationism
    C. rejected the idea that covert operations could be useful
    D. promoted Latin American autonomy

32._____

33. The Allied invasion of Italy in 1943
    A. was bitterly opposed by the Soviet Union
    B. resulted in a quick recapture of Rome and the Italian peninsula
    C. tied up an inordinate amount of Allied resources and was abandoned
    D. began on the island of Corsica

33._____

34. During the peace negotiations after World War I, the Allies could agree that
    A. Germany should pay war reparations
    B. a "war guilt" clause should be included to place blame for the war on Germany
    C. Wilson's Fourteen Points should be imposed
    D. Alsace and Lorraine should be restored to France

34._____

35. The Roosevelt Corollary was announced to ward off European intervention in

    A. the Dominican Republic
    B. Cuba
    C. Panama
    D. Venezuela

35._____

36. Woodrow Wilson's term "peace without victory" implied each of the following, EXCEPT
    A. an equal distribution of conquered territory and resources
    B. the Allied and Central powers should end the war immediately
    C. no nation should be blamed or punished for starting the war
    D. the formation of an international pact to prevent future armed conflicts

37. The 1920s case of Sacco and Vanzetti is most accurately described as
    A. widespread presumption of guilt caused by Red Scare hysteria
    B. a rejection of the idea of internationalism
    C. the beginning of organized U. S. intelligence
    D. the first clear evidence of Communism's threat to U. S. sovereignty

38. The purpose of Franklin Roosevelt's refusal to sell arms to countries in a state of war was to
    A. lure the USSR into the conflict
    B. protect the United States' stance of neutrality
    C. force a diplomatic resolution
    D. impede the expansion of fascism

39. The first sign that the United States was no longer "neutral" in World War II was the
    A. Lend-Lease Acts
    B. Atlantic Charter
    C. Japanese attack on Pearl Harbor
    D. revised Neutrality Act of 1937

40. Each of the following agencies was created out of the circumstances of the Cold War, EXCEPT the
    A. North Atlantic Treaty Organization
    B. National Security Council
    C. United Nations
    D. Central Intelligence Agency

41. The most important consideration at the Yalta Conference of 1945 seemed to be the
    A. territorial spheres of influence of the major powers
    B. punishment of Germany
    C. goals of the Atlantic Charter
    D. method by which European unity could be achieved

42. Each of the following was an event that precipitated the United States to declare war on Germany in 1917, EXCEPT the
    A. loss of seven U.S. merchant ships
    B. discovery of a secret pact between Germany and Mexico
    C. sinking of the Lusitania
    D. German resumption of unrestricted submarine warfare

43. The primary reason for the Allies' opening a second front against the German army in Europe was to
    A. capture the industrial Ruhr region and halt the German war-making machine
    B. liberate and join forces with France
    C. control the traffic of the Rhine River
    D. save the Soviet army from utter desolation

44. In World War I, the insurmountable barrier to genuine American neutrality proved to be 44._____
    A. the economic interdependence of America and the Allies
    B. divided loyalties among America's diverse immigrant populations
    C. secret treaties with certain Allied powers
    D. the British naval blockade

45. In the 1940 presidential campaign, Franklin Roosevelt supported 45._____
    A. war with Germany, but not Japan
    B. a declaration of war on all Axis powers
    C. economic aid to European democracies, but not military intervention
    D. continued U. S. neutrality

46. Eisenhower's response to the Suez War of 1956 was to 46._____
    A. throw U. S. support behind Britain and France
    B. proclaim U. S. neutrality
    C. denounce it as a violation of the principle of self-determination
    D. jointly express, with Soviet premier Krushchev, a desire for the cessation of hostilities

47. Which of the following was NOT an element of the 1941 Atlantic Charter? 47._____
    A. Embargoes on raw materials for Axis powers
    B. Opposition to territorial changes made without the consent of the people
    C. Freedom of the seas
    D. Disarmament of aggressor nations

48. The event which sparked student protests at Kent State University in Ohio during the Vietnam War was 48._____
    A. the reinstatement of the military draft
    B. President Nixon's public announcement that U. S. troops were invading Cambodia
    C. Nixon's "silent majority" speech
    D. the Tet Offensive

49. The "Eisenhower Doctrine" was a Cold War policy aimed at 49._____
    A. the Middle East
    B. Latin America
    C. Southeast Asia
    D. Africa

50. The first Cold War clash between eastern and western powers concerned 50._____
    A. the partitioning of Germany
    B. the governments of the Baltic states
    C. the government of Poland
    D. Hungary's national boundaries

KEY (CORRECT ANSWERS)

1. B	26. B
2. A	27. A
3. B	28. A
4. A	29. B
5. C	30. A
6. C	31. C
7. D	32. A
8. A	33. A
9. C	34. D
10. C	35. A
11. C	36. A
12. A	37. A
13. D	38. D
14. A	39. A
15. A	40. C
16. A	41. A
17. C	42. C
18. C	43. D
19. A	44. A
20. B	45. C
21. A	46. C
22. A	47. A
23. C	48. B
24. D	49. A
25. B	50. C

TEST 3

DIRECTIONS: Each question or incomplete statement is followed by several suggested answers or completions. Select the one that BEST answers the question or completes the statement. *PRINT THE LETTER OF THE CORRECT ANSWER IN THE SPACE AT THE RIGHT*

1. During World War I, African-American Soldiers
   A. were given full equality in the military under an Executive Order
   B. served in segregated units under white officers
   C. served in segregated units, but some were trained as officers
   D. were integrated into white units but treated badly by white soldiers and officers

1.____

2. Immediately after World War I, the most powerful navy in the world belonged to the
   A. United States   C. Britain
   B. Japan   D. Italy

2.____

3. During World War II, Admiral Chester Nimitz's strategy for winning the war in the Pacific was to
   A. launch an invasion of the Japanese mainland from a toehold in Okinawa
   B. force Japan's immediate surrender by dropping two atomic bombs on Hiroshima and Nagasaki
   C. bring Japan to its knees by seizing Tokyo
   D. take control of islands close enough to Japan to launch significant bombing raids

3.____

4. In World War I, which of the following events made the need for U.S. troops more urgent?
   A. Russia's surrender on the Eastern Front
   B. The use of mustard gas on the Western Front
   C. France's surrender on the Western Front
   D. The Arab revolt against the Ottoman Empire

4.____

5. U.S./Soviet relations deteriorated dramatically in 1980 after the Soviet Union invaded
   A. Czechoslovakia   C. Afghanistan
   B. Iran   D. Mongolia

5.____

6. The Treaty of Versailles of 1919 created the reborn state of
   A. Serbia   B. Belgium   C. Poland   D. Austria

6.____

7. Initially, President George W. Bush argued for the 2003 invasion of Iraq based on the
   I. allegation that Saddam Hussein possessed weapons of mass destruction that could be used in terrorist attacks against the United States
   II. allegation that Saddam Hussein had clear ties to the al-Qaeda organization that had carried out terrorist attacks in the United States
   III. idea that the Iraqi people deserved to be rid of the dictatorship of Saddam Hussein and practice democracy and self-determination
   IV. theory that the United States, by invading Iraq, could draw in Islamic terrorists from all around the Middle East to engage in a final and decisive battle

   A. I only
   B. I and II
   C. I, II and III
   D. I, II, III and IV

7.____

8. During World War II, the United States aided China directly by
    A. forcing open the Taiwan Strait by driving out the Japanese Navy
    B. sending ground troops to fight in Manchuria
    C. flying supplies over the Himalayas
    D. maintaining a stronghold at Hong Kong

9. During World War I, Congress passed the _____ Act, which gave the government authority to deport non-citizens who were suspected of subversion.
    A. Revenue
    B. Espionage
    C. Alien
    D. Sedition

10. The Cuban Missile Crisis of 1962 had the beneficial result that
    A. a Washington-Moscow hotline was installed
    B. many Soviet citizens began to take a disapproving view of their government
    C. creating numerous improvements in the U.S. civil-defense system
    D. greater legislative oversight of the CIA

11. In the early years of the Cold War, several labor unions were expelled from the _____ because of their alleged ties to communism.
    A. American Federation of Labor
    B. United Automobile Workers
    C. International Ladies Garment Workers Union
    D. Congress of Industrial Organizations

12. Conservative Republicans in the United States were against the Treaty of Versailles on the grounds that it
    A. limited U.S. sovereignty
    B. barred the Allies from seeking war reparations
    C. limited the U.S. role in maintaining world peace
    D. was a violation of Wilson's own Fourteen Points

13. President Eisenhower's "New Look" military placed an emphasis on
    A. air power and nuclear weapons
    B. overwhelming conventional ground forces
    C. forward-positioned Army bases
    D. United Nations-led peacekeeping forces

14. The foreign policy doctrine of "containment," drafted by George F. Kennan and employed by Harry S. Truman, depended on the idea that
    A. the Soviet Union was not powerful enough to spread communism beyond Eastern Europe
    B. the Soviet Union wanted to avoid an all-out war with the United States
    C. armed confrontation was the only means by which the spread of communism could be halted
    D. there wasn't a single nation in the Western Hemisphere whose people desired a communist government

15. Which of the following opposed American involvement in NATO? 15._____
    A. Robert Taft
    B. Dwight Eisenhower
    C. Douglas MacArthur
    D. George Kennan

16. The Treaty of Versailles of 1919 contained each of the following, EXCEPT 16._____
    A. restoration of Alsace-Lorraine to France
    B. a "war guilt clause" blaming the start of the war on Germany
    C. a provision for the creation of the League of Nations
    D. free trade among nations recovering from the war

17. Major features of President Nixon's foreign policy included 17._____
    I.   increasing but vigilant cooperation with the Soviet Union
    II. reduced military commitment to allies
    III. more engagement with China
    IV. support of military coups against leftist Latin American leaders
    A. I and III
    B. I, II and III
    C. III and IV
    D. I, II, III and IV

18. The Soviet Union built the Berlin Wall as a response to President _____ refusal to accede to Soviet demands. 18._____
    A. Truman's
    B. Eisenhower's
    C. Kennedy's
    D. Johnson's

19. In Woodrow Wilson's January 1917 address, he said the Allied Powers must achieve "peace without victory." By this, he meant 19._____
    A. a peace treaty should be assigned immediately, before any more blood was shed
    B. the relationship of victor/vanquished would leave lingering resentments in Europe that might result in another war
    C. the causes of the war should never be forgotten by those who fought
    D. no matter what measures had to be taken, the Allied Powers could not allow themselves to be defeated by the Central Powers

20. In 2001, President George W. Bush withdrew from the 1972 Anti-Ballistic Missile Treaty with Russia in order to 20._____
    A. re-arm submarines with surface-to-surface ballistic missiles
    B. expand the U.S. nuclear arsenal
    C. expand research on the "Star Wars" missile defense program
    D. reserve the possibility of using ballistic missiles against Afghanistan

21. World War II fighting in North Africa turned in the Allies favor at the Battle of 21._____
    A. Alexandria
    B. El Alamein
    C. Tobruk
    D. Casablanca

22. President Dwight Eisenhower's 1961 farewell address resounds today for its warning about the dangers of
    A. the expanding Soviet bloc
    B. a rising military-industrial complex
    C. the growth of the American counterculture! movement
    D. persistent racial tensions

23. Which of the following did the most to feed Americans' anxiety about Soviet nuclear power?
    A. The launch of *Sputnik*
    B. The "kitchen debates"
    C. News of Stalin's purges
    D. The U2 spy plane incident

24. In 1989, President George H. W. Bush ordered a military invasion and the capture of the dictator of
    A. Haiti
    B. Panama
    C. Grenada
    D. Nicaragua

25. The event of World War II that convinced Americans it was time to begin building up military strength was
    A. the German invasion of Poland in 1939
    B. Hitler's nonaggression pact with Stalin
    C. the fall of France in 1940
    D. Pearl Harbor

26. At the Yalta Conference of 1945, Roosevelt and Churchill unofficially accepted the postwar existence of a Soviet buffer zone that included each of the following, EXCEPT
    A. Estonia
    B. Poland
    C. Lithuania
    D. Czechoslovakia

27. The decline of George Bush, Sr.'s approval ratings toward the end of his administration was due to
    A. the fall of the Soviet Union
    B. a persistent recession
    C. revelations about the mysterious "Gulf War Syndrome" affecting U. S. soldiers
    D. revelations about his involvement in the Iran-Contra affair

28. Domestic opposition to U. S. participation in the Gulf War, which was considerable at the outset of the conflict, gradually fizzled out, mainly because
    A. the United States was winning the war with few casualties
    B. American leaders achieved a strong international consensus before attacking Iraq
    C. members of the news media were restricted to a more limited access to the uglier events of the war
    D. Saddam Hussein's vicious attacks against his own opposition forces were well-publicized

29. At the beginning of his presidency, Ronald Reagan's nuclear defense policy was guided by the principle of
    A. first-strike capability
    B. nuclear deterrence
    C. detente
    D. the Strategic Defense Initiative

29._____

30. In 1943, the Big Three met with Chiang Kai-Shek in Cairo and declared each of the following, EXCEPT that
    A. the war with Japan would continue until the Japanese surrendered unconditionally
    B. Japan would be stripped of all territory acquired since 1895
    C. Chiang's provisional government would administer the occupation of a defeated Japan
    D. Korea would eventually receive independence

30._____

31. The turning point for American public opinion against the Vietnam War was
    A. Buddhist monk Quang Duc's self-immolation in 1963
    B. the Tet Offensive of 1968
    C. the 1969 bombing of Cambodia
    D. Hanoi's spring offensive of 1973

31._____

32. In the fall of 1969, President Nixon reduced the number of draft calls issued to American citizens. His primary motivation for this was to
    A. head off anti-war demonstrations at colleges and universities
    B. demonstrate the effectiveness of "Vietnamization"
    C. direct more resources toward an aerial bombing campaign
    D. win congressional support for his domestic policies

32._____

33. Modern critics of the proposed Strategic Defense Initiative, first mentioned during the Reagan Administration, charge that it
    I.   is an outdated Cold War-era solution to a national security situation that has become much more complex
    II. is an unproven technology that has very little likelihood of achieving its purpose
    III. would be so exorbitantly expensive to implement that it would drain resources from other critical military and domestic programs
    IV. would upset the relatively stable state of international arms control that existed after the fall of the Soviet Union
    A. I only
    B. I, III and IV
    C. II and III
    D. I, II, III and IV

33._____

34. The American Cold War policy of the 1950s can be summed up by the term
    A. first strike
    B. liberation
    C. massive retaliation
    D. détente

34._____

35. Franklin Roosevelt used his "Four Freedoms" to promote
    A. the Lend-Lease Acts
    B. war with Japan
    C. U. S. neutrality
    D. New Deal legislation

35._____

36. The first geographic area to suffer from actual war in the 1930s was?
    A. Poland
    B. Manchuria
    C. Belgium
    D. the Philippines

37. The Women's Army Corps (WAC) was created during World War II, chiefly to
    A. boost the morale of male soldiers
    B. achieve complicity with existing civil rights quotas
    C. provide clerical support for military operations
    D. provide work for women who had been widowed by the war

38. Cold War anti-Americanism in Latin America resulted from each of the following factors, EXCEPT the
    A. tendency of U. S. leaders to support dictators rather than free elections
    B. American reputation for social inequality
    C. widespread belief in communist ideology
    D. dedication to national self-determination

39. "Operation Overlord" refers to the World War II
    A. Allied invasion of France
    B. Allied operation in North Africa
    C. postwar restructuring of the Middle East
    D. postwar reconstruction of Western Europe

40. During World War II, the U.S. government placed caps on each of the following, EXCEPT
    A. wages
    B. individual stock ownership in defense companies
    C. profits made by defense companies
    D. prices

41. During World War I, the primary motive for the war at sea was to
    A. capture and occupy overseas possessions and colonies
    B. impede enemy commerce
    C. destroy the enemy's navy
    D. slow troop transports

42. Britain's entry into World War I was a direct response to
    A. The German invasion of Belgium
    B. The German invasion of France
    C. the assassination of Archduke Ferdinand
    D. The Serbian invasion of Austria-Hungary

43. The main reason the United States refused to recognize Vietnamese independence in 1945 was because
    A. Ho Chi Minh had appropriated and distorted many of the revolutionary ideas of Thomas Jefferson
    B. President Roosevelt had promised France that its colonies would be restored after World War II
    C. Ho Chi Minh was an avowed communist
    D. Ho Chi Minh had collaborated with the Japanese in World War II

44. The 1973 Arab oil embargo was motivated by   44._____
    A. attempts at price control by U.S., British and Dutch petroleum companies
    B. U.S. support for Israel in the Yom Kippur War
    C. U.S price hikes on wheat exports
    D. U.S. support for the Shah of Iran

45. U.S. goals in the 1991 Persian Gulf War included   45._____
    I.   ejection of Iraqi troops from Kuwait
    II. protection of Saudi Arabian oil exports
    III. overthrow of Saddam Hussein's government
    IV. protecting Iraq from being infiltrated by Irani Shiite trouble makers
    A. I only
    B. I and II
    C. I, II and III
    D. I, II, III and IV

46. The Burke-Wadsworth Act of 1940 provided for   46._____
    A. a declaration of war against Germany and Italy
    B. a military buildup that included a draft
    C. aid to Britain and Russia in the form of war goods on a cash basis
    D. aid to Britain and Russia in the form of war goods on a lend-lease basis

47. The Kellogg-Briand Pact of 1928 was an international treaty that   47._____
    A. renounced war as an instrument of national policy
    B. warned Germany not to act on its surging nationalism
    C. condemned the spread of communism
    D. invoked the right of "collective defense" in proposing an pre-emptive attack on Germany

48. During World War II, African-Americans   48._____
    A. experienced a period of racial backlash in the South
    B. won greater access to housing and employment
    C. launched an unprecedented number of small businesses
    D. tended to migrate to northern cities

49. The most significant difference between World War I and World War II federal draft   49._____
    policies was that the
    A. World War I draft offered no exemptions
    B. World War I draft did not recognize conscientious objectors
    C. World War II draft extended to African-Americans
    D. World War II draft was implemented before the United States entered the war

50. The Iran Hostage Crisis of 1979 was directly sparked by   50._____
    A. the Ayatollah Khomeini's fundamentalist revolution
    B. the Soviet invasion of Afghanistan
    C. U.S. admittance of the former Shah of Iran for medical treatment
    D. the election of Ronald Reagan to the presidency

KEY (CORRECT ANSWERS)

1. C	26. D
2. C	27. B
3. D	28. A
4. A	29. B
5. C	30. C
6. C	31. B
7. B	32. A
8. C	33. D
9. C	34. C
10. A	35. A
11. D	36. B
12. A	37. C
13. A	38. D
14. B	39. A
15. A	40. B
16. D	41. B
17. D	42. A
18. C	43. C
19. B	44. B
20. C	45. B
21. B	46. B
22. B	47. A
23. A	48. D
24. B	49. D
25. C	50. C

TEST 4

DIRECTIONS: Each question or incomplete statement is followed by several suggested answers or completions. Select the one that BEST answers the question or completes the statement. *PRINT THE LETTER OF THE CORRECT ANSWER IN THE SPACE AT THE RIGHT*

1. Which of the following was NOT an element of President Eisenhower's policy toward the Middle East?
    A. Support for Britain and France during the Suez Crisis
    B. Use of the CIA to help stage the overthrow of Iranian leader Mohammed Mosaddeq
    C. Economic sanctions against Egypt for its relations with the Soviet Union
    D. The use of U.S. Marines to intervene in a Lebanese coup plot

1._____

2. One result of the Tet Offensive of 1968 was
    A. President Johnson's call for negotiations with North Vietnam
    B. the advice of the Joint Chiefs of Staff to withdraw all U.S. forces from South Vietnam
    C. tacit U.S. approval of the coup that overthrew South Vietnamese President Diem
    D. the fall of Saigon

2._____

3. The Carter Doctrine, announced during Jimmy Carter's 1980 State of the Union Address, proclaimed that the United States would intervene against Soviet aggression in
    A. Latin America and the Caribbean
    B. the Persian Gulf
    C. Southeast Asia
    D. India

3._____

4. The United States' initial belief regarding World War II was that
    A. it would be a short, limited war between a handful of European powers
    B. joining with the Allies would be a way to both fight off fascism and pull the American economy out of the Great Depression
    C. Americans should offer food and medical supplies to Britain, but no money or arms
    D. Americans should not risk provoking Germany by aiding Britain

4._____

5. Of the following, the most controversial response of the George W. Bush administration to the terrorist attacks of September 11, 2001 was to
    A. bar private planes from flying over Washington, D.C.
    B. sign the Homeland Security Act, which created the Department of Homeland Security
    C. approve of a secret domestic surveillance program by the National Security Agency
    D. invade Afghanistan to overthrow the Taliban government

5._____

6. The Stimson Doctrine, which was drafted in response to Japan's invasion of Manchuria in 1932, announced the U.S. policy of
    A. neutrality in the Japan-China conflict
    B. refusing to recognize any territorial changes that were the result of force
    C. arms sales on a cash-and-carry basis to any nation that had been invaded by an aggressor
    D. freezing the American assets of any nation that had aggressively invaded another

6._____

7. The 1957 launch of Sputnik was most directly responsible for the
   A. massive influx of U.S. federal aid to higher education
   B. U-2 incident
   C. Suez Crisis
   D. creation of the Polaris missile

8. In the Five-Power Treaty, or Washington Naval Treaty, of 1922, several world powers agreed to

   I. limit the total ship tonnage of their navies
   II. build no new naval bases
   III. make no improvements to specified existing naval bases
   IV. limit the number of guns carried by an aircraft carrier
   A. I only
   B. I and II
   C. III only
   D. I, II, III and IV

9. In response to Nazi persecution of Jews, the United States first acted decisively with the creation of the War Refugee Board in
   A. 1941
   B. 1942
   C. 1944
   D. 1945

10. At the Tehran Conference of 1943, the chief topic of discussion was
    A. how to divide up the defeated Japanese Empire
    B. the term's of Germany's surrender
    C. how to divide Germany into occupation zones
    D. the opening of a second front in Western Europe

11. "The policy of the United States to support free peoples who are resisting attempted subjugation by armed minorities or by outside pressures" was a direct expression of the
    A. SEATO alliance
    B. Truman Doctrine
    C. Monroe Doctrine
    D. NATO Pact

12. The Berlin Wall was built under Soviet auspices primarily for the purpose of
    A. stopping the "brain drain" from East to West
    B. isolating West Berliners so that they would begin to lobby for a unified Berlin
    C. keeping subversive elements from the West out of East Berlin
    D. provide a defensive palisade against Western Europe

13. The "shuttle diplomacy" of Secretary of State Henry Kissinger in 1975 persuaded
    A. both Israel and Egypt to accept a United Nations peacekeeping force in the Sinai Peninsula
    B. Egypt to recognize the Israeli state
    C. Israeli withdrawal from the Gaza Strip
    D. Israel to recognize an autonomous Palestinian state

14. Of the following countries, which emerged from World War I more powerful than it had been before the war? 14._____
    A. The Soviet Union
    B. Britain
    C. The United States
    D. China

15. John Foster Dulles' foreign policy of "brinkmanship" proposed that the United States should 15._____
    A. isolate opponents both geographically and diplomatically in order to stagnate them
    B. force concessions from the opposition by pushing dangerous situations to the limits of safety
    C. de-escalate threats by reaching diplomatic agreements
    D. build up and maintain military forces and weapons so that opponents would not attack in fear of a larger retaliation

16. The Truman Doctrine was first put into action in response to communist threats in 16._____
    A. Eastern Europe
    B. Germany
    C. Greece and Turkey
    D. Southeast Asia

17. Which of the following was a prominent critic of the Vietnam War in the early 1970s? 17._____
    A. Hubert Humphrey
    B. Edwin Meese
    C. Ronald Reagan
    D. J. William Fulbright

18. During World War II, U.S. and allied forces finally halted Japanese momentum in the Pacific in the Battle of 18._____
    A. Peleliu   C. Okinawa
    B. Tarawa   D. Midway

19. The Bush Doctrine that was used in part to rationalize the invasion of Iraq in 2003 was a departure from previous U.S. foreign policies in its emphasis on. 19._____
    A. containment
    B. fighting against a stateless enemy
    C. deterrence
    D. pre-emptive U.S. military action

20. American opposition to the Treaty of Versailles of 1919 was mostly centered on 20._____
    A. Wilson's inability to secure reparations payments for the United States
    B. its provisions for "collective security"
    C. the protection of French and British empires
    D. the "war guilt" clause

21. During the 1991 Gulf War, U.S. ground forces under General Norman Schwarzkopf forced Iraqi troops from Kuwait in about 21._____
    A. 48 hours
    B. one week
    C. two months
    D. six months

22. Throughout the administrations of Ronald Reagan and George H.W. Bush, an issue of growing public concern was the
    A. threat of war in the Middle East
    B. power vacuum being creating by a failing Soviet Union
    C. growth in the national debt
    D. deep cuts in social services

22.____

23. The most significant lesson of the Tet Offensive of 1968 in the Vietnam War was that
    A. the Viet Cong could launch attacks against major South Vietnamese cities
    B. U.S. forces had committed several atrocities against the people of South Vietnam
    C. the Viet Cong could never win a face-to-face engagement with an army backed by the United States
    D. U.S. air power could be used to "soften" targets for attack

23.____

24. Reasons for the failure of the 1961 Bay of Pigs invasion included the
    I. numerous shortcomings of the CIA's coordination
    II. underestimation of the will and tenacity of the Cuban army
    III. refusal of President Kennedy to authorize air support
    IV. advance warnings to the Cuban government by some Cuban-Americans

    A. I only
    B. I, II and III
    C. III only
    D. I, II, III, and IV

24.____

25. A major cause of the Cold War was the
    A. resolve of Eastern European states to remain neutral after World War II
    B. French defeat and withdrawal from Southeast Asia
    C. American "Red Scare" of the 1950s
    D. power vacuum created in Europe and Asia by the World War II defeats of Germany and Japan

25.____

26. The focal point of Osama bin Laden's grievance in his 1998 fatwa against the United States and its allies was that they were
    A. attempting to destroy Iraq, an Arab nation
    B. continuing to disenfranchise the Palestinians
    C. consuming the bulk of the world's oil resources and contributing to political instability in the Arab world
    D. effectively in control of Islam's holiest sites

26.____

27. The PLO was left without an Arab protector in 1970 when _____ died of a sudden heart attack. 27.____
    A. Hafez al-Assad
    B. Gamal Abdul Nasser
    C. King Hussein of Jordan
    D. Anwar Sadat

Questions 28-29.

DIRECTIONS: Questions 45 and 46 are to be answered on the basis of the statements of the speakers below and on your knowledge of social studies.

Speaker I: The United States should trade with any and all countries on a friendly basis, but should not take sides in other nations' disputes.

Speaker II: We should not get involved in any way with other nations.

Speaker III: We must bear any burden and pay any price to advance the cause of freedom.

Speaker IV: The United States cannot serve as policeman to the entire world. It is not within our ability to do so.

28. Which speaker's statement expresses a viewpoint that led to disputes among the United States, Germany, and Great Britain during the early part of World War I?
    A. I   B. II   C. III   D. IV

29. Which speaker expresses a viewpoint that gained new strength immediately after the Vietnam War?
    A. I   B. II   C. III   D. IV

30. Since Fidel Castro assumed control in 1959, many nations have considered Cuba a threat because the Castro regime
    A. overthrew a democratic Cuban government when taking control
    B. has seriously hindered trade among countries of the Western Hemisphere
    C. has supported revolutions in various parts of the world
    D. has refused to sell sugar or tobacco to industrialized

31. In January of 2006, in his first major policy address after becoming Acting Prime Minister of Israel, Ehud Olmert announced that
    I. Israel would have to relinquish parts of the West Bank in order to maintain its Jewish majority
    II. he supported the creation of a Palestinian state
    III. he would never negotiate with the Palestinian Authority as long as Hamas was involved in Palestinian government
    IV. Israel was in possession of a considerable nuclear arsenal

    A. I only
    B. I and II
    C. III only
    D. II, III and IV

32. The most significant issue in the 1956 war between Egypt and Israel was
    A. the Israeli occupation of the Gaza Strip
    B. the Israeli occupation of the Sinai Peninsula
    C. Palestinian right of return
    D. control of the Suez Canal

33. Following a September 1962 revolution, the Yemen Arab Republic became closely   33.____
    allied with and heavily dependent upon
    A. Muscat and Oman   C. Iraq
    B. Egypt   D. Saudi Arabia

34. Which of the following did Roosevelt and Churchill directly cede to Stalin at the 1945   34.____
    Yalta summit?
    A. Control over the reconstruction of western Berlin
    B. The annexation of Romania
    C. The establishment of socialist governments in the Baltic states
    D. The annexation of parts of eastern Poland

35. Which of the following Soviet cities was captured by the Germans during World War II?   35.____
    A. Stalingrad
    B. Leningrad
    C. Moscow
    D. Kiev

KEY (CORRECT ANSWERS)

1. A	8. D	15. B	22. C	29. D
2. A	9. C	16. C	23. A	30. C
3. B	10. D	17. D	24. B	31. B
4. D	11. B	18. D	25. D	32. D
5. C	12. A	19. D	26. D	33. D
6. B	13. A	20. B	27. B	34. C
7. A	14. C	21. B	28. A	35. D

EXAMINATION SECTION
TEST 1

DIRECTIONS: Each question or incomplete statement is followed by several suggested answers or completions. Select the one that BEST answers the question or completes the statement. *PRINT THE LETTER OF THE CORRECT ANSWER IN THE SPACE AT THE RIGHT.*

1. Generally, the point at which the Soviet population came closest to losing its resolve during the German invasion that began in 1941 was when
    - A. Stalingrad was all but destroyed
    - B. the Germans laid siege to Leningrad
    - C. the port of Odessa was lost
    - D. government leaders fled Moscow

    1._____

2. In the midst of his campaign against the Soviets, Hitler discovered that his offensive would not be a blitzkrieg but a protracted conflict: The primary reason for the slow progress was
    - A. the intense cold of the eastern climate
    - B. the diversion of German troops to the western front in France
    - C. difficulty in maintaining supply lines
    - D. lack of personnel

    2._____

3. In 1982, United States Secretary of State George Shultz outlined a set of conditions which the Soviet Union would be required to meet in order to establish better East-West relations. Which of the following was NOT one of these conditions?
    - A. North Vietnamese withdrawal from Cambodia
    - B. Relaxed tensions in Poland
    - C. Withdrawal of intermediate-range SS-20 missiles aimed at Western Europe targets
    - D. Soviet withdrawal from Afghanistan

    3._____

4. In the period from 1913-1914, which of the following happened FIRST?
    - A. Germany declared war on Russia and France
    - B. Serbia and Bulgaria declared war on each other
    - C. Britain declared war on Austria-Hungary and Germany
    - D. Austria-Hungary declared war on Serbia

    4._____

5. Approximately what percentage of Leningrad's population died during the German siege that lasted from 1941-1944?

    - A. 10
    - B. 25
    - C. 35
    - D. 50

    5._____

6. Which of the following issues was NOT on the agenda of the 1955 Geneva summit?
    - A. Recognition of Communist China
    - B. German reunification
    - C. Improvement of East-West relations
    - D. European security

    6._____

7. By the middle of 1965, relations between the United States and the Soviet Union had one again become strained, this time because of
   A. the escalation of United States involvement in the Vietnam conflict
   B. the Soviets' overtures to France, which had just withdrawn from NATO
   C. the deliberately slow pace at which Soviet missiles were being dismantled in Cube
   D. Soviet involvement in the India-Pakistan conflict

8. Which of the following Soviet Socialist Republics was created by Stalin at the close of War II, largely from land seized from Romania?
   A. Tajikistan   C. Bukovina
   B. Moldavia   D. Bessarabia

9. Which of the following factors contributed to the Bolsheviks' ability to remain in power after the October Revolution?
   I. An outreach to the aristocracy for token policy advice
   II. A type of totalitarianism that eliminated dissent and challenges
   III. Appropriation of the popular policies of their opponents
   IV. Better overall organization than their rivals

   The CORRECT answer is:
   A. I, III   C. II, III, IV
   B. I, II, IV   D. IV only

10. The *turning point* in the war between Germany and Russia that began in 1941, after which the Germans were mostly on the retreat, was the
    A. battle of Stalingrad   C. battle of Moscow
    B. siege of Leningrad   D. battle of Kursk

11. In the initial post-World War II period, each of the following countries had a genuine friendship with the Soviet Union EXCEPT
    A. Czechoslovakia   C. Bulgaria
    B. Romania   D. Yugoslavia

12. The event which most clearly brought an end to the detente process between the United States and the Soviet Union was the
    A. Soviet invasion of Czechoslovakia
    B. demise of the 1972 trade accord
    C. Soviet invasion of Afghanistan
    D. United States deployment of Pershing missiles throughout Western Europe

13. The result of the 1943 discovery of secret grave sites at Katyn, near Smolensk, was the
    A. recognition by the Allies that Jews were being exterminated by the Germans
    B. aggravation of hostilities between Poles and Russians
    C. Allies' granting of Russian annexation of much of eastern Poland
    D. initiation of the Nuremberg trials

14. Which of the following was NOT a member of the Warsaw Pact?
    A. Bulgaria
    B. Hungary
    C. Yugoslavia
    D. Czechoslovakia

15. One of the results of the Potsdam Conference of 1945 was to tacitly establish a fifth, occupation zone in Germany.
    A. Dutch
    B. Czechoslovakian
    C. Polish
    D. Canadian

    15._____

16. The driving force behind the failed coup against Gorbachev's government in 1991 were
    A. fiscal conservatives who believed an economic collapse was imminent
    B. laborers who could not imagine surviving the coming wave of price hikes
    C. liberals who supported Boris Yeltsin
    D. right-wing conservatives who did not want to see the end of the union

    16._____

17. After the Allies had lifted their blockade of the Soviet Union in 1920, the government agreed upon terms proposed by the British. Which of the following was NOT one of these terms?
    A. Repatriation of prisoners of war
    B. Bilateral access to agricultural exports
    C. An end to propaganda warfare
    D. Recognition in principle of debts to private individuals

    17._____

18. The moderate faction of the People's Democratic Party of Afghanistan, which was formed in 1965 and lost control over the Afghani government just prior to the Soviets' 1979 intervention, was the
    A. parcham
    B. hezbollah
    C. khalq
    D. mujahidin

    18._____

19. The effect of World War II on Soviet foreign policy could best be described as a concept of security that involved
    A. military superiority and a determination to fight offensive wars on enemy soil
    B. the rapid achievement of economic superiority and a retrenchment of Soviet borders
    C. the expansion of the Soviet empire and a focus on deterrence
    D. reaching out to defend the interests of ethnic Russian minorities in other countries

    19._____

20. During the India/Pakistan war of 1971, Russia offered military aid to India. Which of the following countries supported Pakistan?
    A. France
    B. The People's Republic of China
    C. Great Britain
    D. The United States

    20._____

21. At the 1943 meeting between Stalin, Churchill, and Roosevelt in Tehran, the most important issue for Stalin was
    A. the establishment of a western European front
    B. the post-war status of Germany
    C. a role in reconstruction
    D. the post-war status of Poland

    21._____

22. The Soviet Union did not veto the 1950 United Nations resolution condemning the North Korean invasion and authorizing military intervention because it
    A. wanted to maintain the pretense that it had known nothing of the invasion in advance
    B. was still exercising caution in light of Eisenhower's overt nuclear threats
    C. wanted to draw the western powers into an armed conflict in Asia
    D. was boycotting the Security Council over the U.N.'s exclusion of communist China

    22._____

23. In which Russian city did industrialists gain most from the World War I effort?   23.____
    A. Vladivostok
    B. Moscow
    C. Odessa
    D. Petrograd (St. Petersburg)

24. At the Yalta summit, Stalin's argument for a dominant Soviet role in postwar Eastern   24.____
    Europe was based on the
    A. fact that the Soviets had fought the Germans and suffered devastating losses
       long before the Allies established a European front
    B. ease with which lines of supply and control could be established through the
       western and southern Soviet cities
    C. cultural and political ties that the Soviet Union already shared with the ethnic
       populations of Eastern European territories
    D. Fact that the Soviet already occupied these areas

25. Which of the following Soviet satellite states publicly criticized the 1968 invasion of   25.____
    Czechoslovakia?
    A. Bulgaria   C. Albania
    B. Hungary   D. Yugoslavia

26. The chief irony of Soviet foreign policy during the 1920s and 1930s was that   26.____
    A. Russia's initial support of the Nazis in Germany was due to a desire for the spread
       of communism there
    B. while the Soviets worked for the eventual demise of capitalism, Moscow actively
       courted foreign investment in the Five-Year Plans
    C. all of its diplomatic relations were aimed entirely at Soviet security
    D. while it was looking to strengthen its borders to the west, China was advancing
       from the east

27. In the 1980s, the People's Republic of China claimed three obstacles that stood in the   27.____
    way of normalized Sino-Soviet relations. Which of the following was NOT one of these?
    The
    A. Soviet occupation of Afghanistan
    B. lack of reparations made to families of the downed KAL commercial airliner
    C. North Vietnamese occupation of Cambodia
    D. presence of Soviet troops along the Russian-Chinese border

28. In the early 1930s, Stalin's policy toward the German Hitler regime was shaped by each   28.____
    of the following factors EXCEPT
    A. the fear of seeing the Communists coming to power and building a more successful
       state in Germany
    B. the conviction that the Nazis were nationalists who were opposed to the Versailles
       system
    C. a fear of seeing capitalism become firmly established in Germany
    D. a hatred of the Social Democrats

29. In 1946, under intense Western pressure, the Soviet Union withdrew its forces from the   29.____
    nation of
    A. Turkey   C. Austria
    B. Iran   D. Czechoslovakia

30. The significance of the battle of Kursk, fought by the Germans and Russians in 1943, was that it
    A. enabled the Russian march to within 60 miles of Warsaw
    B. shattered the myth that the Germans were invincible in warm weather
    C. virtually destroyed the German air force
    D. was the largest infantry battle ever fought

    30.____

31. In the October Revolution of 1917, who planned and executed the actual coup that toppled the government?
    A. Martov
    B. Trotsky
    C. Stalin
    D. Lenin

    31.____

32. For what reason did the Japanese bring their attack on Mongolia to a sudden halt in 1939?
    A. Germany and the Soviet Union had just signed a non-aggression pact.
    B. It was clear that the offensive would fail.
    C. Soviet and Japanese diplomats had just agreed to the terms of a nonaggression pact.
    D. Hitler had just invaded Poland.

    32.____

33. In the summer of 1942, Hitler ordered an attack on the Soviet Union that was designed to Capture the
    A. Baltic states
    B. political and cultural regions in Moscow and Leningrad
    C. *breadbasket* of the Ukraine
    D. industrial regions to the south and eventually the Caucasus

    33.____

34. During the civil war that began in 1918 in Russia, troops from several nations were garrisoned on Russian territory. Which of the following countries did NOT station troops on Russian soil during this time?
    A. Japan
    B. Ottoman Empire
    C. Great Britain
    D. Italy

    34.____

35. The first serious Soviet-Japanese clash that occurred in the latter part of the 1930s occurred at
    A. Lake Khasan, south of Vladivostok
    B. the Khalkha River in Mongolia
    C. Changkufeng hill, south of Vladivostok
    D. the Manchurian border

    35.____

36. Which of the following was the last Soviet city or territory to be liberated from German control during World War II?
    A. Novgorod
    B. The Caucasus
    C. The Ukraine
    D. Odessa

    36.____

37. In 1939, the League of Nations formally condemned the Soviet Union for its aggression against
    A. Romania
    B. Estonia
    C. Finland
    D. Poland

    37.____

38. After the February Revolution of 1917, it was widely taken for granted among Russian revolutionaries that the new state would become a(n)
    A. autocracy
    B. republic
    C. proletarian dictatorship
    D. constitutional monarchy

    38.____

39. Which of the following nations withdrew from the Warsaw Pact in 1968?   39.____
    A. Romania   C. Albania
    B. Hungary   D. Czechoslovakia

40. Which of the following was NOT a reason for the strong resistance to the German   40.____
    invasions of western   Soviet territories in World War II?
    The
    A. devotion to the socialist cause and the Soviet government
    B. Germans' inhumane treatment of prisoners of war
    C. exploitation of the peasantry by the German invaders
    D. Germans' failure to address the political hopes of Soviet minorities

41. Although Russia was the more powerful nation, it lost the Russo-Japanese War of   41.____
    1904-1905. Which of the following was NOT a significant factor contributing to this loss?
    A. British support of the Japanese
    B. Greater popular support in Japan for the war effort
    C. Inadequate Russian infrastructure for material delivery eastward
    D. Japanese naval superiority

42. Which of the following was a result of the Cuban missile crisis?   42.____
    A. The erosion of Krushchev's support within the Communist Party
    B. An economic crisis in Cuba
    C. A loss of respect for Krushchev among Western leaders
    D. An improvement in Sino-Soviet relations

43. Which of the following countries invaded disputed Russian territory in 1920?   43.____
    A. Sweden   C. China
    B. Japan   D. Poland

44. For what reason was St. Petersburg renamed Petrograd during World War I?   44.____
    A. Russian leaders thought St. Petersburg was too Germanic in origin.
    B. The capital had been moved to Moscow.
    C. Lenin wanted to prepare the people for its eventual name, Leningrad.
    D. Leaders wanted to eliminate any implication of religiosity from the name.

45. The aftermath of the Russo-Japanese War (1904-1905) included each of the following   45.____
    conditions in Russia EXCEPT
    A. mounting popular demands for a legislative assembly
    B. an increase in taxation
    C. a surge of nationalist sentiment
    D. a weakening of the prestige of the tsar's government

46. During the Russian civil war of 1918-1920, which of the following countries sent soldiers   46.____
    to occupy Russian territory and aid the White armies?
    A. Japan
    B. Poland
    C. France
    D. The United States

47. The SALT I agreement of 1972, between the United States and the Soviet Union, included   47._____
    limitations on the
    I.   number of missile-carrying planes that could be constructed
    II. number of each nation's offensive nuclear weapons
    III. number of missile-carrying submarines that could be constructed
    IV. deployment of anti-ballistic missiles

    The CORRECT answer is:
    A. I, III
    B. II, IV
    C. II, III, IV
    D. I, IV

48. The unraveling of détente between the U.S. and the Soviet Union was duel to several factors,   48._____
    including the
    I.   Soviet invasion of Afghanistan
    II. perceived loss of U.S. power and prestige during the Iran hostage crisis
    III. election of Ronald Reagan to the U.S. presidency
    IV. circulation of Charter 77 in Czechoslovakia

    The CORRECT answer is:
    A. I and II
    B. I, II and III
    C. II and IV
    D. III and IV

49. Which of the following statements about the Russian Revolution of 1905 is TRUE?   49._____
    A. The most significant factor seemed to be a nationalist humiliation after the Russo-Japanese War.
    B. It resulted from the dissatisfactions of many different groups.
    C. After it was over, the Bolsheviks effectively controlled the government.
    D. It was almost entirely a rural, working-class movement.

50. Compared to the United States' worldwide system of alliances, the Soviet Unions   50._____
    Warsaw Pact
    A. later required membership from its former enemy states
    B. was strictly compulsory arrangement
    C. included nations from both the Eastern and Western hemispheres
    D. had extremely limited global power

KEY (CORRECT ANSWERS)

1. D	26. B
2. C	27. B
3. C	28. C
4. B	29. B
5. D	30. B
6. A	31. B
7. A	32. A
8. B	33. D
9. A	34. B
10. C	35. A
11. B	36. C
12. C	37. C
13. B	38. B
14. C	39. C
15. C	40. A
16. D	41. C
17. B	42. A
18. A	43. D
19. A	44. A
20. B	45. C
21. A	46. A
22. D	47. C
23. D	48. B
24. A	49. B
25. D	50. B

TEST 2

DIRECTIONS: Each question or incomplete statement is followed by several suggested answers or completions. Select the one that BEST answers the question or completes the statement. PRINT THE LETTER OF THE CORRECT ANSWER IN THE SPACE AT THE RIGHT.

1. When the Russian Revolution began, V.I. Lenin was about year of age.   1._____
   A. 25 B. 40 C. 50 D. 65

2. A major reason for the 1979 Soviet invasion of Afghanistan was   2._____
   A. the 1978 coup that overthrew the Afghan government
   B. the recent election of Jimmy Carter to the U.S. presidency
   C. a growing militancy within the Soviet Union's Muslim republics
   D. the desire for more oil revenues to fuel industrialization

3. Essentially, the Warsaw Pact was terminated by the   3._____
   A. formation of NATO
   B. collapse of the Eastern European communist governments in 1989
   C. reunification of Germany in 1990
   D. collapse of the Soviet Union in 1991

4. The event that prompted the formation of the Warsaw Pact was the NATO membership of   4._____
   A. Norway   C. Germany
   B. the United Kingdom   D. Denmark

5. The most important area of Cold War military competition between the Soviet Union and the United States involved the production of   5._____
   A. long-range nuclear missiles
   B. stealth bombers
   C. short-range nuclear missiles
   D. nuclear-armed submarines

6. The most negative aspect of the Cold War era in the Soviet Union was the   6._____
   A. economic sanctions of Western nations
   B. increasing reluctance to engage in international cooperation
   C. fear and discouragement of the general population
   D. conomic toll of maintaining the arms race

7. Each of the following occurred as a result of the end of the Cold War, EXCEPT the   7._____
   A. return of Moldova to Romania
   B. peaceable separation of the Czech Republic and Slovakia
   C. bloody collapse of Yugoslavia
   D. reunification of Germany

8. The Soviet Union was expelled from the League of Nations in December of 1939 because of its   8._____
   A. blockade of Berlin
   B. attack on Finland
   C. invasion of Poland
   D. signing of the Molotov-Ribbentrop Pact with Nazi Germany

9. During World War II, the Soviet Union seized control of the Far Eastern province of_____, which was incorporated into the Russian Soviet Federated Socialist Republic (SFSR).
    A. Mongolia
    B. Tanna-Tuva
    C. Sakha
    D. Tatarstan

10. The Soviet Union achieved superpower status in the period
    A. 1917-1928
    B. 1928-1939
    C. 1945-1985
    D. 1985-1992

11. Each of the following was an example of the Soviet Union attempting to expand its "sphere of influence" during the 1960s, EXCEPT the
    A. Berlin Wall
    B. Cuban Missile Crisis
    C. Six Day War of 1967
    D. principle of "peaceful coexistence"

12. The Soviet republics that generally led the others in pressing for independence from Moscow in the late 1980s were
    A. the Baltics
    B. large Central Asian republics
    C. in the Transcaucasus
    D. on the border with Central Europe

13. The main reason so many Asian and African nations followed a policy of nonalignment in the Cold War era was because they
    A. were working to establish their own democratic institutions
    B. wanted to receive aid from both the United States and the Soviet Union
    C. shared geopolitical goals with both the United States and the Soviet Union
    D. wanted foreign powers to stay out of their internal affairs

14. The first former Warsaw Pact member to join NATO was
    A. Hungary
    B. Poland
    C. the Czech Republic
    D. East Germany as a part of reunified Germany

15. Which of the following is LEAST likely to be considered a factor that contributed to the start of the Cold War?
    A. U.S. weakness at Yalta
    B. Rapid U.S. post-war military demobilization
    C. Soviet quest for spheres of influence
    D. Soviet pressures on the Yugoslavian regime

16. The major factor that led to the end of the Cold War was the
    A. low standard of living and quality of life in the Soviet Union compared to the West
    B. disorder caused by the democratization of the political system
    C. relationship of trust between Ronald Reagan and Mikhail Gorbachev
    D. irreversible decline in Soviet military power

17. In March of 1940, the Soviet Union established the Republic near the border of Finland in order to assert Soviet claims to Finnish land.
    A. Finno-Karelian Soviet Socialist
    B. Finnish Democratic
    C. Karelian Socialist
    D. Karelian Autonomous Soviet Socialist

18. The Soviet policy that caused the most severe escalation in Cold War tensions was the
    A. formation of "people's republics" in Eastern Europe
    B. dissemination of propaganda that blamed "imperialist" powers for international crises
    C. practice of espionage in the West that led to the buildup of its'on nuclear arsenal
    D. refusal to repay its obligations under the Lend-Lease Act

19. In 1990, the Soviet Union refused to recognize a reunited Germany as part of the
    A. International Nuclear Non-proliferation Treaty (NPT)
    B. NATO
    C. Warsaw Pact
    D. European Community

20. In 1939, the Soviet Union fought an undeclared border war with
    A. Japan
    B. India
    C. China
    D. Afghanistan

21. Which of the following was NOT a foreign policy change implemented by Mikhail Gorbachev?
    A. Satellite autonomy programs
    B. Disarmament programs
    C. Greater control of satellite nations
    D. Ddefense spending reductions

22. The root cause of the Soviet Union's resentment for the Allies' conduct of World War II was
    A. the slowness with which the Allies opened a second European front
    B. Stalin's exclusion from the Casablanca Conference
    C. U.S. exclusion of the Soviet Union from the Lend-Lease Act
    D. U.S. refusal to have official contact with a communist regime

23. Which of the following is considered to have been a major Soviet triumph over the United States during the Cold War?
    A. The Prague Spring
    B. The Cuban Missile Crisis
    C. The launch of Sputnik
    D. The response to the Hungarian rebellion

24. Each of the following is widely considered to be a contributing cause of the Cold War, EXCEPT
    A. Russian suspicion of the United Nations
    B. Russian distrust of Allied strategy in World War II
    C. Soviet resentment over its exclusion from postwar politics in Western Europe
    D. disagreements over the interpretation of the Yalta pact

25. During the Cold war, ethnic disputes became a threat to the stability of each of the following Soviet-bloc nations, EXCEPT
    A. Czechoslovakia
    B. East Germany
    C. Yugoslavia
    D. Romania

26. During World War I, two national groups within the Ottoman Empire openly aided the Allied powers. These were the
    A. Persians and Kurds
    B. Greeks and Arabs
    C. Arabs and Armenians
    D. Armenians and Kurds

27. The Sinai Peninsula extends between the gulfs of
    A. Suez and Aden
    B. Hormuz and Suez
    C. Aqabah and Suez
    D. Aqabah and Aden

28. Which of the following countries was NOT involved in the 1956 invasion of the Egyptian Sinai peninsula?
    A. United States
    B. Britain
    C. Israel
    D. France

29. The single most pervasive unifying factor in the Middle East is
    A. A the lack of reliable water resources
    B. common racial characteristics
    C. the Islamic civilization
    D. geography and environment

30. The purpose of the United Nations' Resolution 242, in 1967, was to compel
    A. Syria to acknowledge Israel's partial water rights to the Jordan River
    B. Egypt to allow Israeli navigation of the Strait of Tiran
    C. Israel to return the lands occupied during the Six Day War
    D. the Soviet Union to cease its arms sales to Egypt and Syria

31. Which of the following cities was seized by the British army before Turkish entry into World War I?
    A. Basrah
    B. Amman
    C. Jerusalem
    D. Baghdad

32. Under the mandate system imposed upon the Middle East by European countries after World War I, the British assumed the mandate for each of the following EXCEPT
    A. Iraq
    B. Syria
    C. Palestine
    D. Transjordan

33. Egypt's ability to conduct a successful war against Israel in 1967 was weakened in 1962 when Nasser committed to
    A. a full frontal assault across the Sinai
    B. a secret pact with Syria and Jordan
    C. deterring Saudi-financed royalists in Yemen
    D. a land-for-peace deal with Israel

    33._____

34. Henry Kissinger's efforts to establish peace following the 1973 Arab-Israeli War were hindered by each of the following factors EXCEPT
    A. U.S.-Soviet summit talks
    B. the Turkish invasion of Cyprus
    C. Sadat's refusal to discuss peace
    D. President Nixon's resignation

    34._____

35. During World War I, the Allied powers launched successful assaults in each of the following fronts in the Ottoman Empire EXCEPT
    A. Mesopotamia
    B. Palestine
    C. the Straits
    D. Syria

    35._____

36. What action did the United Nations undertake in 1949 regarding the Arab-Jewish conflict in Palestine?
    It
    A. recommended the partitioning of Palestine into separate Arab and Jewish states
    B. disarmed the militant Zionists
    C. divided Jerusalem between the Arab east and the Jewish west
    D. placed limits on Jewish immigration

    36._____

37. Which of the following is/are reasons for the diminishment of Britain's power in the post-World War II Middle East?
    I. The Cold War
    II. The U.S. sponsorship of Israel
    III. The Baghdad Pact
    A. I *only*
    B. II *only*
    C. I, II
    D. II, III

    37._____

38. The onset of the *intifada* in Israel in 1987 represented
    A. a sustained general uprising among the Arab populations in the West Bank and Gaza against Israeli occupation
    B. an effort organized by the PLO to bring international attention to the plight of Arabs in the occupied territories
    C. a carefully orchestrated terrorist campaign against Israeli occupation, organized and administered by groups such as Hamas
    D. the galvanizing of the Arab nations against Israeli aggression

    38._____

39. During World War I, British negotiations with Sharif Hussein, Prince of Mecca, resulted in Hussein's offer of assistance against the Turks in exchange for the British promise of
    A. an indefinite subsidy
    B. absolute Arab control over the Holy Lands
    C. unrestricted access through the Suez Canal
    D. an independent Arab state

    39._____

40. The reason for the Soviet Union's 1979 invasion of Afghanistan was to
    A. surround Iran for eventual conquest
    B. gain access to the Hindu Kush
    C. increase its oil reserves
    D. prop up a pro-Soviet government

40.____

41. Which of the following nations signed the international Non-Proliferation Treaty of 1968?
    I.   The Soviet Union
    II. France
    III. The United States
    IV. Spain
    V.   India

    The CORRECT answer is
    A. I, III   C. II, III, IV
    B. I, II, III, IV   D. I, II, V

41.____

42. The most likely purpose of the Allies' Balfour Declaration of 1917, backing the Zionists' claim to the Holy Land, was to
    A. strengthen the pro-Allied sentiments of influential Jews
    B. prepare for the post-war deportation of Jews from Western Europe
    C. strengthen alliances with Arab occupants of the Holy Lands
    D. win German Jewish support away from the Kaiser

42.____

43. Throughout the 1940s and 1950s, Gamal Abdul Nasser's popularity among Arabs grew, and he continued to espouse neutralist policies. Which of the following were consequences of this?
    I.   Egypt's relations with Western powers deteriorated.
    II. Israel began to regard Egypt as its biggest external threat.
    III. Egypt's relations with the Soviet Union deteriorated.

    The CORRECT answer is:
    A. I *only*   C. I, II
    B. II *only*   D. I, II, III

43.____

44. Upon Menachem Begin's assumption of the Israeli prime minister position in 1977, the Israeli policy toward its Arab neighbors was evidenced by
    A. accelerated settlement of all the occupied territories
    B. the return of East Jerusalem to Jordan in exchange for Israeli settlement in the West Bank
    C. the return of Golan Heights to Syria in exchange for water rights to the Jordan River
    D. the return of the Sinai to Egypt in exchange for bases in the Suez Canal zone

44.____

45. Though each of the following was a likely purpose of Israel's 1982 invasion of Beirut, only one was publicly Stated or acknowledged. This objective was to
    A. conclude a peace treaty with Lebanon
    B. clear all PLO forces from a 40-km area north of Israel, to put Israel out of range of PLO artillery
    C. arrange for the election of an Israeli-backed Lebanese president
    D. the full destruction of PLO leadership and infrastructure

45.____

46. At the outbreak of World War I in Europe, the great majority of influential leaders in Turkey wanted
    A. Ottoman neutrality in any further wars
    B. to remain neutral until it could be determined which side posed the greatest threat to Anatolia
    C. an Ottoman alliance with the Allied Powers
    D. an alliance with the Central Powers

46._____

47. During the Allied occupation of Iran during World War II, which of the allies wanted the southern provinces to be autonomous after the war?
    A. The Soviet Union
    B. Britain
    C. France
    D. The United States

47._____

48. The earliest roots of the Iran-Iraq war of the 1980s can be traced to
    A. longstanding border disputes
    B. political differences
    C. a desire for greater petroleum resources
    D. Sunni-Shi'a differences

48._____

49. Which of the following was NOT a member of the Central Powers alliance during World War I?
    A. Germany
    B. Iran
    C. The Ottoman Empire
    D. Austria-Hungary

49._____

50. Which of the following statements about Turkey in World War II is TRUE? It
    A. immediately declared its alliance with the Allies
    B. secretly allowed German transport of troops into Iran
    C. remained entirely neutral throughout
    D. declared war on Germany in 1945

50._____

KEY (CORRECT ANSWERS)

1. C
2. C
3. B
4. C
5. A

6. D
7. A
8. B
9. B
10. C

11. A
12. A
13. B
14. D
15. D

16. A
17. A
18. A
19. D
20. A

21. C
22. A
23. C
24. A
25. B

26. C
27. C
28. A
29. C
30. C

31. A
32. B
33. C
34. C
35. C

36. C
37. C
38. A
39. D
40. D

41. D
42. A
43. C
44. A
45. B

46. A
47. B
48. D
49. B
50. D

TEST 3

DIRECTIONS: Each question or incomplete statement is followed by several suggested answers or completions. Select the one that BEST answers the question or completes the statement. *PRINT THE LETTER OF THE CORRECT ANSWER IN THE SPACE AT THE RIGHT.*

1. Ronald Reagan's 1982 Arab-Israeli peace initiative was flatly rejected by the Israeli government of Menachem Begin, for the reason that the proposal
    A. would be discussed openly with the PLO
    B. deviated from the Camp David agreements by endorsing specific outcomes
    C. would not include King Hussein of Jordan, who was thought to be sympathetic to Israel
    D. called for the creation of an independent Palestine state

    1._____

2. In 1988, King Hussein of Jordan relinquished his country's claims to the West Bank and Gaza, which it had maintained since 1949. The feeling among U.S. and Israeli leaders was that
    A. at last the *intifada* in the West Bank and Gaza might come to an end
    B. the move was a blow because it meant a smaller role for Hussein in Middle East diplomacy
    C. Israel now had sole claim to the area
    D. Hussein was setting a peaceful precedent for the PLO

    2._____

3. At the outbreak of World War I, Zionist activities were centered in
    A. Russia
    B. France
    C. Germany
    D. Poland

    3._____

4. Which of the following was NOT a result of the 1982-1985 Israeli occupation of Lebanon? The
    A. installment of a pro-Israel president
    B. weakening of Syrian influence in Lebanon
    C. PLO retained political influence among Palestinians
    D. growth in strength of Shi'i forces in Beirut and south Lebanon

    4._____

5. During World War I, the Bolshevik Revolution in 1917 had the greatest effect on the_____ front.
    A. Straits
    B. Mesopotamian
    C. Palestine
    D. Caucasus

    5._____

6. The United Nations' Resolution 181, recommending the partitioning of Palestine into Jewish and Arab states, was adopted in
    A. 1939
    B. 1947
    C. 1949
    D. 1954

    6._____

7. Which of the following countries was NOT a participant in the 1955 anti-Soviet Baghdad Pact?
    A. Britain
    B. Turkey
    C. United States
    D. Iran

    7._____

69

8. 1954, the Soviet Union made its first successful Cold inroad in Middle Eastern affairs through arms sales to
   A. Turkey
   B. Iraq
   C. Iran
   D. Egypt

9. In the years following the 1967 Six-Day War, one of the most important new features of the Arab-Israeli conflict proved to be
   A. U.S. patronage of Israel
   B. the emergence of a Palestinian-based guerrilla movement
   C. an aggressive Israeli military philosophy
   D. Soviet patronage of Egypt and Syria

10. Which of the following did NOT exist in the Middle East at the outbreak of World War I?
    A. Iran was divided between Russian and French zones of interest.
    B. Great Britain completely dominated the southern and Persian Gulf coasts of the Arabian peninsula.
    C. The Ottoman Empire had shifted into the German sphere of influence.
    D. Egypt was in effect a British protectorate.

11. During World War II, the turning point that marked the beginning of an Axis decline in the Middle East was
    A. the removal of Egyptian prime minister Ali Maher from power
    B. the Allied recapture of Crete
    C. Rommel's defeat at the Battle of El Alamein
    D. the Allied occupation of Iran

12. Which of the following best describes the effect of the 1970 Soviet invasion of Afghanistan on Middle Eastern affairs?
    A. Soviet-Middle Eastern affairs deteriorated as many Gulf states moved toward a closer relationship with the United States.
    B. Many Middle Eastern terrorist groups launched attacks within Soviet territory, especially in Russia.
    C. With a larger Middle Eastern border, the Soviets expanded their influence through arm sales.
    D. Fear of the Soviets caused many leaders to steer clear of the appearance of close relations with the United States.

13. Iraq's invasion of Kuwait in 1990 was generally considered to be an international rather than a regional issue, for several reasons. Which of the following was NOT one of these reasons?
    A. Iraq's government had shown an appetite for conquest and military brutality.
    B. Iraq's chemical and biological weapons, and its attempts to acquire nuclear weapons, made it a longterm threat to the entire Middle East.
    C. The involvement of a Syrian or Libyan pro-Iraqi ally could seriously threaten the existence of Israel.
    D. Kuwait's importance to the world economy was greater

14. During World War I (1915), the Ottoman Empire ordered the transfer of all non-Muslims away from points of military concentration, and disarmed all non-Muslims in the military forces. The purpose of this order was to
    A. insulate the Ottoman forces from Allied spies
    B. rid the country of Armenian rebels
    C. dismantle the *millet* system
    D. stem the surge of German infiltration into Ottoman governmental matters

14._____

15. The Western world's contemporary perception of the Middle East appears to be dominated by certain common aspects. Which of the following is NOT one of these?
    A. The political tensions arising from the Arab-Israeli confrontation
    B. Enormous petroleum reserves
    C. A remarkable commercial crossroads between East and West
    D. Extremism among zealous Muslims, Jews, and Christian

15._____

16. Which Middle Eastern country suffered the most significant long-term effects from the Palestine disaster of the 1940s?
    A. Turkey
    B. Iraq
    C. Egypt
    D. Saudi Arabia

16.____

17. The basic idea behind the 1979 Camp David agreements was that
    A. Israel, Egypt, and Jordan would work together to establish an elected self-governing authority in the West Bank and Gaza
    B. Israel must find a way to withdraw from all occupied territories without endangering its security
    C. the United States would commit a small peacekeeping force to oversee the Israeli withdrawal from occupied territories
    D. Israel, Egypt, Jordan, and Syria would observe a cease-fire until the issue of Israeli occupation was settled diplomatically

17._____

18. The longer the 1981 cease-fire between Israel and the PLO lasted, the more it seemed to alarm Menachem Begin and the Israeli Government. Which of the following was NOT a reason for this?

    A. gave the PLO time to form cooperative defense treaties with countries such as Egypt and Syria
    B. enhanced Arafat's stature as a responsible political figure who could control his organization
    C. gave the PLO time to build up forces in Lebanon
    D. implied an indirect Israeli recognition of the PLO

18._____

19. Which of the following was the first Middle Eastern country to be admitted to the North Atlantic Treaty Organization (NATO)?
    A. Israel
    B. Iran
    C. Turkey
    D. Lebanon

19._____

20. Which of the following was an element or proposal of the 1982 Reagan Peace Initiative, offered to Israel and the Arabs?
The United States would
    A. exclude the PLO from participation in diplomatic discussions
    B. support the creation of an independent Palestinian state
    C. support government by the Palestinians in the occupied territories
    D. support further Israeli settlement in the occupied territories

21. The country that played the most significant role in provoking the 1967 Six-Day War was
    A. Syria
    B. Egypt
    C. Jordan
    D. Israel

22. 1973 the Organization of Arab Petroleum Exporting Countries (OAPEC) announced a general boycott of oil sales to the United States in response to
    A. U.S. support of U.N. Resolution 242
    B. the Camp David agreements
    C. evidence of U.S. military involvement in the Arab-Israeli War
    D. U.S. appropriations for an Israeli military arms package

23. The event that precipitated the 1956 invasion of the Sinai was Nasser's
    A. involvement of the Soviet Union in the Aswan dam project
    B. announcement of the nationalization of the Suez Canal Company
    C. announcement of support for Palestinian Arabs
    D. attack on British troops in the Canal Zone

24. Which of the following statements about *political* and *practical* Zionists is TRUE?
    A. Political Zionists sought to secure a Jewish homeland through the intervention of the Great Powers.
    B. Political Zionists believed that the new Jewish state would have to be entirely secular.
    C. Practical Zionists adhered to a strict code of nonviolence.
    D. Practical Zionists were determined to establish a presence in Palestine at any cost, and then find a way of establishing its legitimacy.

    The CORRECT answer is:
    A. I only
    B. I, III
    C. II, III
    D. I, IV

25. The 1969 *War of Attrition* was waged by
    A. Syria, against Israel over possession of the Golan
    B. the Soviet Union, against Afghanistan over Indian Ocean access
    C. Egypt, against Israel over possession of the Sinai
    D. Jordan, against Israel over possession of the West Bank

26. The purpose of the Treaty of London, signed in 1915, was into the Allied powers.
    A. Russia
    B. France
    C. Italy
    D. the United States

27. Which of the following was NOT a significant factor that led to the Iran-Iraq War? 27._____
    A. Conflicting Baathist and pan-Islamic ideologies
    B. Iranian claims to Kuwait
    C. Control of the Shatt al-Arab waterway
    D. Aid to Iraqi Kurds

28. Israel's objective for its 1978 invasion of Lebanon was to 28._____
    A. expel the PLO
    B. expand its Mediterranean coastline
    C. clear an area that would serve as a security zone
    D. capture Beirut

29. Each of the following was a condition that was imposed upon the resolution of the 1956 Suez Crisis EXCEPT 29._____
    A. a general peace treaty between Egypt and Israel
    B. the Israeli evacuation of the Sinai
    C. the Israeli right to navigate the Strait of Tiran
    D. the Israeli evacuation of Gaza

30. Toward the end of World War I, the Turkish war effort turned from a fight for territorial integrity and peace agreements to a fight for national survival. This turning point was marked most clearly by the Turkish response to the 30._____
    A. Gallipoli campaign
    B. Bolshevik publication of the secret Allied treaties and their division of Ottoman territory
    C. Arab revolt of 1916
    D. Russian invasion of the Caucasus

31. The 1942 movement to establish a pan-Arab state under the leadership of Ibn Saud was an ultimate failure, primarily because of the 31._____
    A. movement's failure to address the status of Palestinian Jews
    B. refusal of the Hashemites to be ruled by a Saudi
    C. Western world's low regard for Ibn Saud
    D. exclusion of Egypt

32. For what reason did Egypt become involved in the 1967 Six-Day War? 32._____
    A. Syria's and Jordan's challenge to assert its leadership in the Arab world
    B. Soviet encouragement
    C. The Israeli invasion of the Sinai
    D. Israeli harassment of ships in the Strait of Tiran

33. Except for the Roman Empire, which was governed from the outside, the major pre-modern empires in the Middle East centered successively in four focal points of power. Which of the following was NOT one of these? 33._____
    A. The Iranian Plateau
    B. Jerusalem and the Levant
    C. Mesopotamia
    D. The Nile Valley

34. Ottoman control in North Africa was effectively ended in 1911 with the 34._____
    A. Yemeni revolt
    B. Italian seizure of Libya
    C. second Balkan War
    D. assassination of Archduke Ferdinand

35. The Allied forces' reason for occupying Iran during World War II was
    A. the presence and unfriendly activities of Germans there
    B. Iranian support of imperial Japan
    C. the growing German dependence on Iranian oil
    D. Iran's known arms trade with the Germans

36. Which of the following countries supported Iraq in the Iran-Iraq War?
    A. Libya
    B. Syria
    C. Saudi Arabia
    D. Algeria

37. Throughout the late 20th century, the principal basis for the PLO's legitimacy has come from its
    A. military capability
    B. specific and often reiterated geographic claims
    C. broad range of international support as the institutional symbol of Palestinian nationalism
    D. its longtime acts of terrorist aggression against Western, Israeli, and Islamic civilians leading to appeasement of its nationalistic and political desires

38. Bulgaria was recruited as a member of the Central powers during World War I to
    A. divert Allied divisions from the German western front
    B. provide a direct line of communication between the Central powers and the Ottoman territory
    C. blunt the threat of Greek nationalists to the west of the Ottoman Empire
    D. guard the Dardanelles

39. Which of the following did NOT prove to be a difference between Anwar Sadat and his predecessor, Gamal Abdul Nasser?
    Sadat
    A. was more focused on pan-Arabian interests than on purely Egyptian matters
    B. had a less dynamic personality
    C. was less ideological
    D. had a more relaxed leadership style

40. In the first three decades following the breakup of the Ottoman Empire in 1918, which of the following states of the Arab East was fully independent?
    A. Iraq
    B. Yemen
    C. Bahrain
    D. Iran

41. Of the following Arab-Israeli issues, which existed BEFORE the 1967 Six-Day War?
    The
    A. return of the Sinai peninsula to Egypt
    B. final settlement of Israel's borders
    C. status of Jerusalem
    D. return of the Golan Heights to Syria

42. In the peace agreements following World War I, the city of Constantinople was initially placed under_____control.
    A. Italian
    B. Turkish
    C. Russian
    D. British

43. The Free Officers of Egypt, led by Mohammad Neguib and Nasser, had each of the following ideas at the core of their 1952 revolution EXCEPT
    A. eliminating the power of the landlords
    B. ridding the country of British influence
    C. establishing a representative democracy
    D. ending the corruption of political life

44. Because it distracted many British troops from the war effort for several years, the most significant Ottoman military contribution to the Central powers' effort during World War I was the campaign in
    A. the Caucasus
    B. upper Mesopotamia
    C. the Dardanelles
    D. the Sinai

45. After World War II had ended, the Soviets wanted certain conditions met before their withdrawal from Iran. Which of the following were included in these demands?
    I. The creation of an Irano-Soviet Oil Company with 51% Soviet ownership
    II. A peaceful Irani settlement with the Azerbaijan and Kurdish movements
    III. The rejection of any diplomatic relations with Britain

    The CORRECT answer is:
    A. I only
    B. II only
    C. I, II
    D. II, III

46. After the outbreak of the 1973 Arab-Israeli War, Israel's strategy regarding Syria became
    A. to consolidate its forces at the Golan Heights summit
    B. the conquest of Damascus
    C. the cession of part of the Golan Heights
    D. a full retreat from the Golan Heights

47. The last French soldiers to withdraw from the Levant departed in
    A. 1024
    B. 1939
    C. 1946
    D. 1967

48. The PRIMARY goal of the Palestinian Liberation Organization (PLO) has been to
    A. establish a home state for Palestinian Arabs
    B. eliminate communist influence in the Arab nations
    C. bring about a peaceful settlement of the conflicts between Egypt and Palestinian Arabs
    D. control the Organization of Petroleum Exporting Countries (OPEC)

49. In the 1980's, the MAJOR ostensible source of the conflict between Israel and Palestinian Arabs was
    A. the presence of Israeli ships in the Suez Canal
    B. the interference of Libya in Middle Eastern affairs
    C. the demand of Palestinian Arabs for their own homeland
    D. Soviet support of radical Arab groups in occupied territories

50. A common goal of both Zionists and Palestinian Arabs in the Middle East was to
    A. unite the Middle East under their religion
    B. improve their relations with the Soviet Union
    C. become leaders in the world economy
    D. have their own independent country

KEY (CORRECT ANSWERS)

1. B
2. B
3. C
4. B
5. D
6. B
7. C
8. D
9. B
10. A
11. C
12. A
13. C
14. B
15. C
16. C
17. A
18. A
19. C
20. A
21. B
22. D
23. B
24. D
25. C
26. C
27. B
28. C
29. A
30. B
31. B
32. A
33. B
34. B
35. A
36. C
37. D
38. B
39. A
40. B
41. B
42. C
43. C
44. D
45. C
46. B
47. C
48. A
49. C
50. D

TEST 4

DIRECTIONS: Each question or incomplete statement is followed by several suggested answers or completions. Select the one that BEST answers the question or completes the statement. *PRINT THE LETTER OF THE CORRECT ANSWER IN THE SPACE AT THE RIGHT.*

1. Which statement BEST describes the Middle East during the 1980's?   1._____
   A. Palestinians in the occupied territories wanted greater integration into Israeli society.
   B. The nations of the Middle East adopted a common foreign policy.
   C. Arab unity had not been achieved.
   D. International cooperation brought about an era of peace.

2. Which statement BEST explains why Great Britain and France joined Israel in attacking Egypt when Egypt nationalized the Suez Canal in 1956?   2._____
   A. The European nations wanted control of the oil fields around the Suez Canal.
   B. The Suez Canal was an important link between European nations and their Asian trading partners.
   C. Great Britain and France were allies of Israel, which had originally controlled the Suez Canal.
   D. Seizure of the Suez Canal indicated Egypt's rejection of democratic principles.

3. In the Middle East, and IMMEDIATE effect of World War I was the   3._____
   A. unification of Arab countries against the League of Nations
   B. division of large sections of the area among the Allies
   C. revival of Islamic fundamentalism in Arab nations
   D. creation of the state of Israel

4. The LARGEST producer of oil in the Middle East is   4._____
   A. Saudi Arabia
   B. Kuwait
   C. Iran
   D. Iraq

5. One result of the Suez Canal Crisis of 1956 was   5._____
   A. a decision by the United Nations to use a police force to restore order
   B. rejection by the United States of Nasser's request for funds to construct the Aswan Dam
   C. a Paris summit conference to improve East-West relations
   D. increased solidarity among members of the North Atlantic Treaty Organization

6. Which of the following countries share a disputed border area?   6._____
   A. Afghanistan-Pakistan
   B. Iraq-Soviet Union
   C. Iran-Syria
   D. Turkey-U.S.S.R.

7. The Middle East, with its wealth of oil deposits,   7._____
   A. is hampered by the scarcity of cultivable land in the area
   B. is self-sufficient with respect to coal and iron
   C. is considered potentially capable of industrial development comparable to that of Western Europe
   D. has surpassed the United States as the world's leading oil production region

8. Of the following, the motive MOST responsible for Iraq's attack on Iran was Iraq's desire for control of the
    A. oil fields of eastern Iran
    B. Shatt at Arab
    C. strategic mountain passes in Northern Iran
    D. southern Persian Gulf oil routes

8.____

9. Of the following, the MAJOR cause of the current lack of unity among the Arab nations of the Middle East is
    A. their language differences
    B. the interference of major world powers
    C. nomadic tribal allegiances
    D. historic conflicting economic and political interests

9.____

10. An IMPORTANT consequence of the war between Iraq and Iran has been that
    A. Iraq has gained control of the strategic Shatt al Arab
    B. the standard of living of the people of Iraq has suffered greatly
    C. Iran is facing immediate economic collapse
    D. the combined oil production of Iran and Iraq has been cut about 50%

10.____

11. Arab objections to the 1977 Israeli-Egyptian peace settlement have centered chiefly on the status of
    A. the Sinai Peninsula
    B. the Suez Canal
    C. the West Bank
    D. West Jerusalem

11.____

12. Which problem has proved historically to be the MAJOR stumbling block to settlement of the Arab-Israeli conflict in the Middle East?
    A. Claims by both sides to the same territory
    B. Interference by outside religious groups
    C. Failure of the United Nations to become involved
    D. Desire of both sides to control the oil resources in the area

12.____

13. The Gulf war was supported by all of the following countries EXCEPT
    A. Egypt
    B. Syria
    C. Jordan
    D. the United Arab Emirates

13.____

14. The term "Intifada" refers to
    I. the 1987-1993 uprising by Palestinians against Israeli occupation in the West Bank and Gaza Strip
    II. the Palestinian uprising that began after September 20, 2000, after the visit of the Israeli right-wing politician Ariel Sharon to the holy site known (to Jews) as the Temple Mount or (to Arabs) the Harame sh-Sherif
    III. a holy war undertaken as a sacred duty by Muslims
    IV. any action undertaken by Muslims to expel an oppressive or imperial occupying force
    A. I only
    B. I and II
    C. II only
    D. I, II, III and IV

14.____

15. From 1917 to 1920, when it occupied Palestine, Britain tried to reconcile the conflicting aspirations of Zionism and Arabism by facilitating discussions between Amir Faisal and the Zionist Chaim Weizmann. Elements of their 1919 agreement included 15._____
    I. Arab recognition of the Balfour Declaration, allowing Jewish immigration
    II. British recognition of the independence of the Greater Syria
    III. Jewish/Arab cooperation in the economic development of Palestine
    IV. the establishment of a Jewish state in Palestine
    A. I and II
    B. I, II and III
    C. II and III
    D. I; II, III and IV

16. In the early 21st century, armed conflict between Islamic fundamentalists and other groups have destabilized governments in each of the following countries EXCEPT 16._____
    A. Turkey
    B. Yemen
    C. Algeria
    D. Jordan

17. The first Middle Eastern states to be drawn into the Cold War rivalry that followed World War II were 17._____
    A. Egypt and Iran
    B. Turkey and Syria
    C. Turkey and Iran
    D. Iran and Iraq

18. The conflict in Palestine, which began during World War I, was rooted in each of the following EXCEPT 18._____
    A. Zionism
    B. French colonialism
    C. British imperialism
    D. Arab nationalism

19. The reason for Israel's 1982 invasion of Lebanon was that 19._____
    A. it was a haven for armed factions of the Palestinian Liberation Organization
    B. it was a virtual protectorate, under Syrian control
    C. the Lebanese government was growing stronger and more threatening
    D. Hezbollah guerillas were making persistent attacks on Israeli border towns

20. Britain's willingness to favor the establishment of a Jewish national home in Palestine, expressed in the Balfour Declaration of 1917, was influenced by a desire to 20._____
    A. live up to the agreements established in the McMahon-Husayn correspondence
    B. punish the Ottomans for World War I
    C. control southern Iraq
    D. control the territory adjacent to the Suez Canal

21. Suleyman I's Ottoman Empire contained each of the following ethnic groups, EXCEPT 21._____
    A. Tatars
    B. Armenians
    C. Russians
    D. Magyars

22. After the 1990 Persian Gulf War, Iraq used environmental warfare to retaliate against two ethnic groups who had resisted the rule of Saddam Hussein. These groups were the
    A. Kuwaitis and Saudis
    B. Sunnis and Shi'as
    C. Kurds and Shi'as
    D. Kurds and Assyrians

23. The first Israeli prime minister who was publicly committed to the annexation of the West Bank and Gaza Strip was
    A. Menachem Begin
    B. Yitzhak Shamir
    C. David Ben-Gurion
    D. Golda Meir

24. Each of the following participated in the Arab-Israeli War of 1948-49 EXCEPT
    A. Iraq
    B. Lebanon
    C. Syria
    D. Egypt

25. The most significant effect of World War I on the Arab world was to
    A. provide the Arabs with a common goal jihad against the Western world
    B. signal the end of European colonial ambitions in the Middle East
    C. break apart the presumed unity that Arabs had felt under Ottoman rule
    D. led directly to the establishment of an Israeli state

26. Saddam Hussein's armed invasion of Iran in 1980 was backed by every Arab country in the world, except Syria. Syria's opposition to the invasion was rooted in Hafez al-Assad's
    A. view that the Khomeini government was a protest against the United States and Israel
    B. fear that if the invasion of Iran was successful, Hussein's ambitions might grow to include Syria
    C. longstanding feud with King Hussein of Jordan
    D. sense that the invasion was a violation of Iran's right to self-determination

27. In the post-World War I era, as Kemal Ataturk attempted a rebellion against the legally constituted government in Istanbul, the event that did the most to unify the resistance forces was the
    A. Greek invasion of Anatolia
    B. signing of the Treaty of Sevres
    C. dismissal of Kemal from the military
    D. loss of the Levantine provinces

28. The "June War" of 1967 resulted in
    I. the Egyptians being driven from the Sinai Peninsula
    II. Jordan retreating across the Jordan River, abandoning the West Bank
    III. Syrian cession of the Golan Heights to Israel
    A. the closure of the Suez Canal for the next eight years I and II
    B. I, II and III
    C. II and III
    D. I, II, III and IV

29. British military strategy in the Middle East during World War I was shaped by the need to
    I. protect the oil fields of Iran
    II. defend the approaches to India
    III. penetrate the Dardanelles and threaten Istanbul
    IV. ward off Syrian attempts to control the Suez Canal
    A. I and it
    B. I, II and IV
    C. II and III
    D. I, II, III and IV

29._____

30. Traditionally, Pakistan has maintained an informal alliance with
    A. the United States
    B. Afghanistan
    C. China
    D. Iran

30._____

31. In November of 1947, the General Assembly of the United Nations voted on the proposal of its Special Committee on Palestine (UNSCOP), that recommended the partition of Palestine into two states, one Arab and one Jewish, with Jerusalem designated an international district. Which of the following nations voted AGAINST the proposal?
    A. India
    B. United States
    C. China
    D. Soviet Union

31._____

32. The Arab revolt against Ottoman rule in 1916 is most accurately characterized as a
    A. broad-based, pan-Arab response
    B. Bedouin movement that gathered support as it achieved success
    C. Hashemite-dominated enterprise relying on tribal loyalties
    D. doomed effort fueled by French deceptions

32._____

33. During the 1991 Persian Gulf War, Iraq launched missiles against targets in
    I. Saudi Arabia
    II. Israel
    III. Iran
    IV. Bahrain
    The Correct answer is
    A. I and II   C. I, II and IV
    B. II only   D. I, II, III and IV

33._____

34. Which of the following movements, founded in the late 1950s, espoused a Palestinian nationalist ideology in which Palestine would be liberated by the actions of Palestinians?
    A. Hezbollah   C. Ansar al-Islam
    B. Hamas   D. Fatah

34._____

35. In the early 21' century, about 25 percent of the world's oil reserves lay within the nation of
    A. Iran
    B. Kuwait
    C. Saudi
    D. Kazakhstan

35._____

36. The Ottoman Empire's advance through the Balkans was essentially ended in   36._____
    A. 1683   C. 1878
    B. 1712   D. 1914

37. In 1980, Saddam Hussein's closest confidante in the Arab world was   37._____
    A. Anwar Sadat   C. Osama bin Laden
    B. King Hussein of Jordan   D. Hafez al-Assad

38. The major factor that has contributed to terrorist activities in the Middle East, even after   38._____
    the launch of Operation Iraqi Freedom in 2003, has been
    A. the presence of U.S. military bases on the soil of several Arab nations
    B. decreasing world oil prices and the resulting economic hardships
    C. among OPEC nations political instability in most Arab nations
    D. the conflict between Israelis and Palestinians

39. In 1996 Osama bin Laden was expelled from the nation of_____, under pressure from   39._____
    the United States, Saudi Arabia, and Egypt.
    A. Afghanistan   C. Sudan
    B. Syria   D. Pakistan

40. In 1985,_____ declared armed struggle to end the Israel occupation of Southern Lebanon.   40._____
    A. the PLO   C. the South Lebanon Army
    B. Hamas   D. Hezbollah

41. Which of the following was NOT a "Phase I" element of President George W Bush's Road   41._____
    Map for Peace between Israel and the Palestinians, which he announced in June of 2002?
    A. "Right of return" for Palestinian refugees
    B. A freeze on Israeli settlement expansion
    C. Palestinian elections
    D. An end to Palestinian violence

42. To help rid this Arab nation of chemical-weapons facilities in 2005, President George   42._____
    Bush waived existing U.S. export restrictions.
    A. Iraq   C. Uzbekistan
    B. Libya   D. Iran

43. The Arab claims in the War of 1948 were broadly backed by   43._____
    A. France   C. Japan
    B. China   D. the Soviet Union

44. In 2003, the Arab League voted 21-1 in favor of a resolution demanding the immediate   44._____
    and unconditional removal of U.S. and British soldiers from Iraq. The lone dissenting
    vote was cast by
    A. Yemen   C. Jordan
    B. Kuwait   D. Bahrain

45. The 1973 "Yom Kippur War" began when launched a surprise joint attack on the Jewish   45._____
    day of fasting.
    A. Jordan and Syria
    B. Syria and Egypt
    C. Syria and Lebanon
    D. Iraq and Egypt

46. The official reason given by Saddam Hussein for his 1990 invasion of Kuwait was that Kuwait
    A. had illegally ruled over a portion of Iraqi territory since 1923
    B. Was harboring Iranian militants who had launched attacks on Iraq
    C. had formed an alliance with its enemy, the United States
    D. Was illegally slant-drilling petroleum across the Iraq-Kuwait border

47. In March of 2005, Israeli troops transferred control_____ of to the Palestinians in order to help Mahmoud Abbas convince Palestinian militants to adhere to a cease-fire.
    A. Bethlehem
    B. Ramallah
    C. Jericho
    D. Qalqiya

48. In January of 2005, the *New Yorker* magazine reported that squads of U.S. commandoes had been infiltrated the nation of_____ for several months, scouting targets for possible airstrikes.
    A. North Korea
    B. Pakistan
    C. Iran,
    D. Syria

49. The first peace treaty between Israel and an Arab nation was signed in1979, between Israel and
    A. Jordan
    B. Saudi Arabia
    C. Egypt
    D. Iraq

50. As he rose to power in Iraq after the 2003 U.S. invasion, the leader of al Qaeda in Iraq, Abu Musab al-Zarqawi, denounced the government of_____ as tyrants who allowed Westerners to loot the riches of
    A. Iraq
    B. Kuwait
    C. Saudi Arabia
    D. Bahrain

KEY (CORRECT ANSWERS)

1. C	26. A
2. B	27. A
3. B	28. D
4. B	29. B
5. A	30. C
6. A	31. A
7. A	32. C
8. B	33. A
9. D	34. D
10. D	35. C
11. A	36. A
12. A	37. B
13. C	38. D
14. B	39. C
15. B	40. D
16. D	41. A
17. C	42. B
18. B	43. B
19. A	44. B
20. D	45. B
21. C	46. D
22. C	47. C
23. A	48. C
24. A	49. C
25. C	50. C

EXAMINATION SECTION
TEST 1

DIRECTIONS: Each question or incomplete statement is followed by several suggested answers or completions. Select the one that BEST answers the question or completes the statement. *PRINT THE LETTER OF THE CORRECT ANSWER IN THE SPACE AT THE RIGHT.*

1. Which one of the following statements BEST describes the nature of the Japanese Peace Treaty of 1951?
   It
   A. provided for the permanent disarmament of Japan
   B. was a general peace settlement signed by the major allied powers as well as by Communist China
   C. neutralized Japan in the Cold War
   D. left most of the basic economic problems of Japan unsolved

   1._____

2. The event of 1914 that transformed the conflict between Serbia and Austria-Hungary into a general war was the
   A. Russian mobilization
   B. German invasion of Belgium
   C. German ultimatum to France
   D. British support of Belgium

   2._____

3. Which one of the following statements CORRECTLY describes the effect of the Treaty of Versailles (1919) upon Germany?
   It
   A. stripped Germany of many of her colonies, but permitted her to retain those colonies that chose to remain a part of the German Empire
   B. prohibited conscription in Germany, but permitted her to keep a volunteer army and a navy adequate for defense against attack by her European neighbors
   C. preserved the Reich as a united nation, though it deprived Germany of territory in Europe inhabited by conquered alien population
   D. levied a moderate sum in reparations, subject to reduction later if Germany carried out the remaining provisions of the treaty

   3._____

4. Which one of the following was LEAST concerned with political decisions during World War II?
   A. Bretton Woods Conference
   B. Yalta Conference
   C. Atlantic Charter
   D. Moscow Conference

   4._____

5. Which of the following countries are members of the North Atlantic Treaty Organization?
   I. Greece   II. Netherlands   III. Ireland   IV. Canada   V. Turkey

   The CORRECT answer is:
   A. I, II, III
   B. II, IV, V
   C. I, III, IV, V
   D. II, III, IV

   5._____

85

6. Which group of states was neutral in BOTH world War I and World War II? 6._____
   A. Portugal, Denmark, Luxembourg
   B. Portugal, Sweden, Norway
   C. Spain, Luxembourg, Denmark
   D. Denmark, Sweden, Spain

7. Which one of the following was NOT violated by Japan when she seized control of 7._____
Manchuria in 1931?
   A. Covenant of the League of Nations
   B. Nine Power Treaty
   C. Locarno Pact
   D. Kellogg-Briand Pact

8. In which one of the following respects did Hitler's rise to power resemble that of Mussolini? 8._____
   A. He was appointed Chancellor and Mussolini was appointed Premier because their respective parties had won a majority of the seats in Parliament.
   B. He used his army of Brown Shirts and Mussolini his Black Shirts to seize the Parliament buildings and oust their opponents.
   C. Both of them organized a successful revolution against the Communist governments of their respective countries.
   D. Both of them executed coups d'etat while going through the motions of legality.

9. Which is the CORRECT order of occurrence for the following events?

   9._____
   I.   Nazi-Soviet Non-Aggression Pact
   II. Hitler's invasion of Poland
   III. Nazi occupation of Austria
   IV. Munich Pact

   The CORRECT answer is:
   A. I, II, III, IV   C. III, IV, I, II
   B. II, III, IV, I   D. IV, III, II, I

10. Which of the following statements regarding the United Nations are CORRECT? 10._____
    I.   The Atomic Energy Commission is responsible to the Security Council.
    II. The Secretariat is directly responsible to the Security Council.
    III. The Economic and Social Council is responsible to the General Assembly.
    IV. The Specialized agencies are directly responsible to the Economic and Social Council.
    V.   The Trusteeship Council is directly responsible to the Economic and Social Council

    The CORRECT answer is:
    A. II, III, V   C. I, III, IV
    B. II, IV, V   D. I, II

11. Which of the following African states was NOT dominated by a foreign power in 1914? 11._____
    A. South Africa
    B. Ethiopia
    C. Libya
    D. Egypt

12. Which one of the following did NOT result from the Manchurian Incident of 1931? It
    A. stimulated a new unity and an intensified boycott of Japanese goods on the part of the Chinese
    B. inspired the United States to announce that it would not recognize changes made in violation of treaties
    C. caused the League of Nations to apply sanctions against Japan
    D. influenced the U.S.S.R. to sell its half-interest in the Chinese Eastern Railroad in Manchuria

13. The Republican government of Germany in the 1920's lacked stability because it(s)
    A. was elected by narrow margins
    B. did not back Stresemann's foreign policy
    C. was a coalition government without a consistent policy on internal reforms
    D. political support rested on the leadership of the landed aristocracy

14. The policy of the Communist regime in the U.S.S.R., that met with the MOST internal resistance between World Wars I and II was
    A. NEP
    B. collectivization of farms
    C. plans for industrialization
    D. foreign policy

15. In which of the following areas was a plebiscite held as a means of self-determination after World War I?
    A. Saar
    B. Danzig
    C. Memel
    D. Trieste

16. Which of the following statements in regard to World War II conferences is INCORRECT? The
    A. Casablanca Conference of January 1943 laid down the aim of unconditional surrender.
    B. Quebec meeting of 1943 was chiefly concerned with the possibility of a world organization of nations in the interest of global peace
    C. Dumbarton Oaks Conference drew the blueprint for the organization of the United Nations
    D. Yalta Conference considered the problem of the occupation of conquered European territory

17. Two international agencies of the United Nations which did NOT exist under the League of Nations are a(n)
    A. Trusteeship Council and an International Labor Office
    B. Economic and Social Council and an International Court of Justice
    C. Educational, Scientific, and Cultural Council and a Economic and Social Council
    D. International Labor Office and an Educational, Scientific, and Cultural Council

18. Which one of the following crises is NOT matched correctly with the two countries it affected?
    A. Fashoda Crises (1898) - Britain and France
    B. Moroccan Crises (1905-6) - France and Spain
    C. Moroccan Crises (1911) - France and Germany
    D. Serbian Crisis (1914) - Austria - Hungary and Russia

19. Which one of the following European countries did NOT attempt to expand to other continents between 1870-1914? 19.____
    A. Austria-Hungary
    B. Belgium
    C. Portugal
    D. Russia

20. In which one of the following pairs does the cause PRECEDE the effect? 20.____
    A. Twenty-One Demands - Overthrow of the Manchu Dynasty
    B. Interference in the affairs of Korea - Sino-Japanese War of 1895
    C. Stimson Doctrine - Invasion of Manchuria
    D. Boxer Rebellion - Open Door Policy

21. Which one of the following items consists of states that were independent in 1914? 21.____
    A. Liberia - Korea
    B. Thailand - Ethiopia
    C. Indo-China - Libya
    D. Malaya - Nigeria

22. Which one of the following suffered the GREATEST territorial loss in Europe after World War I? 22.____
    A. Austria-Hungary
    B. Turkey
    C. Russia
    D. Germany

23. The Treaty of Rapallo (1922) 23.____
    A. reflected the anti-Communist orientation of the German officer corps
    B. marked a relaxation of the isolation of the Soviet Union after World War I
    C. made it difficult for Germany to evade some of the provisions of the Treaty of Versailles
    D. completed the encirclement of the Soviet Union by hostile powers after World War I

24. A bibliography for a student who is to report on the experiences of the ordinary person during the Second World War might include all of the following EXCEPT 24.____
    A. BURMA SURGEON - Gordon S. Seagrave
    B. HIROSHIMA - John Hersey
    C. REVOLT IN THE DESERT - Thomas E. Lawrence
    D. THUNDER OUT OF CHINA - White and Jacoby

25. Which one of the following is NOT true of the Washington Arms Conference of 1921-22? 25.____
    A. The five major naval powers agreed to reduce the tonnage of capital ships.
    B. The Four Power Pact superseded the Anglo-Japanese Alliance of 1902.
    C. Nine powers officially gave support to the Open Door Policy.
    D. The Escalator Clause which was adopted allowed signatories to evade some of the treaty provisions.

26. Which one of the following is NOT true of India in the 20th century? 26.____
    A. Gandhi, as a pacifist, refused to support Great Britain in both World Wars I and II.
    B. India is not a member of SEATO.
    C. In 1950, India became a member of the Commonwealth of Nations.
    D. India, after being liberated, at first chose dominion status, but later decided to become a republic.

27. Which one of the following statements BEST describes the nature of the Japanese Peace Treaty of 1951?
    It
    A. provided for the permanent disarmament of Japan
    B. was a general peace settlement signed by the major allied powers as well as by
    C. Communist China
    D. neutralized Japan in the Cold War
    E. left most of the basic economic problems of Japan unsolved

27._____

28. The event of 1914 that transformed the conflict between Serbia and Austria-Hungary into a general war was the
    A. Russian mobilization
    B. German invasion of Belgium
    C. German ultimatum to France
    D. British support of Belgium

28._____

29. Which one of the following statements CORRECTLY describes the effect of the Treaty of Versailles (1919) upon Germany?
    It
    A. stripped Germany of many of her colonies, but permitted her to retain those colonies that chose to remain a part of the German Empire
    B. prohibited conscription in Germany, but permitted her to keep a volunteer army and a navy adequate for defense against attack by her European neighbors
    C. preserved the Reich as a united nation, though it deprived Germany of territory in Europe inhabited by conquered alien population
    D. levied a moderate sum in reparations, subject to reduction later if Germany carried out the remaining provisions of the treaty

29._____

30. Which one of the following was LEAST concerned with political decisions during World War II?
    A. Bretton Woods Conference
    B. Yalta Conference
    C. Atlantic Charter
    D. Moscow Conference

30._____

31. Which group of states was neutral in BOTH World War I and World War II?
    A. Portugal, Denmark, Luxembourg
    B. Portugal, Sweden, Norway
    C. Spain, Luxembourg, Denmark
    D. Denmark, Sweden, Spain

31._____

32. Which one of the following was NOT violated by Japan when she seized control of Manchuria in 1931?
    A. Covenant of the League of Nations
    B. Nine Power Treaty
    C. Locarno Pact
    D. Kellogg-Briand Pact

32._____

33. In which one of the following respects did Hitler's rise to power resemble that of Mussolini? 33._____
    A. He was appointed Chancellor and Mussolini was appointed-Premier because their respective parties had won a majority of the seats in Parliament.
    B. He used his army of Brown Shirts and Mussolini his Black Shirts to seize the Parliament buildings and oust their opponents.
    C. Both of them organized a successful revolution against the Communist governments of their respective countries.
    D. Both of them executed coups d'etat while going through the motions of legality.

34. Which is the CORRECT order of occurrence for the following events 34._____
    I. Nazi- Soviet Non-Aggression Pact
    II. Hitler's invasion of Poland
    III. Nazi occupation of Austria
    IV. Munich Pact

    The CORRECT answer is:
    A. I, II, III, IV
    B. II, III, IV, I
    C. III, IV, I, II
    D. IV, III, II, I

35. Which of the following statements regarding the United Nations are CORRECT? 35._____
    I. The Atomic Energy Commission is responsible to the Security Council.
    II. The Secretariat is directly responsible to the Security Council.
    III. The Economic and Social Council is responsible to the General Assembly.
    IV. The Specialized agencies are directly responsible to the Economic and Social Council.
    V. The Trusteeship Council is directly responsible to the Economic and Social Council.

The CORRECT answer is
    A. II, III, V
    B. II, IV, V
    C. I, III, IV
    D. I, II

36. Which one of the following did NOT result from the Manchurian Incident of 1931? 36_____
    It
    A. stimulated a new unity and an intensified boycott of Japanese goods on the part of the Chinese
    B. inspired the United States to announce that it
    C. would not recognize changes made in violation of treaties
    D. caused the League of Nations to apply sanctions against Japan
    E. influenced the U.S.S.R. to sell its half-interest in the Chinese Eastern Railroad in Manchuria

37. The Republican government of Germany in the 1920's lacked stability because it(s) 37._____
    A. was elected by narrow margins
    B. did not back Stresemann's foreign policy
    C. was a coalition government without a consistent policy on internal reforms
    D. political support rested on the leadership of the landed aristocracy

38. Which of the following statements in regard to World War II conferences is INCORRECT? The
    A. Casablanca Conference of January 1943 laid down the aim of unconditional surrender
    B. Quebec meeting of 1943 was chiefly concerned with the possibility of a world organization of nations in the interest of global peace
    C. Dumbarton Oaks Conference drew the blueprint for the organization of the United Nations
    D. Yalta Conference considered the problem of the occupation of conquered European territory

39. During World War II, the straits at the entrance to the Black Sea were controlled by
    A. Bulgaria
    B. Germany
    C. Great Britain
    D. Russia
    E. Turkey

40. A MAJOR test of the power of the League of Nations to prevent aggression came in 1931 at the time of the
    A. border dispute between Russia and Poland
    B. occupation of Manchuria by Japan
    C. German recovery of the Saar
    D. invasion of Ethiopia by Italy
    E. bombardment of Corfu

41. The Balfour Declaration (1917) stated that Britain
    A. favored a Jewish national homeland in Palestine
    B. favored the division of Palestine between the Arabs and Jews
    C. favored a restrictive quota system for Jewish immigration to Palestine
    D. would establish a protectorate in Palestine at the end of the war
    E. would recognize an independent state of Palestine under the complete control of the Arabs.

42. Which country's support of Serbia against Austria-Hungary in 1914 contributed to World War I?
    A. Germany
    B. Great Britain
    C. Japan
    D. Russia
    E. The United States

43. Upon the establishment of the West German state (Federal Republic of Germany), its government had
    I. accepted the principle of Western Allied control of the industrial Ruhr
    II. entered the Schuman Pact together with France, Italy, Belgium, Holland, Luxemberg, and Great Britain
    III. been accepted as a full and equal member of the Council of Europe
    IV. consistently opposed participation in a European army under a supra-national authority

The CORRECT answer is:
   A. I, II, III, IV
   B. I, II, IV
   C. II, IV
   D. I, III
   E. I, II

44. The Nazi-Soviet Pact of 1939 was based on the same principles as those involved in the   44._____
    A. Treaty of Lausanne of 1923
    B. Locarno Treaties
    C. Treaty of Rapallo of 1922
    D. Treaty of Trianon

45. Hitler's policies were similar to Bismarck's post 1871 policies in that both   45._____
    A. favored a union of Germany and Austria
    B. favored an alliance with Italy
    C. sought agricultural *living-space* in Eastern Europe
    D. sought to expand German naval power

46. One of the purposes of the Triple Entente of 1907 was the protection of   46._____
    A. Austria-Hungary against Germany
    B. England against Russia
    C. France against England
    D. Russia against Austria-Hungary

47. In the Russo-Chinese Pact of 1945, the Soviet government agreed to   47._____
    A. give military supplies and moral support to the Nationalist government
    B. recognize Chinese rule over Outer Mongolia
    C. support the Chinese Communists in their fight to gain control of China
    D. give China complete control of the Chinese Eastern Railway

48. The Yalta and Potsdam Conferences in 1945 sought to solve the problem of Germany   48._____
    by agreeing to the
    A. permanent division of Germany into four occupation zones
    B. four-zone division of Germany until order was restored and the unification of Germany could be established in a peace treaty
    C. settlement of Germany's post-war boundaries and the extent of reparation payments
    D. establishment of a central German government and the determination of the amount of military production to be permitted

49. Adolf Hitler became Chancellor of Germany in 1933 by   49._____
    A. a coup d'etat after the *Reichstag Fire*
    B. gaining support of the army
    C. appointment by Von Hindenburg
    D. having his party win a majority of the Reichstag seats

50. The post-World War II period has seen all of the following events in international relations   50._____
    EXCEPT:
    A. Italy allying herself with the Western democracies
    B. the United States making regional agreements with Western Europe and Southeast Asia
    C. France liquidating her empire in Southeast Asia and Africa
    D. England returning to the pre-war policy of non-participation in formal alliances

KEY (CORRECT ANSWERS)

1. D	26. A
2. B	27. D
3. A	28. D
4. B	29. C
5. A	30. B
6. D	31. D
7. C	32. C
8. D	33. D
9. C	34. C
10. C	35. C
11. B	36. C
12. C	37. C
13. C	38. B
14. B	39. E
15. A	40. B
16. B	41. A
17. C	42. D
18. B	43. D
19. A	44. C
20. B	45. B
21. B	46. D
22. C	47. C
23. B	48. B
24. C	49. C
25. D	50. D

TEST 2

DIRECTIONS: Each question or incomplete statement is followed by several suggested answers or completions. Select the one that BEST answers the question or completes the statement. *PRINT THE LETTER OF THE CORRECT ANSWER IN THE SPACE AT THE RIGHT.*

1. The imperialist rivals of Russia in the late 19th and early 20th centuries were
    A. Germany and Italy
    B. Japan and Great Britain
    C. France and the Netherlands
    D. Germany and Belgium

    1._____

2. What is the CORRECT chronological order of the actions of Adolf Hitler in violation of the Treaty of Versailles?
    I. Reoccupation of the Rhineland
    II. Rearmament of Germany
    III. Seizure of Czechoslovakia
    IV. Seizure of Danzig

    2._____

    The CORRECT answer is:
    A. I, II, III, IV
    B. II, I, III, IV
    C. II, III, IV, I
    D. II, III, I, IV

3. The Treaty of Rapallo (1922)
    A. reflected the anti-Communist orientation of the German officer corps
    B. marked a relaxation of the isolation of the Soviet Union after World War I
    C. made it difficult for Germany to evade some of the provisions of the Treaty of Versailles
    D. completed the encirclement of the Soviet Union by hostile powers after World War I

    3._____

4. Which one of the following is NOT true of the Washington Arms Conference of 1921-22?
    A. The five major naval powers agreed to reduce the tonnage of capital ships.
    B. The Four Power Pact superseded the Anglo-Japanese Alliance of 1902.
    C. Nine powers officially gave support to the Open Door Policy.
    D. The Escalator Clause which was adopted allowed signatories to evade some of the treaty provisions.

    4._____

5. Which one of the following post-World War I treaties or agreements is INCORRECTLY paired with the subject with which it deals?
    A. Dawes Plan (1924) - War reparations
    B. Kellogg-Briand Pact (1928) - Renunciation of war as a part of national policy
    C. Pact of Locarno (1925) - Limitation of armaments
    D. Munich Pact (1938) - Status of Czechoslovakia

    5._____

6. In which one of the following pairs is there NO causal relationship between the two items?
    A. War of the Austrian Succession - Decembrist Revolt
    B. The Crimean War - Reforms of Alexander TI
    C. The Russo-Japanese War - Revolution of 1905
    D. World War I - Revolution of 1917

    6._____

7. During the period 1920-1930, which one of the following political leaders instituted one of the MOST revolutionary programs ever enacted in so short a span of time?
   A. Adolph Hitler
   B. David Lloyd George
   C. Mahatma Gandhi
   D. Mustapha Kemal

7._____

8. In the Locarno treaties of 1925,
   A. Germany guaranteed the frontiers of Poland and Czechoslovakia
   B. Great Britain promised military aid to Czechoslovakia and Poland in the event of the violation of their frontiers by Germany
   C. Great Britain guaranteed the frontiers of France and Belgium against Germany
   D. France, Britain, and Germany agreed to settle all international disputes by binding arbitration

8._____

9. In entering into the Triple Entente with France and Russia in 1907, England agreed to
   A. demarcate British and Russian spheres of influence in Persia
   B. give France a free hand in the Sudan
   C. give Russia control of the Straits
   D. assign France a sphere of influence in Syria

9._____

10. Which one of the following was TRUE of the government of the German Empire (1871-1918)?
    A. It had a centralized form of government.
    B. Voting by states gave Prussia a veto in the Reichstag.
    C. The ministerial responsibility was to the Emperor and not to the elected member.
    D. Voting for the Reichstag was restricted to property owners.

10._____

11. Hitler observed legal treaty obligations in the
    A. remilitarization of the Rhineland
    B. reunion of the Saar with Germany
    C. Anschluss of Austria and Germany
    D. annexation of danzig

11._____

12. Which one of the following is TRUE of the Hungarian Uprising of 1956?
    It
    A. proved that the Uniting for Peace Resolution had made the General Assembly more effective
    B. provided a rare instance of United States and Russian cooperation in the United Nations
    C. demonstrated Soviet willingness to permit a Titoisttype of regime in Hungary
    D. showed that a disagreement between the United States and the Union of Soviet Socialist Republics could paralyze action in the General Assembly

12._____

13. At the beginning of World War II, the Fascist government of Spain MOST closely resembled that of
    A. Italy
    B. France
    C. Denmark
    D. the Soviet Union

13._____

14. Which agreement made in Europe prior to the outbreak of World War II was supposed to have brought "peace in our time?"
    A. Rome-Berlin-Tokyo Axis
    B. Russo-German Non-Aggression Pact
    C. Munich Pact
    D. Atlantic Charter

14._____

15. That World War II shifted the balance of power is illustrated by the
    A. rise of France to first-class status
    B. increase in Britain's colonial empire
    C. position of isolation of the United States
    D. emergence of Soviet Russia as a world leader

15._____

16. The incident that led to World War I occurred in
    A. Germany
    B. Italy
    C. the Balkan Peninsula
    D. the Scandinavian Peninsula

16._____

17. A policy followed by both Great Britain and France in making concessions to dictators to keep the peace in the 1930's was called
    A. collective security
    B. containment
    C. arbitration
    D. appeasement

17._____

18. Which nation maintained a democratic government for the LONGEST time during the period between World War I and World War II?
    A. Czechoslovakia
    B. Germany
    C. Poland
    D. Spain

18._____

19. During the period 1920-39, the history of Europe supports the generalization that
    A. the policy of appeasement was successful
    B. the League of Nations successfully checked aggression
    C. European nations gave up their African colonies
    D. economic distress contributed to the rise of fascism

19._____

20. Which country, created after World War I, remained for two decades one of the MOST prosperous and democratic states in Europe in spite of an inland position, a vague frontier, and large national minorities?
    A. Czechoslovakia
    B. Poland
    C. Switzerland
    D. Italy

20._____

21. In seizing and maintaining power, the Communists, Fascists, and Nazis were careful to
    A. establish good relations with churches
    B. blame their nations' troubles on scapegoats
    C. respect treaties made earlier in the history of their nations
    D. encourage private enterprise in economic life

21._____

22. The unifications of Germany and Italy were similar in that   22._____
    A. unification was encouraged by the Pope
    B. unification was completed by plebiscite
    C. war was used as a means of uniting various states
    D. the assistance of France was essential

23. Defeat in World War I ended the political existence of   23._____
    A. Germany
    B. France
    C. Austria-Hungary
    D. Alsace-Lorraine

24. The desire of Germany to take over areas held by other nations provoked crises in the 1930's in   24._____
    A. Austria and Spain
    B. the Saar and Albania
    C. the Rhineland and Schleswig
    D. the Sudetenland and Danzig

25. Which were totalitarian nations in the period just prior to World War II?   25._____
    A. Italy, Russia, Germany
    B. Spain, Germany, France
    C. Germany, France, Russia
    D. Japan, Italy, Great Britain

26. Which one of the following occurred in the year that Woodrow Wilson was elected President of the United States? The   26._____
    A. Manchu Dynasty was ended and the Chinese Republic proclaimed
    B. Meiji Restoration took place
    C. British put down the Sepoy Rebellion
    D. British got the mandates for Palestine and Mesopotamia-Iraq

27. In 1919, Bela Kun temporarily seized power in Hungary, while the Spartacists attempted an armed insurrection in Berlin.   27._____
    These actions were evidence that
    A. fascism was on the rise
    B. the Russian Revolution was giving impetus to communist movements in other countries
    C. the monarchist groups were trying to hold on to their power in post-war Europe
    D. there was strong opposition to the Treaty of Versailles

28. Which one of the following describes Europe in the period 1905-1914? The   28._____
    A. middle and upper classes lost their political and cultural leadership
    B. discontent of subject nationalities declined
    C. working class became more militant in an effort to satisfy its grievances
    D. role of the state was reduced with rising living standards

29. Which one of the following was TRUE of the Paris Peace Settlements of World War I?   29._____
    A. The wishes and aspirations of Slavic nationalities were ignored.
    B. Russia and Germany were integrated into the new European political structure.
    C. France's demand for a security pact was satisfied.
    D. There was serious neglect of the long-range economic problems of Europe.

30. Which one of the following Communist governments has established diplomatic relations with West Germany?   30._____
    A. Albania
    B. Czechoslovakia
    C. Poland
    D. Rumania

31. A territorial change that was in accordance with the Treaty of Versailles was the   31._____
    A. award of the Saar to Germany
    B. annexation of Danzig by Germany
    C. union of Austria and Germany
    D. annexation of the Sudentenland by Germany

32. Serbia's role in the creation of Yugoslavia was similar to that of   32._____
    Sardinia in the unification of Italy
    A. Austria in the establishment of the German Empire
    B. Russia in the creation of an independent Poland
    C. Croatia in the formation of Hungary

33. Hitler became Chancellor in Germany as a result of   33._____
    A. a coup d'etat
    B. a majority of votes in the election of 1932
    C. a political arrangement with other parties
    D. the longstanding political support of President Hindenburg

34. Which one of the following was the FIRST major act of aggression which challenged the ability of the League of Nations to keep peace?   34._____
    A. Italy's invasion of Ethiopia
    B. Franco's rebellion against the Spanish Loyalists
    C. Japan's invasion of Manchuria
    D. Hitler's Aschluss with Austria

35. Which one of the following provisions of the Treaty of Versailles implemented one of Wilson's Fourteen Points?   35._____
    A. Loss of Germany's colonial possessions
    B. German reparation payments for civilian war damage
    C. Reconstitution of an independent Poland with access to the sea
    D. Unilateral limitation of German armed forces

36. The Treaty of Rapallo (1922) was SIGNIFICANT because it   36._____
    A. reflected the anti-Communist orientation of the German officer corps
    B. marked a relaxation of the isolation of the Soviet Union after World War I
    C. made it more difficult for Germany to evade some of the provisions of the Treaty of Versailles
    D. completed the encirclement of the Soviet Union by hostile powers after World War I

37. Which one of the following contributed to Hitler's accession to power?   37._____
    A. Support given by Ebert and Noske to the Spartacists
    B. Lack of presidential power under the Weimar Constitution
    C. Election of the Reichstag on the basis of proportional representation
    D. Failure of the Weimar Constitution to guarantee private property

38. Which one of the following was expelled from the League of Nations for its acts of aggression?
    A. Japan   B. Germany   C. Italy   D. Russia

39. During the period immediately preceding the outbreak of World War II, which is the CORRECT chronological order of the following events?
    I. Absorption by Germany of Bohemia and Moravia as a protectorate
    II. Annexation to Germany of Austria
    III. Annexation to Germany of the Sudentenland
    IV. Nazi-Soviet non-aggression pact

    The CORRECT answer is:
    A. II, III, I, IV
    B. IV, III, II, I
    C. III, II, I, IV
    D. I, IV, II, III

40. What is the MAIN idea of this quotation? The
    A. Soviet Union has expanded its influence throughout eastern Europe
    B. Soviet Union has helped the nations of eastern Europe improve their standard of living
    C. democratic nations of western Europe have stopped the expansion of Soviet influence in the world
    D. Soviet Union will support communist revolutions in Southeast Asia

41. The Russian peasants supported the Bolsheviks in the 1917 revolutions MAINLY because the Bolsheviks promised to
    A. establish collective farms
    B. maintain the agricultural price-support system
    C. bring modern technology to Russian farms
    D. redistribute the land owned by the nobility

42. Which has been a MAJOR change in the political situation in Western Europe in the last half of the 20th century?
    A. Nationalism has increased rivalry between Western European nations.
    B. Western European nations have gained power through control of world oil resources.
    C. Western European nations have worked cooperatively for security and prosperity.
    D. Powerful dictatorships have emerged throughout Western Europe.

43. Which statement BEST describes Europe just before World War I?
    A. The formation of opposing alliance systems increased international distrust.
    B. European leaders resorted to a policy of appeasement to solve international disputes.
    C. The communist nations promoted violent revolution throughout Western Europe.
    D. The isolationist policies of England and France prevented their entry into the hostilities.

44. Karl Marx believed that a proletarian revolution was MORE likely to occur as a society became more
    A. Religious
    B. militarized
    C. industrialized
    D. democratic

45. The events that took place in Hungary in the 1950's and in Czechoslovakia in the 1960's demonstrated the Soviet Union's
    A. support of nationalism among satellite nations
    B. influence on the economies of developing nations
    C. determination to maintain political control over Eastern Europe at that time
    D. attempts to promote its artistic and literary achievements in Western Europe

45.____

46. The political reorganization of Russia after the Communist Revolution of 1917 resulted in
    A. the establishment of a two-party political system
    B. increased political power for ethnic minorities
    C. a limited monarchy with the Czar as a figurehead
    D. a federation of socialist republics

46.____

47. A study of the causes of the American, French, and Russian Revolutions indicates that revolutions USUALLY occur because the
    A. society has become dependent on commerce and trade
    B. society has a lower standard of living than the societies around it
    C. existing government has been resistant to change
    D. lower classes have strong leaders

47.____

48. A MAJOR reason many Russian people supported the Bolsheviks in the November 1917 revolution was that the Bolsheviks called for
    A. an immediate peace settlement with Germany
    B. a heavy investment in industry
    C. the collectivization of agriculture
    D. the abolition of all religion

48.____

49. Communist philosophy teaches that people should
    A. revere their ancestors and religious traditions
    B. obey their rulers because they have authority from heaven
    C. reject technology and Western values
    D. place the interests of the group before the interests of the individual

49.____

50. A study of Yugoslavia, the People's Republic of China, and the Soviet Union during the 1980's would BEST indicate that Marxism
    A. achieved its goal of a classless society
    B. was formally discontinued by all three countries
    C. is often reshaped to meet the particular needs of the government
    D. is practiced strictly in accordance with Karl Marx's ideas

50.____

KEY (CORRECT ANSWERS)

1. B	26. A
2. B	27. B
3. B	28. C
4. D	29. D
5. C	30. C
6. A	31. A
7. D	32. A
8. C	33. C
9. A	34. C
10. C	35. C
11. B	36. B
12. D	37. C
13. A	38. D
14. C	39. A
15. D	40. A
16. C	41. D
17. D	42. C
18. A	43. A
19. D	44. C
20. A	45. C
21. D	46. D
22. D	47. C
23. A	48. A
24. D	49. D
25. A	50. C

TEST 3

DIRECTIONS: Each question or incomplete statement is followed by several suggested answers or completions. Select the one that BEST answers the question or completes the statement. PRINT THE LETTER OF THE CORRECT ANSWER IN THE SPACE AT THE RIGHT.

1. Joseph Stalin's leadership of the Soviet Union can BEST be characterized as a period of
    A. democratic reform and nationalism
    B. humanism and democracy
    C. religious freedom and tolerance
    D. censorship and terror

    1._____

2. Which is GENERALLY a characteristic of a communist economy?
    A. Investment is encouraged by the promise of large profits
    B. The role of government in the economy is restricted by law
    C. Government agencies are involved in production planning
    D. Entrepreneurs sell shares in their companies to the government

    2._____

3. In the 1980's, the MAJOR ostensible source of the conflict between Israel and Palestinian Arabs was
    A. the presence of Israeli ships in the Suez Canal
    B. the interference of Libya in Middle Eastern affairs
    C. the demand of Palestinian Arabs for their own homeland
    D. Soviet support of radical Arab groups in occupied territories

    3._____

4. In the 1970's, when Iran was ruled by the Shah, the Ayatollah Khomeini's MAJOR criticism was of the
    A. Shah's friendship with the Soviet Union
    B. return to traditional Islamic law
    C. lack of political and social rights for women
    D. non-Islamic influences on the culture and economy

    4._____

5. Which generalization is BEST supported by developments in trade such as Japanese investments in Southeast Asia, the sale of United States grain to the Soviet Union, and the reliance of many Western European nations on oil from the Middle East?
    A. Most of the nations of the world are adopting socialist economies.
    B. Nations that control vital resources are no longer able to influence world markets.
    C. The goal of the world's economic planners is to decrease national self-sufficiency.
    D. The nations of the world have become interdependent.

    5._____

6. The withdrawal of France from Indochina, the involvement of the Soviet Union in Cuba, and the United States support of the Contras in Nicaragua illustrated that nations
    A. consistently discard traditional foreign policy goals after changes in administration
    B. tend to base foreign policy decisions on what they believe to be their self-interests
    C. no longer use warfare as a means to resolve international conflict
    D. tend to refer foreign policy conflicts to the United Nations

    6._____

7. A study of revolutions would MOST likely lead to the conclusion that pre-revolutionary governments
    A. are more concerned about human rights than the governments that replace them
    B. are refuse to modernize their armed forces with advanced technology
    C. attempt to bring about the separation of government from religion
    D. fail to meet the political and economic needs of their people

8. The North Atlantic Treaty Organization, the Cuban Missile Crisis, and the Korean War are examples of
    A. attempts to prevent the spread of communist power
    B. United States efforts to gain foreign territory
    C. the failure of capitalism and free market economies
    D. United Nations interference in the internal affairs of member nations

9. During the 1980's, a nation that was nonaligned and economically developing would MOST likely have
    A. entered into an exclusive trade agreement with the United States
    B. joined the other members of the Warsaw Pact
    C. formed a military alliance with the Soviet Union
    D. accepted aid from both the Soviet Union and the United States

10. Which statement BEST described the political situation in Eastern Europe during the 1980's?
    A. Nationalism was a strong force for change.
    B. Communist governments gained power through democratic elections.
    C. Ethnic rivalries were eliminated throughout the region.
    D. United States influence was used to keep communist governments in power.

11. The Soviet Union's reaction to the 1968 revolt in Czechoslovakia was to
    A. permit limited political and economic reforms in Czechoslovakia
    B. withdraw Soviet troops from Eastern Europe
    C. send Soviet troops to occupy Czechoslovakia
    D. bring the matter to the attention of the United Nations

12. Which statement BEST describes most Eastern European countries immediately after World War II?
    They
    A. adopted democratic reforms in their political systems
    B. became satellite states of the Soviet Union
    C. became dependent on aid provided by the Marshall Plan
    D. emerged as world economic powers

13. A MAJOR cause of the Russian Revolution of 1917 was the
    A. defeat of Germany in the Russian campaign
    B. marriage of Czar Nicholas II to a German princess
    C. existence of sharp economic differences between social classes
    D. appeal of Marxism to the Russian nobility

14. Which was a characteristic of Germany under Adolf Hitler and the Soviet Union under Josef Stalin?
    A. An official foreign policy of isolationism
    B. Governmental control of the media
    C. Public ownership of business and industry
    D. The absence of a written constitution

15. Which statement BEST describes the relationship between World War I and the Russian Revolution?
    A. World War I created conditions within Russia that helped trigger a revolution.
    B. World War I postponed the Russian Revolution by restoring confidence in the Czar.
    C. The Russian Revolution inspired the Russian people to win World War I.
    D. World War I gave the Czar's army the needed experience to suppress the Russian Revolution

16. The Cold War ended under the presidency of
    A. John F. Kennedy
    B. Richard Nixon
    C. Jimmy Carter
    D. Ronald Reagan

DIRECTIONS: Question 17 is to be answered on the basis of the cartoon shown below and on your knowledge of social studies.

17. What is the MAIN idea of the cartoon? Communism
    A. Is open to all classes of society
    B. Has become increasingly more powerful
    C. Has lost sight of its original goals
    D. Is no longer taken seriously

18. A BASIC economic difference between capitalism and socialism concerns the issue of to
    A. role of the government in controlling public education
    B. role of trade in achieving national prosperity
    C. ownership of the means of production and distribution
    D. Amount of resources spent on industrial expansion

19. During the decade following World War II, the _____ was a MAJOR cause of tension in Europe.
    A. formation of Soviet-dominated Communist governments in many Eastern European nations
    B. failure of the non-Communist countries to support the United Nations
    C. cutbacks in fuel supplies by oil-producing nations
    D. return of United States military forces to pre-World War II levels

20. Recognition by both the United States and the Soviet Union of their mutual ability to destroy the world had encouraged both nations at times to
    A. place greater emphasis on the United Nations as a peacemaker
    B. engage in direct combat with each other using conventional weapons
    C. seek ways of controlling the spread of nuclear weapons
    D. place great emphasis on civil defense programs

21. Détente, as applied to interaction between the United States and the Soviet Union, was BEST described as a
    A. joint policy to reduce tensions and improve relations
    B. joint policy to improve peace prospects in the Middle East
    C. United States policy of protection for Soviet dissidents
    D. Soviet policy of seeking loans and trade with the United States

22. A basic difference between communism and capitalism is that, in a communist economic system,
    A. there is a small demand for consumer goods
    B. major industries are under the direction of labor unions
    C. industry planning is controlled by the government
    D. monopolies are illegal

23. After the end of World War II, United States government policy toward the Soviet Union was influenced PRIMARILY by the
    A. existence of Soviet control in Eastern European countries
    B. close alliance between the United States and China
    C. abundance of Soviet aid during the war
    D. cooperation between Soviet and American scientists on nuclear projects

24. A significant cultural aspect of life in many Communist nations had been the
    A. Organized social and economic discrimination against women
    B. emphasis upon athletics and other forms of non-economic competition
    C. restraints upon the development of social welfare programs
    D. encouragement of free creative efforts of writers and composers

25. Which quotation about the nature of history BEST describes Karl Marx's basis for communism?
    A. The history of the world is but the biography of great men.
    B. History is made out of the failures and heroism of each significant moment.
    C. The history of all hitherto existing society is the history of class struggles.
    D. Those who cannot remember the past are condemned to repeat it.

26. The event that BEST illustrates the application of the Monroe Doctrine in United States foreign policy is the
    A. establishment of the North Atlantic Treaty Organization (NATO)
    B. Berlin airlift
    C. Cuban missile crisis
    D. declaration of war against Germany in World War II

27. Which one of the following conferences provided for restoration of territory to Russia which she had lost as a result of the Treaty of Portsmouth?
    A. Yalta
    B. Potsdam
    C. Cairo
    D. Teheran

28. During the period immediately preceding the outbreak of World War II, which is the CORRECT chronological order of the following events?
    I. Absorption by Germany of Bohemia and Moravia as a protectorate
    II. Annexation to Germany of Austria
    III. Annexation to Germany of the Sudentenland
    IV. Nazi-Soviet non-aggression pact

    The CORRECT answer is:
    A. II, III, I, IV
    B. IV, III, II, I
    C. III, II, I, IV
    D. I, IV, II, II

29. In which one of the following pairs dealing with the Cold War was the FIRST item a cause of the SECOND?
    A. Attack on South Korea - Formation of NATO
    B. Guerrilla war in Greece - Truman Doctrine
    C. Hungarian revolt - Geneva Conference of 1954
    D. U-2 Incident - Agency of International Development

30. The *cordon sanitaire* refers to the
    A. belt of states from Finland to Rumania formed to prevent the westward expansion of Communism after World War I
    B. coalition of Arab states formed to encircle Israel after World War II
    C. boycott organized to weaken the Japanese economy and thus strike at Japanese aggression in China in the 1930's
    D. belt of states formed in eastern Europe to protect the Union of Soviet Socialist Republics against anti-Communist agitation after World War II

31. The Treaty of Rapallo (1922) was SIGNIFICANT because it
    A. reflected the anti-Communist orientation of the German officer corps
    B. marked a relaxation of the isolation of the Soviet Union after World War I
    C. made it more difficult for Germany to evade some of the provisions of the Treaty of Versailles
    D. completed the encirclement of the Soviet Union by hostile powers after World War I

32. Which one of the following formulated the theory on which the government's policy of containment was based?
    A. George F. Kennan
    B. Arthur H. Vandenberg
    C. George C. Marshall
    D. John Foster Fulles

33. Which one of the following events occurred FIRST in time? The
    A. organization of the North Atlantic Treaty Organization
    B. Marshall Plan for European economic recovery
    C. Communist coup in Czechoslovakia
    D. enactment of the Point-Four Program

34. The Estonian, Latvian, and Lithuanian Republics were
    A. Independent before the First World War but were added to the former U.S.S.R between 1918-1939
    B. Part of czarist Russia before the First World War and were independent 1918-1939
    C. Part of Russia from 1815 to the present time
    D. Independent from 1815 until their annexation by the former Soviet Union following the Second World War in 1945

35. Which of the following agreements at Yalta became a MAJOR source of later disagreement between the Allies and the Soviet Union?
    The
    A. division of East Prussia between the Soviet Union and Poland
    B. future organization of the Polish government
    C. entry of the Soviet Union into the war in the Far East
    D. cession of Far Eastern territories to the Soviet Union

36. The Revolution of 1905 in Russia resembled the French Revolution of 1789 because in both revolutions
    A. a middle class minority sought representative government
    B. socialism played an important role for industrial workers
    C. the interests of peasants were ignored
    D. rulers were able to prevent the establishment of a representative assembly

37. Which one of the following describes Europe in the period 1905-1914? The
    A. middle and upper classes lost their political and cultural leadership
    B. discontent of subject nationalities declined
    C. working class became more militant in an effort to satisfy its grievances
    D. role of the state was reduced with rising living standards

38. Which one of the following was TRUE of the Paris Peace Settlements of World War I?
    A. The wishes and aspirations of Slavic nationalities were ignored.
    B. Russia and Germany were integrated into the new European political structure.
    C. France's demand for a security pact was satisfied.
    D. There was serious neglect of the long-range economic problems of Europe.

39. In entering into the Triple Entente with France and Russia in 1907, England agreed to
    A. Demarcate British and Russian spheres of influence in Persia
    B. Give France a free hand in the Sudan
    C. Give Russia controls of the straits
    D. Assign France a sphere of influence in Syria

40. Which one of the following occurred FIRST?
    A. Uprising of the Petrograd Soviet
    B. Decembrist Revolt
    C. Bloody Sunday
    D. November Revolution

41. Prior to the nuclear test ban treaty of 1963, the LAST written agreement signed by the Union of Soviet Socialist Republics and the United States was the
    A. United Nations Charter
    B. Peace Treaty with Japan
    C. Peace Treaty with Austria
    D. Potsdam Agreement

42. Which one of the following is TRUE of the Hungarian Uprising of 1956?
It
    A. proved that the Uniting for Peace Resolution had made the General Assembly more effective
    B. provided a rare instance of United States and Russian cooperation in the United Nations
    C. demonstrated Soviet willingness to permit a Titoist-type of regime in Hungary
    D. showed that a disagreement between the United States and the former Union of Soviet Socialist
       Republics could paralyze action in the General Assembly

43. *Red Sunday* is a term referring to the slaughter of
    A. Girondists in the French Revolution
    B. peasants in Russia's Revolution of 1905
    C. Huguenots in the French religions war
    D. Nazis in the first beer-hall putsch

44. Between the end of World War II and 1965, the United States and the Soviet Union a reed upon all of the following EXCEPT the
    A. conclusion of an Austrian peace treaty
    B. formation of a treaty on Antarctica
    C. condemnation of the Anglo-Grench-Israeli attack on Egypt in 1956
    D. assessment on United Nations members to support United Nations Congo military operations

45. Which one of the following constituted a violation by the Soviet Union of agreements made at the Yalta Conference?
    A. Acquiring the Kurile Islands from Japan
    B. Entering the war against Japan
    C. Preventing free democratic elections in Eastern Europe
    D. Occupying the eastern zone of Germany

46. Which one of the following suffered the GREATEST territorial loss in Europe after World War I?
    A. Austria-Hungary   C. Russia
    B. Germany   D. Turkey

47. Which is the CORRECT chronological order of the following events?
    I.   Communist coup in Czechoslovakia
    II. Communist victory on China mainland
    III. Communists gain control of Poland , e CORRECT answer is:
    IV. Russia blockades West Berlin

    A. III, I, IV, II
    B. III, II, I, IV
    C. III, II, I, IV
    D. None of the above

48. In June 1950, the Security Council of the United Nations was able to act quickly to brand North Korea the aggressor because the
    A. General Assembly happened to be in session
    B. Soviet Union was boycotting its meetings
    C. veto does not apply in the case of armed conflict
    D. President of the United States had already ordered American armed forces to support South Korea

48._____

49. In which one of the following ways did the Bolsheviks secure power in Russia By
    A. overthrowing the Czar
    B. being voted into office by the all-powerful Soviets
    C. staging a coup d'etat against the Provisional government
    D. making a united front with the Mensheviks in the Constituent Assembly

49._____

50. Which one of the following was one of the provisions of the Yalta Agreement of 1945?
    A. It restored to the Union of Soviet Socialist Republics the imperialist rights the Czar had lost in the Far East.
    B. In recognition of the Soviet losses in the war, the Soviet Union was granted the option joining the fight against Japan.
    C. It gave the Russians eight votes in the United Nations General Assembly to counterbalance the votes of the British Commonwealth.
    D. It provided for the recognition of the Soviet-controlled Polish government by Franklin D. Roosevelt and Winston Churchill.

50._____

KEY (CORRECT ANSWERS)

1. D	26. C
2. C	27. A
3. D	28. A
4. D	29. B
5. D	30. A
6. B	31. B
7. D	32. A
8. A	33. B
9. D	34. B
10. A	35. B
11. C	36. A
12. B	37. C
13. C	38. D
14. B	39. A
15. A	40. B
16. D	41. C
17. C	42. D
18. C	43. B
19. A	44. D
20. C	45. C
21. A	46. C
22. C	47. A
23. A	48. B
24. B	49. C
25. C	50. A

TEST 4

DIRECTIONS: Each question or incomplete statement is followed by several suggested answers or completions. Select the one that BEST answers the question or completes the statement. PRINT THE LETTER OF THE CORRECT ANSWER IN THE SPACE AT THE RIGHT.

1. The term that BEST characterizes the foreign policy of the United States since World War II is
    A. Appeasement
    B. containment
    C. isolationism
    D. non-intervention

    1._____

2. Stalin's 1939 non-aggression treaty with Hitler was intended to provide
    A. Stalin with time to consolidate his power in Russia and avoid an invasion against his unprepared nation
    B. Russia with much needed technical and capital equipment to assure success of the Five Year Plan for industrialization
    C. the world with another respite from the prospect of World War II
    D. Russia greater leverage in its negotiations with Britain and France for a collective security pact

    2._____

3. In the Russo-Chinese Pact of 1945, the Soviet government agreed to
    A. give military supplies and moral support to the Nationalist government
    B. recognize Chinese rule over Outer Mongolia
    C. support the Chinese Communists in their fight to gain control of China
    D. give China complete control of the Chinese Eastern Railway

    3._____

4. Which of the following statements is TRUE concerning Russia's foreign relations?
    A. After the American Revolution, Russia was the first power to recognize the United States as a sovereign power.
    B. Russia refused to cooperate with the Quintuple Alliance in suppressing the liberal uprisings in Latin America.
    C. During our Civil War, Russia sent her fleets to the harbors of New York and San Francisco.
    D. Russia agreed to submit the Bering Sea controversy to arbitration.
    Russia forced Japan to restore Shantung to China after the Sino-Japanese War.

    4._____

5. The U.S.S.R had attempted to secure control of or gain rights in all of the following ports EXCEPT
    A. Petsamo
    B. Dairen
    C. Bergen
    D. Vladivostok
    E. Port Arthur

    5._____

6. During World War II, the straits at the entrance to the Black Sea were controlled by
    A. Bulgaria
    B. Germany
    C. Great Britain
    D. Russia
    E. Turkey

    6._____

111

7. All of the following statements express policies of the United States government during the Cold War EXCEPT:
    A. Our policy with regard to Europe was not to interfere with her internal concerns but consider each European government de facto as the legitimate government and cultivate friendly relations with it
    B. Even though Soviet leaders professed to believe that the conflict between capitalism and communism was irreconcilable and must eventually be resolved by the triumph of the latter, was our hope that a fair and equitable settlement would be reached when they realize that we were too strong to be beaten and too determined to be frightened
    C. If we find it impossible to enlist Soviet cooperation in the solution of world problem's, we should be prepared to join with the British and other Western countries in an attempt to build up a world of our own
    D. The role of this country should consist of friendly aid in the drafting of a European economic program to get Europe on its feet and to provide financial support for such a program so far as it may be practical for us to do so
    E. The United States seeks no territorial expansion or selfish advantage and has no plans for aggression against any other state, large or small, but is committed to the mutual security of non-Communist nations in Europe

8. One of the MOST widely publicized policies of the State Department, the policy of *containment*, was attributed to George F. Kennan.
   Of th following, the MOST correct statement of this policy is that
    A. the encroachments of the Russians can be halted by helping nations to develop their economies and thus raise their standards of living
    B. the Russians should be confronted with unalterable counterforce at each point where they show signs of encroaching upon the interests of a peaceful and stable world
    C. containment is not possible unless the Russians are made to understand that furher encroachments will result in an American attack on Russia itself
    D. The United States should ally itself with any country, no matter what its government s, provided that it is willing to join in preventing Russia from expanding
    E. imperialist Russia can be contained by providing the free world with the means of defense

9. There is here a stark reality upon which our foreign policies must be based. With any foreseeable land forces from non-Communist nations, even including the United States, a land offensive against the Communist world could bring no military victory, no political conclusion ...our foreign policies must be based on the defense of the Western Hemisphere.
   This statement represented MOST NEARLY the viewpoint of
    A. Charles Bohlen
    B. Dean Acheson
    C. Dwight D. Eisenhower
    D. Herbert Hoover
    E. Thomas E. Dewey

10. Stalin's IMMEDIATE response to the German invasion of the Soviet Union in 1941 was to
    A. coordinate a secret counteroffensive through the Caucasus
    B. go into seclusion for several days
    C. appeal to the Allies for assistance
    D. publicly rally the population around the socialist cause

11. The food crisis that existed when the Bolsheviks seized power in 1917 persisted for several years afterward, mostly because
    A. a widespread drought was killing off many Russian crops
    B. surplus stores of grain were hoarded by thuggish overlords in rural areas
    C. most Russian grain was being exported to support the expansion of Bolshevik power
    D. peasants were given no incentive to produce under War Communism's requisition policies

11._____

12. In 1986, the Soviet Union and Japan had no working peace agreement because of
    A. lingering tensions from the Soviet destruction of a commercial airliner just north of Japan
    B. the Soviet occupation of four northern Japanese islands since World War II
    C. the Japanese refusal to cede all of Sakhalin Island
    D. the lack of a formal treaty after the Russo-Japanese War

12._____

13. In 1926, a United Opposition was formed within the Communist Party. Against whom was this opposition united?
    A. Stalin
    B. Gorky
    C. Trotsky
    D. Zinoviev and Kamenev

13._____

14. The Rapallo Treaty of 1922 marked the establishment of diplomatic relations between the Soviet Republic and
    A. Orgburo
    B. Central Committee
    C. Politburo
    D. Supreme Soviet

14._____

15. The short-term effect of the 1967 Six-Day War on Soviet foreign relations was
    A. Arab skepticism of Soviet resolve
    B. improved diplomatic relations with Israel
    C. increased Soviet involvement in building the Arab militaries
    D. a strengthening of cooperation with the West

15._____

16. Which of the following was NOT an idea that was characteristic of the *changing landmarks* movement of the 1920s? The
    A. Bolsheviks were the embodiment of the Russian spirit and would achieve the ultimate stability of the nation
    B. revolution had been halted by the Soviet government, which was proceeding to carry out programs
    C. evolution from radicalism to empire would proceed as it had after the French revolution
    D. Russian revolution was fundamentally a nationalist revolution with Slavic roots

16._____

17. Among the factors that permitted the Bolsheviks' relatively bloodless takeover of the Winter palace in the fall of 1917, the most significant was

    A. their appeal to the peasantry
    B. the lack of resistance from the military
    C. their ability to appease the landed aristocracy
    D. the brilliance of Lenin and Trotsky

17._____

18. The 1961 Vienna meetings between Kennedy and Krushchev were focused primarily on the issue of
    A. the Cuban missile crisis
    B. nuclear arms reduction in general
    C. Communist China's world role
    D. Germany and Berlin

19. Each of the following was an issue that received significant attention at the 1967 Glassboro Summit between Lyndon Johnson and Premier Kosygin EXCEPT
    A. The Middle East
    B. nuclear nonproliferation
    C. Germany and Berlin
    D. Vietnam

20. At the Potsdam conference of 1945, United States President Truman was not as conciliatory toward Stalin as his predecessor, Roosevelt, had been. The main reason for this was that
    A. Truman was generally a more forceful personality than Roosevelt
    B. the new British Prime Minister, Clement Attlee, was urging Truman to exclude the Soviets from the war effort against Japan
    C. Truman knew the atomic bomb had been developed
    D. Stalin's designs on Eastern Europe had been made clearer

21. Which of the following contributed to the overall failure of the revolutionary movement of 1905?
    I. Inability to mobilize support in rural areas
    II. The splitting of the opposition over the issue of the Duma
    III. The return of loyalist armed forces from the Far East
    IV. The disabling of communications networks effected by general strikes
    The CORRECT answer is:
    A. I, II   B. II, III   C. I, III, IV   D. I, II, III, IV

22. The original Union of Soviet Socialist Republics, established in 1922, included the republic.
    A. Estonian   B. Ukrainian   C. Uzbek   D. Georgian

23. Which of the following countries did NOT declare war on the Ottoman Empire in 1912?
    A. Greece   B. Bulgaria   C. Romania   D. Serbia

24. Approximately what percentage of the total population of the Soviet Union was killed during World War II?
    A. 3   B. 7   C. 12   D. 20

25. Which of the following groups was a Turkic minority within the Soviet Union?
    A. Ingush   B. Kalmyks   C. Azeris   D. Karachai

26. For what reason was the Soviets' 1956 invasion of Hungary not protested strongly by the international community?
    A. It was a secret invasion that lasted only several hours.
    B. Hungary was already thought to be lost to Communism.
    C. It was a relatively bloodless suppression.
    D. Most governments were already preoccupied with the invasion of the Suez Canal

27. The March Revolution of 1917 began spontaneously in
    A. Kiev
    B. Moscow
    C. the peasant countryside
    D. Petrograd

28. In his 1941 address to the Soviet people after the German invasion, Stalin justified his previous nonaggression pact with Hitler on the grounds that
    A. it ensured a strong Soviet presence in Eastern Europe after the war was over
    B. it had bought the country time to build its defenses
    C. he had believed Germany to be the lesser of two evils in the conflict
    D. he had been deceived by the fascist leader

29. Which of the following were members of the White forces during the civil war that began in 1918?
    I. Monarchists
    II. Liberals
    III. Conservatives
    IV. Mensheviks

    The CORRECT answer is:
    A. I, III
    B. II, IV
    C. I, III, IV
    D. I, II, III, IV

30. The post-revolutionary civil war in Russia began in 1918 when White forces under General Alexander Kolchak gathered in
    A. the Transcaucasus
    B. the Crimea
    C. Siberia
    D. Petrograd

31. In the period that passed between the failed coup of August 1991 and the formation of the Commonwealth of Independent States (CIS), how many of the former Soviet republics declared their independence?
    A. 5   B. 9   C. 12   D. 15

32. Which of the following was a result of the 1921 Treaty of Riga?
    A. Poland was granted control of border regions in the Ukraine and Belorussia.
    B. Japan was granted control of southern Sakhalin Island.
    C. The Baltic states remained independent.
    D. The Transcaucasus was divided into three republics.

33. Which of the following was the first Soviet republic to declare its independence from the USSR?
    A. Chechnya
    B. Lithuania
    C. Georgia
    D. Ukraine

34. Immediately upon entering World War I in 1914, Russia's initial goals were to
    I. fulfill its defense obligation to France
    II. acquire the Turkish Straits
    III. block German and Austrian ambitions in the Balkans
    IV. acquire Constantinople

    The CORRECT answer is:
    A. I, III
    B. II, III
    C. II, IV
    D. III, IV

35. The 1991 coup against the Gorbachev government failed because of a number of blunders or the part of the plotters. Their most significant mistake was probably
    A. taking inadequate steps to control the media
    B. over estimating the loyalty of military officers
    C. failing to arrest or silence Boris Yeltsin
    D. de laying the deployment of military support for the coup

35._____

36. The *secret additional protocol* of the 1939 nonaggression pact between Germany and the Soviet Union concerned an agreement to
    A. divide up Eastern Europe at the end of the war
    B. lend Russian naval support in the German offensive against Britain
    C. overlook the German extermination of Eastern European Jews
    D. launch a joint commercial venture in the oil-rich regions of the Middle East

36._____

37. Which of the following was NOT a factor in the 1920 victory of the Bolsheviks over White forces in the civil war?
    A. Support from several eastern European neighbors
    B. Control of most of the important railroad lines
    C. The refusal of the White forces to adopt a policy of land reforms
    D. Their success at creating an army

37._____

38. The United States Senate's ratification of the first international Non-Proliferation Treaty was postponed by the
    A. Tet offensive
    B. Soviet invasion of Czechoslovakia
    C. Cuban missile crisis
    D. Soviet invasion of Afghanistan

38._____

39. After the surrender of Japan to the United States in 1945, the Soviet Union was allowed each of the following EXCEPT
    A. a role in the postwar administration of Japan
    B. the occupation of Manchuria
    C. the occupation of all of Sakhalin Island
    D. the occupation of the Kuril Islands

39._____

40. Each of the following nations supplied troops to aid the 1968 Soviet invasion of Czechoslovakia EXCEPT
    A. Poland   C. Bulgaria
    B. East Germany   D. Romania

40._____

41. Alter the Potsdam conference of 1945, the Allies seemed to be moving inevitably toward
    A. a sustained offensive against the Japanese mainland
    B. the cession of Eastern Europe to Soviet influence
    C. the occupation of Spain
    D. the partitioning of Germany

41._____

42. The last German offensive against Russia in the Second World War was launched in 1943 against the city of
    A. Harkov
    B. Stalingrad
    C. Kursk
    D. Smolensk

42._____

43. Which of the following best explains why Roosevelt and Churchill accepted the vagueness of Stalin's promises at the 1945 Yalta conference to establish democratically elected leadership in Eastern Europe?
They
   A. Did not discern the insincerity of Stalin's promise
   B. Under that the only way to dislodge the Soviet from these countries would be through a direct offensive
   C. Wanted to hasten the onset of reconstruction in order to prevent further hostility in Western Europe
   D. Perceived a desperate need for Russian involvement in the war with Japan

43.____

44. Which of the following was NOT occupied by the Red Army when World War II ended in Europe?
   A. Hungary
   B. Albania
   C. Syria
   D. Austria

44.____

45. The purpose of the 1957 Eisenhower Doctrine was to
   A. block Communist expansion in Southeast Asia
   B. prevent the construction of the Berlin Wall
   C. pave the way for improved East-West relations
   D. block Communist expansion in the Middle East

45.____

46. After the October Revolution, Lenin's efforts to bring all of Russia under Bolshevik authority centered on
   A. appeasement of the peasantry
   B. using the Red Army to put down opposition
   C. redistributing the lands of the nobility among the proletariat
   D. gaining control of the local soviets

46.____

47. Which of the following Eastern European countries had practiced democracy in its government prior to World War II?
   A. Czechoslovakia
   B. Hungary
   C. Yugoslavia
   D. Poland

47.____

48. In the 1960s, when it was clear that the United States was escalating its involvement in Vietnams the Soviets initial reaction was to

   A. urge the North Vietnamese to negotiate an end to the conflict
   B. establish a supply route to the North Vietnamese through China
   C. mobilize troops as a show of support for the North Vietnamese
   D. sit back and wait for China to become involved

48.____

49. Each of the following was a desire expressed by Roosevelt and Churchill at the 1945 Yalta Conference EXCEPT
   A. Soviet participation in the war against Japan
   B. Soviet responsibility for the reconstruction of the Baltic states
   C. an agreement on the occupation of Germany
   D. Soviet guarantees of free elections in Eastern Europe

49.____

50. After taking power, the Bolsheviks undertook many actions which demonstrated their repudiation of democratic principles. The first indication occurred in 1917 when the party
    A. seized all private property
    B. established the Cheka, or political police
    C. outlawed strikes
    D. disbanded the first elected Constituent Assembly

50.____

KEY (CORRECT ANSWERS)

1. C	26. D
2. A	27. C
3. C	28. C
4. C	29. D
5. C	30. C
6. E	31. D
7. A	32. A
8. B	33. B
9. D	34. A
10. B	35. C
11. D	36. A
12. B	37. A
13. A	38. B
14. A	39. A
15. A	40. D
16. A	41. D
17. B	42. C
18. D	43. B
19. C	44. C
20. C	45. D
21. B	46. D
22. B	47. A
23. C	48. A
24. C	49. B
25. D	50. D

EXAMINATION SECTION
TEST 1

DIRECTIONS: Each question or incomplete statement is followed by several suggested answers or completions. Select the one that BEST answers the question or completes the statement. *PRINT THE LETTER OF THE CORRECT ANSWER IN THE SPACE AT THE RIGHT.*

1. Which of the following resulted from the Russian Revolution of 1905?
    A. Emancipation of the serfs
    B. Legalization of the Bolshevik party
    C. Universal suffrage
    D. A free press
    E. The creation of the Duma

2. Which of the following resulted from the close relationship between science and government in industrialized nations during the Second World War?
    A. The pace of discovery and invention noticeably slowed.
    B. Specialization decreased.
    C. Much scientific research became financially dependent on military funding.
    D. Fewer students were interested in scientific training.
    E. The benefits of scientific advances were no longer questioned.

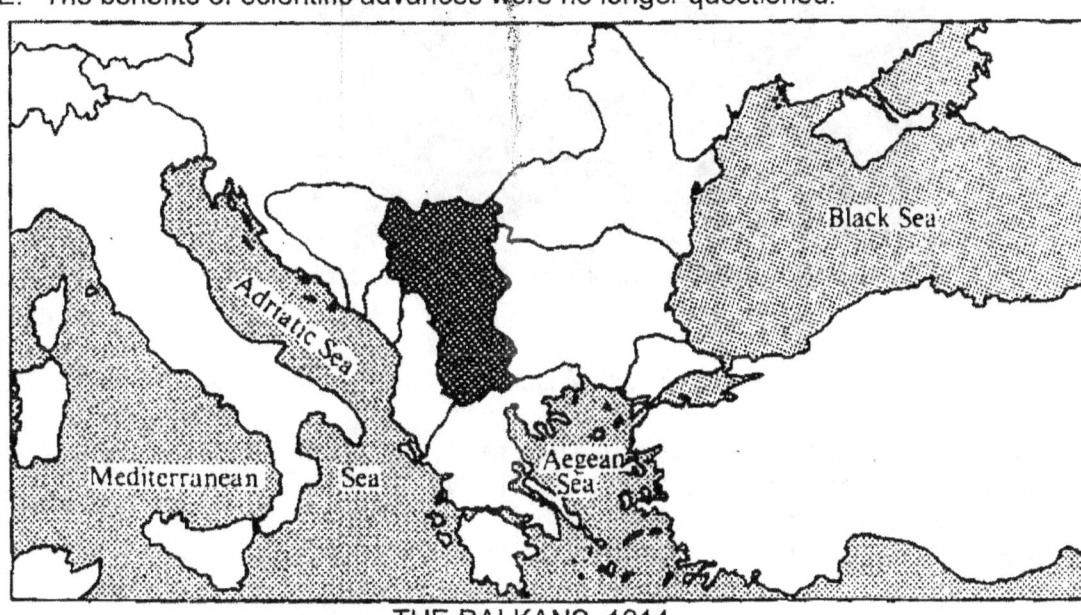

THE BALKANS. 1914

3. On the map above, the shaded state is

    A. Poland B. Hungary C. Greece
    D. Serbia E. Bulgaria

4. The Nazi party's ideal role for *Aryan* women in Germany was that they
    A. were to be mothers, wives, and homemakers
    B. were to serve in equal numbers with men in state and party bureaucracies at all levels
    C. were to enjoy economic power equal to that of men
    D. were to have no political or legal rights
    E. would be a reserve military force, available for frontline duty when there was a shortage of male soldiers

Imperial War Museum

5. The purpose of the British poster shown above was to
    A. shame able-bodied men into volunteering for military service
    B. encourage fathers to remain at home with their children
    C. discourage enlistment by white-collar workers
    D. commemorate those who had died in the First World War
    E. highlight the differences between the First and the Second World Wars

6. "... we are for a socialism that is proper to a highly developed country and is devoid of those repulsive features imposed upon our country by a handful of narrow-minded, dogmatic, power-hungry careerists and unscrupulous despots. We have no reason to assume an anti-Soviet attitude insofar as the Soviet Union's internal policy is concerned. We object only to brutal interference in the affairs of other nations."
This passage reflects the attitude of
    A. Italian fascist in 1925
    B. German communist in 1929
    C. Spanish anarchist in 1936
    D. British Tory in 1937
    E. Czech dissident in 1969

PERCENTAGE INCREASE IN THE POPULATION
OF GERMANY, 1816-1914

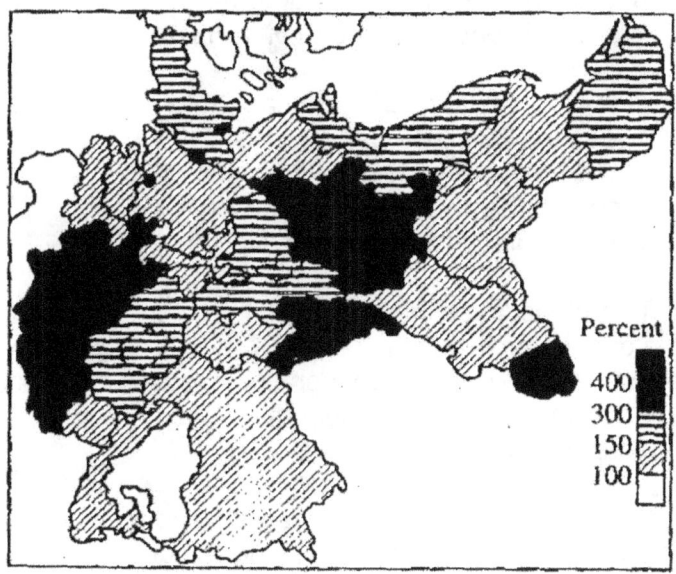

7. The map above BEST supports which of the following statements?
    A. Religious affiliation explains the growth in population.
    B. Immigration to the Western Hemisphere decimated the population of central Germany.
    C. The Franco-Prussian and Austro-Prussian wars left Germany divided and depopulated.
    D. The population of industrial regions grew most rapidly.
    E. The influx of Russians and Eastern Europeans made Germany the largest multinational state in Europe

8. A student report has in it the quotation, "The only thing we have to fear is fear itself."
    A. The report is related to the topic of
    B. the bombing of Pearl Harbor in 1941
    C. the placement of Soviet missiles in Cuba in 1962
    D. economic conditions in the U.S. in 1933
    E. the U.S. involvement in Vietnam in 1967

9. In recent years, the MOST dramatic example of our Constitution's subordination of the military to civilian control was seen in the
    A. election of. Dwight Eisenhower as President in 1952
    B. Bay of Pigs operation
    C. widespread opposition to American involvement in Vietnam
    D. removal in 1951 of General MacArthur from all Far East commands

10. Of the wars listed below in which the United States was a participant, the one authorized by a declaration of war by Congress was
    A. the Korean War
    B. World War II
    C. the Vietnam War
    D. the Naval War with France 1798-1800

11. Of the following men, the one *correctly* associated with the idea he believed in is

    A. Mohandas K. Gandhi: non-violent non-cooperation
    B. Yasir Arafat: passive resistance
    C. Ayatollah Khomeini: a constitutional monarchy for Iran
    D. Mao-Tse Tung: peaceful coexistence with the Soviet Union

11._____

12. United States membership in the Organization of American States (OAS) is an example of
    A. close cooperation between the U.S. and Canada
    B. abandonment of the Good Neighbor policy.
    C. domination of the western hemisphere by the United States
    D. rejection of the Roosevelt Corollary to the Monroe Doctrine

12._____

13. The SALT accords were important because they
    A. provided an example of the effectiveness of the. UN.
    B. provided an example of Soviet-American cooperation in space exploration
    C. were an important step toward limiting a nuclear missle arms race
    D. had strong bipartisan support in the U.S. Senate

13._____

14. In the Russo-Chinese Pact of 1945 the Soviet government agreed to
    A. give military supplies and moral support to the Nationalist government
    B. recognize Chinese rule over Outer Mongolia
    C. support the Chinese Communists in their fight to gain control of China
    D. give China complete control of the Chinese Eastern Railway

14._____

15. The pair of Americans associated with the idea of forging a good-neighbor relationship between the United States and Latin America is
    A. James G. Blaine and Richard Olney
    B. Theodore Roosevelt and John Hay
    C. Franklin D. Roosevelt and Cordell Hull
    D. Lyndon Johnson and Dean Rusk

15._____

16. Of the following developments, the one which BEST accounts for the growth of world population in the last four decades is
    A. the opening of new lands for settlement and agriculture
    B. new food supplies and material well-being made possible by industrial and technological development
    C. international disease control and modern medicine
    D. the decline of wars

16._____

17. The Yalta and Potsdam Conferences in 1945 sought to solve the problem of Germany by agreeing to the
    A. permanent division of Germany into four occupation zones
    B. four-zone division of Germany until order was restored a peace treaty and the unification of Germany could be ,established in
    C. settlement of Germany's post-war, boundaries and the extent of reparation payments
    D. establishment of a central German government and the determination of the amount of military production to be permitted.

17._____

18. A combination of these four situations: defeat in a great war, serious food shortages, failure to sign a peace treaty, and a workers' council rebellion - led to the
    A. Chinese Revolution of 1911
    B. Russian Revolution of 1905
    C. victory of the Chinese Communists over the Chinese Nationalists
    D. Russian Revolution of 1917

19. The Nigerian Civil War of 1967-1970 had as its BASIC cause
    A. Arab vs. African racial antagonisms
    B. Tribal conflicts
    C. Communist agitation
    D. Claims of white supremacists

20. Arab objections to the 1977 Israeli-Egyptian peace settlement have centered chiefly on the status of
    A. the Sinai Peninsula
    B. the Suez Canal
    C. the West Bank
    D. West Jerusalem

21. Of the following terms, the one *correctly* matched with its significance is:
    A. Three People's Principles- peace, Buddhism and elimination of foreigners
    B. Great Leap Foward- peaceful coexistence with the West
    C. Long March- Mao's escape to Yenan from Chiang-Kai Shek
    D. Tai Ping Rebellion- Sun Yat-Sen's leadership

22. Of the following, the *only* indigenous polity in Africa that escaped a generation of colonialism during the era of imperialism was
    A. Ethiopia
    B. Chad
    C. Rwanda
    D. Morocco

23. The President correctly matched with the phrase used to express his foreign policy is:
    A. Franklin Pierce - 54°40' or fight
    B. James Madison - No entangling alliances
    C. Woodrow Wilson - Watchful waiting
    D. Harry Truman - With malice toward none

24. The most far-reaching attempt to redraw the map of Europe along the lines of nationality was made at the peace settlement following
    A. the Napoleonic Wars
    B. World War I
    C. World War II
    D. the Franco-Prussian War of 1870-71

25. The quotation, "The nation began to make itself over according to Western standards," "describes:
    A. India, immediately after the Sepoy Rebellion
    B. Russia, following the Russo-Japanese War
    C. China, immediately following the Opium War
    D. Japan, following the overthrow of the shogunate

26. In the period between the two World Wars, a profound pacifism, expressed as an almost doctrinaire insistence on peace, was seen MOST widely in
    A. the Soviet Union and Germany
    B. Germany and Italy
    C. France and Germany
    D. Great Britain and France

26._____

27. The 1978 treaty between the United States and Panama reversed the relationship between these countries established by the
    A. Clayton-Bulwer Treaty (1850)
    B. Treaty of Paris (1899)
    C. Hay-Pauncefote Treaty (1900)
    D. Hay-Bunau-Varilla Treaty (1903)

27._____

28. When President Carter visited Mexico in 1979, President Lopez-Portillo expressed his distrust of the United States. To prove his point about occasional lack of harmony between the two countries in the past, he could have cited all of the following EXCEPT:
    A. the Vera Cruz affair
    B. the Pancho Villa raids
    C. U.S. immigration policy
    D. the Zimmerman note

28._____

29. During the period immediately preceding the outbreak of World War II, which is the CORRECT Chronological order of the following events?
    I. Absorption by Germany of Bohemia and Moravia as a protectorate
    II. Annexation to Germany of Austria
    III. Annexation to Germany of the Sudentenland
    IV. Nazi -Soviet non-aggression pact

    The CORRECT answer is
    A. II, III, I, IV
    B. IV, III, II, I
    C. III, II, I, IV
    D. I, Iv, II, III

29._____

30. The MOST common barrier to economic progress in developing countries is a shortage of
    A. raw materials
    B. agricultural land
    C. capital
    D. unskilled workers

30._____

31. Of the following, the motive MOST responsible for Iraq's attack on Iran was Iraq's desire for control of the
    A. oil fields of eastern Iran
    B. Shaft al Arab
    C. strategic mountain passes in Northern Iran
    D. southern Persian Gulf oil routes

31._____

32. Of the following, the statement about nationalism which is MOST accurage is that it
    A. prevents the rise of militarism
    B. is an idea which can be used to unite people
    C. encourages diversity of thinking within nations
    D. preserves the ethnic identities of different groups within a country

32._____

33. All of the following nations probably have the ability to make atomic bombs at present EXCEPT
    A. Israel
    B. India
    C. Pakistan
    D. Libya

34. A student report on Camp David Summit Conference on Egyptian-Israeli relations should refer to all of the following EXCEPT an agreement to
    A. set up a Palestinian State
    B. sign an Egyptian-Israeli Peace Treaty in the near future
    C. return the Sinai Desert region to Egypt
    D. decide within 5 years the fate of Palestinians living in the West Bank

35. All of the following are factors in the Lebanese crises EXCEPT the
    A. Lebanese Christian refusal to give up Israeli aid
    B. extent to which Syrian troops make up the peace-keeping force
    C. Russian involvement on the side of the Lebanese Christians
    D. Syrian development of missiles on Lebanese soil

36. Of the following, the problem which is common to most industrial nations of the world is
    A. little fluctuation in the volume of currency in each nation
    B. energy needs which are greater than present resources
    C. unstable political conditions
    D. a decreasing standard of living

37. Of the following nations, the one which shares a border with both China and the Soviet Union is
    A. Iran
    B. India
    C. Afghanistan
    D. Pakistan

38. The lack of modern economic development of the Amazon Basin of Brazil is due to all of the following reasons EXCEPT
    A. lack of evolopment capital
    B. lack of a developed infrastructure
    C. failure to find mineral deposits
    D. failure of government policy in recognizing the area's wealth

39. From 1949 to the development of Nixon's policy of detente, the leaders of mainland China have viewed United States policy as one of encirclement and a threat to the existence of the People's Republic.
    This view was a result of
    A. United States support of the Nationalists on Taiwan, involvement in the wars in Korea and Vietnam, and the presence of military bases in Japan and the Philippines
    B. United States policies such as the Marshall Plan and NATO which were designed to reconstruct and rebuild Western Europe as a bulwark against Russian expansion
    C. the failure of the United States and its allies to prevent the Russians from enforcing the Brezhnev Doctrine in Czechoslovakia
    D. the United States policy of exporting nuclear technology for economic purposes only and its refusal to accept unilateral nuclear disarmament

40. The nation which benefited MOST from the successful revolution against Spain in South America in the early nineteenth century was
    A. the United States, which initiated a series of mutual defense pacts with the new nations
    B. France, whose revolutionary ideas ignited many of these liberation movements
    C. Russia, which realized the indigenous social and economic systems were conducive to the spread of radical ideals
    D. England, which dominated the trade and commerce of the new nations

40._____

41. The problem of providing food for the world's population in the future
    A. will not be important because the birth rate declines in all nations as they develop, industrialize and modernize
    B. is unsolvable unless drastic action is taken through the science of eugenics to reduce the world's population
    C. will be solved by the inevitable havoc of a nuclear war
    D. may be met by such measures as extracting protein from non-edible plants, increased use of protein-rich fish meal, and the domestication of wild animals

41._____

42. The term that BEST characterizes the foreign policy of the United States since World War II is
    A. appeasement
    B. isolationism
    C. containment
    D. non-intervention

42._____

43. President Johnson's policy in 1965-8 was to press for the implementation of the Great Society Program in the realm of domestic affairs while
    A. seeking an all-out victory in Vietnam
    B. pursuing the policy of containment by means of a limited war in Vietnam
    C. attempting to disentangle the United States from the quagmire of Vietnam
    D. risking general war with both China and Russia over Vietnam

43._____

44. The rapid transformation of Japan from a feudal domain to a modern industrial state in a brief period of half a century was brought about by the
    A. assistance rendered to the emerging new Japanese government by the United States
    B. desire of the Japanese people to protect themselves against Western encroachment
    C. bountiful natural resources found in Japan, which speeded the process of modernization
    D. splendid isolation offered by Japan's situation as an island apart from mainland Asia

44._____

45. The policy of appeasement for the sake of avoiding general war with an aggressor power is associated with
    A. Chamberlain's policy at Munich in 1938
    B. Roosevelt's and Churchill's policy agreed upon at the Atlantic Conference
    C. Woodrow Wilson's policies incorporated in the Treaty of Versailles in 1919
    D. Truman's policy governing our relations with the Soviet Union in 1947

45._____

46. Stalin's 1939 non-aggression treaty with Hitler was intended to provide   46._____
    A. Stalin with time to consolidate his power in Russia and avoid an invasion against
       his unprepared nation
    B. Russia with much needed technical and capital equipment to assure success of
       the Five Year Plan for industrialization
    C. the world with another respite from the prospect of World War II
    D. Russia greater leverage in its negotiations with Britain and France for a collective
       security pact

47. The MAIN purpose of the July 1981 meeting in the Bahamas of the representatives   47._____
    of the United States, Mexico, Canada and Venezuela was to
        A. discuss ways to remove Castro as leader of Cuba
        B. establish methods of economic cooperation in the Caribbean Basin
        C. discuss methods of amending the Charter of the Organization of American
           States
        D. set up defense alliances against Communist penetration into the Caribbean
           Basin

48. The FIRST national draft law in American history was enacted during   48._____
        A. the Revolutionary War
        B. the Civil War
        C. World War II
        D. the Korean War

49. The dismissal of General Douglas MacArthur by President Harry Truman during the   49._____
    Korean War was a result of
        A. disagreements between the two men as to Chinese intervention
        B. the President's desire to replace MacArthur with General Dwight D. Eisenhower
        C. the challenge by General MacArthur to run for the Republican nomination for
           President in 1952
        D. the insubordination displayed by a general to his commander-in-chief

50. The fight for ratification of the Treaty of Versailles in 1919 found President Wilson on   50._____
    one side and the Senate Republicans on the other.
    The so-called Lodge reservations to the Treaty were designed to
        A. release the United States from certain entanglements, and to safeguard historic
           policies such as the Monroe Doctrine
        B. permit American participation in the League of Nations as-a consultative nation
        C. allow the United States to sign a separate treaty of peace with Germany
        D. insure a Republican victory in the Presidential election of 1920

KEY (CORRECT ANSWERS)

1. E	26. D
2. C	27. D
3. D	28. D
4. A	29. A
5. A	30. C
6. E	31. B
7. D	32. B
8. C	33. D
9. D	34. A
10. B	35. C
11. A	36. B
12. D	37. C
13. C	38. D
14. C	39. A
15. C	40. D
16. B	41. D
17. B	42. C
18. D	43. B
19. B	44. B
20. C	45. A
21. C	46. A
22. C	47. D
23. C	48. B
24. B	49. D
25. D	50. A

TEST 2

DIRECTIONS: Each question or incomplete statement is followed by several suggested answers or completions. Select the one that BEST answers the question or completes the statement. *PRINT THE LETTER OF THE CORRECT ANSWER IN THE SPACE AT THE RIGHT.*

1. A MAJOR reason for Chiang Kai-shek's defeat by Chinese Communists was　　　　1.____
   A. the failure of the United States to give him any assistance
   B. the alliance between Sun Yat-sen and Mao Tse-tung
   C. Japan's success in conquering all of China
   D. the failure of the Kuomintang Party to offer a program to gain peasant support

2. The statement which BEST explains Pakistan's decision to develop nuclear weapons is that　　2.____
   A. its economy can easily afford the cost of developing nuclear capability
   B. it feels that other nations who possess nuclear capability are a threat to its security
   C. its dominant religion stresses military and national pride
   D. the United Nations encouraged it to develop these weapons

3. An IMPORTANT consequence of the war between Iraq and Iran had been that　　3.____
   A. Iraq has gained control of the strategic Shatt al Arab
   B. the standard of living of the people of Iraq has suffered greatly
   C. Iran is facing immediate economic collapse
   D. the combined oil production of Iran and Iraq has been cut about 50%

4. A new role for most African and Asian nations which developed in the 1960's and 1970's is　　4.____
   A. supplying the world with scarce natural resources
   B. having a voice in making world decisions
   C. serving as the site for the continuing struggle by the major powers, for world
   D. supremacy
   E. being the source of different forms of literacy and artistic expression

5. The imperialist rivals of Russia in the late 19th and early 20th centuries were　　5.____
   A. Germany and Italy
   B. Japan and Great Britain
   C. France and the Netherlands
   D. Germany and Belgium

6. What is the CORRECT chronological order of the actions of Adolf Hitler in violation of the Treaty of Versailles?　　6.____
   I. Reoccupation of the Rhineland
   II. Rearmament of Germany
   III. Seizure of Czechoslovakia
   IV. Seizure of Danzig

The CORRECT answer is:
   A. I, II, III, IV
   B. II, I, III, IV
   C. II, III, IV, I
   D. II, III, I, IV

7. Which one of the following was a MAJOR reason why Italy joined the Triple Alliance?
    A. She needed help to complete her independence.
    B. She wanted to participate in the partitioning of China.
    C. France had seized Tunisia.
    D. She feared the loss of her African colonies.

8. Adolf Hitler became Chancellor of Germany in 1933 by
    A. a coup d'etat after the *Reichstag Fire*
    B. gaining support of the army
    C. appointment by Von Hindenburg
    D. having his party win a majority of the Reichstag seats

9. The post-World War II period has seen all of the following events in international relations EXCEPT
    A. Italy allying herself with the Western democracies
    B. the United States making regional agreements with Western Europe and Southeast Asia
    C. France liquidating her empire in Southeast Asia and Africa
    D. England returning to the pre-war policy of non-participation in formal alliances

10. President Truman said that the peace treaty with Japan *was a treaty of reconciliation which looks to the future and not to the past.*
    This idea is expressed in which one of the following treaty provisions?
    A. The Japanese overseas empire acquired prior to World War I be left intact.
    B. Japan be relieved completely of responsibility for reparations
    C. All Allied Powers occupation forces be withdrawn.
    D. A new constitution restoring the emperor's powers be promulgated.

11. The reason President Truman gave for relieving General MacArthur of command in Korea was General MacArthur's
    A. military blunders
    B. insubordination
    C. refusal to negotiate with the Chinese Communists
    D. emergence as a candidate for the presidency

12. Under the Constitution of the Fifth French Republic, the emergency powers granted to the President resemble closely the emergency powers given to the
    A. President of the United States
    B. President of Germany under the Weimar Constitution
    C. Prime Minister of England
    D. President of Italy under the Constitution of 1947

13. The function of the National Security Council is to
    A. keep check on subversives in government employment
    B. formulate basic foreign policies for the United States
    C. supervise the selective service law
    D. recommend changes in the social security laws

14. Which one of the following statements BEST represents the geographic character of the Middle East?
    A. Contrary to popular impression, it is not strategically located for the merging of continents and oceans.
    B. Although oil is the best known resource, other mineral resources are of greater importance.
    C. The greatest limiting factor to cultivation is not water but fertile oil.
    D. While the image of the area is one unrelieved aridity and deserts, there are significant variations of climate and topography.

15. The Hallstein Doctrine held that
    A. West Germany should sever diplomatic relations with any country, except the U.S.S.R., which recognized East Germany
    B. the re-unification of Germany was a pre-condition for the recognition of the Oder-Neisse line as the German-Polish boundary
    C. the West German Republic acknowledged moral, but not legal, responsibility for Nazi treatment of the Jews
    D. prosecution of Nazi war criminals was limited by a twenty-year statute of limitations

16. Which one of the following measures was NOT adopted by the Federal government in the conduct of both World War I and World War II?
    A. The sale of bonds to finance the Wars
    B. Conscription
    C. Control of production
    D. Government operation of railroads

17. In which one of the following groups is a Secretary of State CORRECTLY paired with a policy he advocated?
    A. Frank B. Kellogg - Opposition to American participation in an international enunciation of war
    B. Elihu Root - Membership of the United States in the World Court
    C. John F. Dulles - Support of the British invasion of the Sinai Peninsula in 1956
    D. William J. Bryan - Insistence on respect for our rights as neutrals from 1914-1917 at the risk of war

18. Which one of the following pairs is NOT in a cause-and-effect relationship?
    A. The Napoleonic Wars - Decembrist Revolt
    B. The Crimean War - Reforms of Alexander II
    C. The Russo-Japanese War - Revolution of 1905
    D. World War I - Revolution of 1917

19. Which one of the following was one of the provisions of the Yalta Agreement of 1945?
    A. It restored to the Union of Soviet Socialist Republics the imperialist rights the Czar had lost in the Far East.
    B. In recognition of the Soviet losses in the war, the Soviet Union was granted the option of joining the fight against Japan.
    C. It gave the Russians eight votes in the United Nations General Assembly to counterbalance the votes of the British Commonwealth.
    D. It provided for the recognition of the Soviet-controlled Polish government by Franklin D. Roosevelt and Winston Churchill.

20. The *Uniting for Peace* resolution of 1950 increased the power of the United Nations General Assembly by
    A. giving it the power to wage war in Korea
    B. curtailing the prerogatives of the United Nations Security Council as the agency with the primary *responsibility for the maintenance of peace and security*
    C. allowing it to take action on threats to peace if the Security Council is hampered by the veto
    D. allowing virtually all peace-loving nations of the world to join the United Nations

21. In which one of the following are the events arranged in CORRECT chronological order?
    I. Russo-Japanese War
    II. Sino-Japanese War
    III. Japan's annexation of Formosa
    IV. Russia's getting concession in Liaotung Peninsula

    The CORRECT answer is:
    A. II, I, IV, III
    B. III, IV, I, II
    C. II, III, IV, I
    D. IV, II, I, III

Question 22-25
DIRECTIONS: Questions 22 through 25 are to be answered on the basis of the following map

22. Which one of the following is the CORRECT date for the map?
    A. 187   B. 1913   C. 1922   D. 1939

23. Which of the areas listed below were parts of the same nation as of the date of the map above?
    A. D & R
    B. G & I
    C. W, T, & V
    D. H, H & Q

24. If a map twenty years prior to the date of the map above were to be examined, which one of the following areas would NOT be shown as an independent nation?
    A. D   B. F   C. L   D. Q

25. Which one of the areas listed below was the FIRST to lose 100. its independence in subsequent political revisions?
    A. G   B. H   C. Q   D. V

26. Which one of the following was NOT provided for in the Treaty of Rome (1957) which established the European Economic Community?
    A. Common action will be taken to improve living and working conditions for employees.
    B. Monetary policies of the members are to be coordinated.
    C. The colonies and associated territories of the members are to be excluded from the Common Market.
    D. Trade barriers are to be gradually eliminated among the six members over a period of years.

27. Which one of the following crises is NOT matched CORRECTLY with the two countries it affected?
    A. Fashoda Crisis (1898) - Britain and France
    B. Moroccan Crisis (1905-06) - France and Spain
    C. Moroccan Crisis (1911) - France and Germany
    D. Serbian Crisis (1914) - Austria-Hungary and Russia

28. Which one of the following European countries did NOT attempt to expand to other continents between 1870 and 1914?
    A. Austria-Hungary
    B. Belgium
    C. Portugal
    D. Russia

28.____

29. In which one of the following pairs does the cause precede the effect?
    A. Twenty-one Demands - Overthrow of the Manchu Dynasty
    B. Interference in the affairs of Korea - Sino-Japanese War of 1895
    C. Stimson Doctrine - Invasion of Manchuria
    D. Boxer Rebellion - Open Door Policy

29.____

30. Which one of the following items consists of states that were independent in 1914?

    A. Liberia - Korea
    B. Siam - Ethiopia
    C. Indo-China - Libya
    D. Malaya - Nigeria

30.____

31. Which one of the following suffered the GREATEST territorial loss in Europe after World War I?
    A. Austria-Hungary
    B. Germany
    C. Russia
    D. Turkey

31.____

32. The Treaty of Rapallo (1922)
    A. reflected the anti-Communist orientation of the German officer corps
    B. marked a relaxation of the isolation of the Soviet Union after World War I
    C. made it difficult for Germany to evade some of the provisions of the Treaty of Versailles
    D. completed the encirclement of the Soviet Union by hostile powers after World War I

32.____

33. A bibliography for a student who is to report on the experiences of the ordinary person during the Second World War might include all of the following EXCEPT
    A. BURMA SURGEON - Gordon S. Seagrave
    B. HIROSHIMA - John Hersey
    C. REVOLT IN THE DESERT - Thomas E. Lawrence
    D. THUNDER OUT OF CHINA - White and Jacoby

33.____

34. Which one of the following is NOT true of the Washington Arms Conference of 1921-22?
    A. The five major naval powers agreed to reduce the tonnage of capital ships.
    B. The Four Power Pact superseded the Anglo-Japanese Alliance of 1902.
    C. Nine powers officially gave support to the Open Door Policy.
    D. The Escalator Clause which was adopted allowed signatories to evade some of the treaty provisions.

34.____

35. Which one of the following is NOT true of India in the 20th century?
    A. Gandhi, as a pacificist, refused to support Great Britain in both World Wars I and II.
    B. In 1950, India became a member of the Commonwealth of Nations.
    C. India, after being liberated, at first chose dominion status, but later decided to become a republic.
    D. India is not a member of SEATO.

35.____

36. Which one of the following statements BEST describes the nature of the Japanese Peace Treaty of 1951?
    It
    A. provided for the permanent disarmament of Japan
    B. was a general peace settlement signed by the major allied powers as well as by Communist China
    C. neutralized Japan in the Cold War
    D. left most of the basic economic problems of Japan unsolved

37. Which one of the following statements BEST explains Theodore Roosevelt's reasons for helping to bring the Russo-Japanese War to an end? He wanted to
    A. prevent an upset in the balance of power in the Far East
    B. thwart the ambitions of Great Britain in the Far East
    C. help Japan continue her westernization
    D. repay a debt of gratitude to Russia for having sold Alaska to the United States

38. Which one of the following MOST correctly describes our military position in 1917?
    A. Modern equipment compensated for the small size of our army and navy.
    B. Both our army and navy were weak.
    C. While our army was strong, our navy was weak.
    D. Our navy was relatively stronger than our army.

39. In 1919, Senator Lodge, chairman of the Senate Committee on Foreign Relations, urged that the Treaty of Versailles be
    A. rejected and a new treaty drawn up
    B. ratified with reservations
    C. ratified without the League Covenant
    D. rewritten by the Senate Committee on Foreign Relations

40. Which one of the following BEST describes the Kellogg-Briand Pact of 1928?
    It
    A. contributed materially to international peace
    B. outlawed all wars, regardless of cause
    C. was popularly known as the Locarno Pact
    D. permitted war for purposes of defense

41. Which one of the following statements is NOT true of the election campaign of 1940?
    A. Both major candidates favored *all-out* aid to Great Britain *short of war*.
    B. Both major candidates advocated a conscription law.
    C. Roosevelt favored, and Wilkie opposed, a program of full preparedness.
    D. Both major candidates promised not to send American forces overseas.

42. Which one of the following was the MOST direct cause for the promulgation of the Truman Doctrine?
    The
    A. decision of Britain to withdraw its forces from Greece
    B. demands made on the United States during the Korean War
    C. need to strengthen the Marshall Plan
    D. decision to build up the military strength of NATO

43. In June 1950, the Security Council of the United Nations was able to act quickly to brand North Korea the aggressor because the
    A. General Assembly happened to be in session
    B. Soviet Union was boycotting its meetings
    C. veto does not apply in the case of armed conflict
    D. President of the United States had already ordered American armed forces to support South Korea

44. Through which body of water would an oil tanker pass FIRST en route from Kuwait to France via the Suez Canal?
    A. Arabian Sea
    B. Indian Ocean
    C. Persian Gulf
    D. Red Sea

45. Which one of the following statements is NOT in accord with the Malthusian theory?
    A. Population tends to increase more rapidly than subsistence.
    B. Man's lot can be improved by the discovery of more efficient means of supplying his food needs.
    C. Famine, wars, and disease are positive checks on the growth of population.
    D. Population is limited by the means of subsistence.

46. During the period 1920-1930, which one of the following political leaders instituted one of the MOST revolutionary programs ever enacted in so short a span of time?
    A. Adolph Hitler
    B. David Lloyd George
    C. Mahatma Gandhi
    D. Mustapha Kemal

47. In which one of the following pairs of items concerning Italy does the cause precede the result?
    A. March on Rome - Seizure of factories by workers
    B. Imposition of League sanctions - Invasion of Ethiopia
    C. Non-intervention policy - Mussolini's aid to Franco
    D. Establishment of a corporate state - Restriction of free enterprise

48. Which one of the following post-World War I treaties or agreements is INCORRECTLY paired with the subject with which it deals?
    A. Dawes Plan (1924) - War reparations
    B. Kellogg-Briand Pact (1928) - Renunciation of war as a part of national policy
    C. Pact of Locarno (1925) - Limitation of armaments
    D. Munich Pact (1938) - Status of Czechoslovakia

49. Which one of the following statements is TRUE of Korea in the 20th century?
    A. Korea was annexed by Japan by the Treaty of Portsmouth ending the Russo-Japanese War.
    B. Korean independence was guaranteed at the Cairo Conference of 1943 with the United States, Great Britain, China, and the Soviet Union as participants.
    C. Although South Korea has the bulk of the peninsula's population, North Korea is much more industrialized.
    D. The Soviet Union attempted but was not able to block action of the Security Council when North Korea invaded South Korea.

50. The effect of the ascendancy of Chiang-Kai-shek in China in 1927 was to
    A. reaffirm the policy of extraterritoriality
    B. strengthen the ties between China and the Soviet Union
    C. prevent the seizure of Manchuria by Japan
    D. free the Kuomintang of Communist control

KEY (CORRECT ANSWERS)

1. D	26. C
2. B	27. B
3. D	28. A
4. C	29. B
5. B	30. B
6. B	31. B
7. C	32. B
8. C	33. C
9. D	34. D
10. C	35. A
11. B	36. D
12. B	37. A
13. B	38. D
14. D	39. B
15. A	40. D
16. D	41. C
17. B	42. A
18. A	43. B
19. A	44. C
20. C	45. B
21. C	46. D
22. C	47. D
23. A	48. C
24. D	49. C
25. A	50. D

TEST 3

DIRECTIONS: Each question or incomplete statement is followed by several suggested answers or completions. Select the one that BEST answers the question or completes the statement. *PRINT THE LETTER OF THE CORRECT ANSWER IN THE SPACE AT THE RIGHT.*

1. Which one of the following describes MOST accurately Japanese foreign policy in the years 1931 to 1939? Japan
    A. established the state of Manchukuo, a protectorate over Outer Mongolia, and extended her influence into Inner Mongolia
    B. accepted the Stimson Doctrine, withdrew from the League of Nations, and purchased Soviet rights in the Chinese Eastern Railroad
    C. approved the Nine Power Treaty, accepted the Lytton Report, and invaded China in 1937
    D. attempted to establish a New Order in Asia, indemnified the United States for the bombing of the Panay, and terminated the agreements made at the Washington and London Naval Conferences

1._____

2. Which one of the following constituted a violation by the Soviet Union of agreements made at the Yalta Conference?
    A. Acquiring the Kurile Islands from Japan
    B. Entering the war against Japan
    C. Preventing free democratic elections in Eastern Europe
    D. Occupying the eastern zone of Germany

2._____

3. Which one of the following groups consists ENTIRELY of works of fiction dealing with World War II?
    A. BELL FOR ADANO - FAREWELL TO ARMS - TALES OF THE SOUTH PACIFIC
    B. ALL QUIET ON THE WESTERN FRONT - THE NAKED AND THE DEAD - THE WALL
    C. FOR WHOM THE BELL TOLLS - THE MOON IS DOWN - THE YOUNG LIONS
    D. ARCH OF TRIUMPH - CAINE MUTINY - MOUNTAIN ROAD

3._____

4. Which one of the following principles is NOT a charter obligation of United Nations members? To
    A. settle their international disputes by peaceful means
    B. refrain from using force in their international relations in any manner inconsistent with the purposes of the United Nations
    C. hold free elections
    D. refrain from giving assistance to any state against which the United Nations is taking preventive action

4._____

5. Which one of the following is NOT true of the post-World War II period?
    A. Italy allied herself with the Western powers.
    B. The United States gave up the policy of isolation by making regional agreements in the North Atlantic and Southeast Asian areas.
    C. France liquidated her empire in Southeast Asia.
    D. England returned to the principle of *balance of power* by refusing to join any formal alliances.

5._____

6. Which one of the following items is linked INCORRECTLY with its origin?
    A. Economic Commission for Europe - United Nations
    B. European Coal and Steel Community - Schuman Plan
    C. European Economic Community - Rome Treaties
    D. Organization for European Economic Cooperation Point IV

7. Which one of the following countries is NOT a member of NATO and the Common Market Trade group, *Inner Six*?
    A. Belgium   B. France   C. Italy   D. Spain

8. Which one of the following territorial adjustments was made at the Geneva Conference of 1954?
    A. Burma was separated from India.
    B. Indonesia was divided into Dutch and Indonesian zones.
    C. Korea was divided at the 38th parallel.
    D. Vietnam was divided along the 17th parallel.

9. In which one of the following groups is the person PROPERLY associated with the country?
    A. Sekou Toure - Congo Republic
    B. Ferhat Abbas - Tunisia
    C. William V.S. Tubman - Rhodesia
    D. Kwame Nkrumah - Ghana

10. Which one of the following pairs expresses an INCORRECT association?
    A. Algeria - National Liberation Front (FLN)
    B. Kenya - Mau Mau
    C. Morocco - Habib Bourguiba
    D. Union of South Africa - Albert Luthuli

11. Which one of the following groups consists ENTIRELY areas which have been in the French Community?
    A. Algeria - Gabon Republic - Senegal Republic
    B. Algeria - Morocco - Tunisia
    C. France - Malagasy Republic - Republic of the Co
    D. Dahomey - Laos - Martinique

12. Which one of the following groups included ONLY members of the Organization of American States?
    A. Brazil - Canada - Mexico
    B. Argentina - Chile - United States
    C. Colombia - Cuba - West Indies Federation
    D. British Honduras - Panama - Uruguay

13. The Alliance for Progress MOST likely gave attention to the northeastern section of Brazil because this region is
    A. the part of South America closest to Cuba
    B. possessed of strategic materials in large quantities
    C. characterized by poverty and low standard of living
    D. in the temperate zone

14. Which of the following Arab countries did not have a civil uprising in 2012?
    A. Egypt   C. Yemen
    B. Libya   D. Lebanon

15. From 1899 to 1914, the whole structure of American foreign policy in the Far East rested on
    A. executive acts and executive agreements sanctioned by the Congress
    B. treaty commitments sanctioned by the United States Senate
    C. executive acts and executive agreements without congressional sanction
    D. international agreements binding on Asiatic, European, and American powers

16. As a result of the Washington Arms Conference of 1921-2, the United States
    A. agreed to modify its Open Door Policy in China
    B. granted naval parity to England and Japan
    C. received all the German island possessions south of the Equator
    D. secured the abrogation of the Anglo-Japanese Alliance of 1902

17. The Neutrality Acts adopted by the United States during Franklin D. Roosevelt's administration were
    A. similar to those adopted during World War I
    B. a reaffirmation of our historic policy toward the rights of neutrals
    C. a reversal of our historic policy toward the rights of neutrals
    D. a restatement of the doctrine of freedom of the seas

18. If the Neutrality Laws of the 1930's had been in effect at the time, which one of the following incidents would NOT have been significant?
    A. De Lome Letter
    B. Black Tom Explosion
    C. Lusitania Affair
    D. Panay Incident

19. Of the following, which one was the MOST important issue in the election of 1900?
    A. Tariff reduction
    B. Currency reform
    C. Imperialistic expansion
    D. Regulation of business

20. The Roosevelt Corollary was FIRST applied when
    A. Panama declared its independence from Colombia in 1903
    B. violent revolution broke out in the state of Haiti in 1915
    C. Cuban revolutionary disturbances erupted in 1906
    D. the Dominican Republic was unable to pay its debts in 1905

21. Which statement BEST describes the Treaty of Versailles? It(s)
    A. was based on Wilson's Fourteen Points
    B. was a compromise between the Fourteen Points and the secret treaties
    C. economic provisions carried out explicitly the pre-armistice agreement with Germany
    D. was divorced from the Covenant of the League of Nations

22. The Progressive Movement in the United States (1900-1916) GENERALLY
    A. believed that economic and social problems could be solved by the natural play of economic forces without government intervention
    B. favored the intervention of a strong government to realize the ideals of equality and democracy
    C. believed in a theory of economic determinism to explain the abuses of industrialism
    D. believed in a return to the states' rights theories of Thomas Jefferson

23. A MAJOR economic trend characteristic of large American corporations after World War II has been
    A. a decrease in investments abroad
    B. increased control by stockholders
    C. increased self-financing through retained earnings
    D. a decline in the number of consolidations

24. The decade, after World War I resembled the decade after the Civil War in that both periods
    A. were characterized by considerable political and business corruption
    B. had a continuation of wartime controls of the economy
    C. had an increase in public debt and taxes
    D. had an increase in social reform

25. In the Stimson Doctrine, the United States
    A. protested the violation of the Nine-Power Treaty
    B. threatened to impose economic sanctions against Japan
    C. rejected the findings of the Lytton Commission
    D. proposed joint United States-British military action

26. Which one of the following was a critic of Franklin D. Roosevelt's policy of aiding the Allies short of war (1939-1941)?
    A. Charles A. Lindbergh
    B. Henry L. Stimson
    C. William Allen White
    D. Wendell L. Willkie

27. A MAJOR purpose of both the Yalta and Potsdam Conferences was to
    A. establish the United Nations
    B. call for unconditional surrender of Germany
    C. set terms for the surrender of Italy
    D. discuss problems of post-war Germany

28. The Truman Doctrine was originally announced in connection with developments in
    A. Nationalist China
    B. Greece
    C. West Berlin
    D. Czechoslovakia

29. Which one of the following statements regarding the Alliance for Progress is CORRECT?
    A. A cooperating nation must devise a development program before funds are allocated.
    B. Like the Marshall Plan, it is a government-to-government program involving grants from the United States Treasury without private participation.
    C. Funds needed for economic reconstruction will be provided entirely by non-governmental private investment.
    D. Latin American nations must coordinate their defenses with those of the United States in order to be eligible for aid.

30. Hitler's racial theories were in accord with the beliefs of
    E. Heinrich Heine
    F. Houston Stewart Chamberlain
    G. Erich Maria Remarque
    H. Ellsworth Huntington

31. Which one of the following was TRUE of the European Common Market?
    A. The annual increase of the gross national product of the European Economic Community exceeded that of either the United States or the Soviet Union.
    B. It had fallen somewhat behind its original schedule of internal customs tariff cuts on industrial goods.
    C. It had admitted the members of the European Free Trade Association to associate membership.
    D. It had already reached its goal of eliminating internal duties on the agricultural products of member states.

32. The United Nations played a leading role in
    A. arranging a truce in Indo-China in 1954
    B. arranging for the British withdrawal from Cyprus
    C. establishing an independent Indonesia
    D. settling the Kashmir dispute between Pakistan and India

33. Which one of the following statements is TRUE of the Korean War of 1950?
    A. The Security Council of the United Nations ordered troops to Korea over the veto of Russia.
    B. The Chinese Communists invaded Korea following the American crossing of the Yalu River.
    C. No significant boundary changes resulted from the War.
    D. General MacArthur was dismissed for bombing Chinese targets north of the 38th parallel.

34. Nicolai Lenin's New Economic Policy provided for the
    A. relinquishment of state ownership of basic industries
    B. suppression of big individual farmers or kulaks
    C. substitution of a *planned economy* for the remnants of free enterprise.
    D. restoration of private enterprise for profit

35. Between the end of World War II and 1965, the United States and the Soviet Union agreed upon all of the following EXCEPT the
    A. conclusion of an Austrian peace treaty
    B. formation of a treaty on Antarctica
    C. condemnation of the Anglo-French-Israeli attack on Egypt in 1956
    D. assessment on United Nations members to support United Nations Congo military operations

36. Which one of the following nations became independent After World War II?
    A. Egypt   B. Iraq   C. Sudan   D. Thailand

37. In which one of the following pairs did the FIRST event precede the SECOND?
    A. Re-militarization of the Rhineland - Germany leaves   the League of Nations
    B. Invasion of Poland - Signing of the Nazi-Soviet Pact
    C. Formation of Rome-Berlin-Tokyo Axis - Italian invasion of Ethiopia
    D. Munich Crisis - Partition of Czechoslovakia

38. The *Spirit of Locarno* of 1925 referred to
    A. French efforts to build a cordon sanitaire against Russia
    B. the stabilization of Germany's western boundary
    C. British efforts to protect Czechoslovakia against Germany
    D. America's efforts to ease German reparations

39. Which one of the following is TRUE of Adolph Hitler's accession to power in Germany?
    A. The Communist Party supported the Weimar Republic.
    B. The Nazi Party gained a majority of the votes in the Reichstag.
    C. An alliance with the Nationalist Party gave Hitler a Parliamentary Majority
    D. Hitler became chancellor by a coup d"etat.

40. Mussolini's Corporate State
    A. provided for a parliament with representation according to occupation
    B. abolished private ownership of the means of production
    C. permitted lockouts but made strikes and boycotts illegal
    D. fixed profits but permitted wages to rise freely

41. The United States and British systems of government are alike in that both   41._____
    A. provide for popular election of the chief executive
    B. place constitutional authority for executive action on the shoulders of a single individual
    C. allow for legislative control over executive programs through the power of the purse
    D. assure the executive of majority support in the legislature

42. On the question of the obligation of members of the United Nations to pay special   42._____
    assessments for maintaining peace, the World Court has ruled that
    A. members are not obligated to pay since such operations are not expenses of the United Nations within the meaning of its Charter
    B. the General Assembly may float bond issues in order to raise funds for this purpose
    C. all United Nations members are legally obligated to pay such assessments
    D. members two years behind in their financial contributions shall lose their vote in the General Assembly

43. Which one of the following organizations is an official agency of the United Nations?   43._____
    The
    A. Economic Commission for Europe
    B. European Coal and Steel Community
    C. European Community of Atomic Energy
    D. Organization for European Economic Cooperation

44. The Five Power Treaty signed at the Washington Conference of 1921-22 was   44._____
    SIGNIFICANT in that it
    A. provided a program of international armaments limitation for the first time in history
    B. became the basis for the later Locarno Pacts
    C. kept Japanese militarists content with the naval status quo until the mid-thirties
    D. committed the signatories to uphold the Open Door Policy

45. Which one of the following was TRUE of the Weimar Republic?   45._____
    A. Officials of the old German Empire remained in their positions.
    B. Sweeping land reform was undertaken.
    C. All property of the Kaiser and other imperial nobility was confiscated.
    D. Important industries were nationalized.

46. Which one of the following occurred under the Soviet New Economic Policy?   46._____
    A. Soviet collectivization of farms made great strides.
    B. Middlemen were removed from private trading.
    C. The big individualist farmers (Kulaks) became less important.
    D. Peasant proprietors engaged in capitalistic agriculture.

47. Which one of the following occurred during the Eisenhower Administration?   47
    A. Nikita Khrushchev became the dictator of the Soviet Union.
    B. Congress passed the McCarran Immigration and Nationality Act.
    C. The Castro Regime was declared incompatible with the principles of the Organization of American States.
    D. The 22nd Amendment was ratified by the required 36 states.

48. In the Locarno treaties of 1925,
    A. Germany guaranteed the frontiers of Poland and Czechoslovakia
    B. Great Britain promised military aid to Czechoslovakia and Poland in the event of the violation of their frontiers by Germany
    C. Great Britain guaranteed the frontiers of France and Belgium against Germany
    D. France, Britain, and Germany agreed to settle all international disputes by binding arbitration

49. The creation of the North Atlantic Treaty Organization was a DIRECT result of the
    A. defection of Yugoslavia from the Communist bloc
    B. erection of the Berlin Wall
    C. Communist coup in Czechoslovakia
    D. formation of the Warsaw Pact

50. Hitler observed legal treaty obligations in the
    A. remilitarization of the Rhineland
    B. reunion of the Saar with Germany
    C. Anschluss of Austria and Germany
    D. annexation of Danzig

KEY (CORRECT ANSWERS)

1. D	26. A
2. C	27. D
3. D	28. B
4. C	29. A
5. D	30. B
6. D	31. A
7. D	32. C
8. D	33. C
9. D	34. D
10. C	35. D
11. A	36. C
12. B	37. D
13. C	38. B
14. D	39. C
15. C	40. A
16. D	41. C
17. C	42. C
18. C	43. A
19. C	44. A
20. D	45. A
21. B	46. D
22. B	47. A
23. C	48. C
24. A	49. C
25. A	50. B

TEST 4

DIRECTIONS: Each question or incomplete statement is followed by several suggested answers or completions. Select the one that BEST answers the question or completes the statement. *PRINT THE LETTER OF THE CORRECT ANSWER IN THE SPACE AT THE RIGHT.*

1. In which one of the following did both events of the post-World War II period occur at about the same time?
   The
   A. seizure of power in China by the Communists - The start of the Algerian Revolt against France
   B. outbreak of the Korean War - The Castro Revolution in Cuba
   C. invasion of Sinai by Israel - The Hungarian Revolt against Soviet control
   D. construction of the Wall in Berlin - The creation of the German Democratic Republic

   1._____

2. In which one of the following is the diplomatic conference CORRECTLY matched with its agenda?
   A. Casablanca - Formation of an international peace organization
   B. Potsdam - Polish administration of territories east of the Oder-Niesse line
   C. Teheran - Preparation for an Allied North African invasion
   D. Yalta - Opening of a western front by the Allies against Germany

   2._____

3. Which one of the following is CORRECT about the Korean War?
   A. United Nations forces failed to make important penetrations into North Korea.
   B. The multiplicity of United Nations military contingents inhibited unified action.
   C. The armistice restored the pre-war territorial status quo.
   D. The Soviet veto in the Security Council failed to block United Nations action.

   3._____

4. Which of the following decisions were made during the Kennedy Administration?
   A. The United States firmly asserted that it would not tolerate Soviet interference in the Congo.
   B. The United States refused to provide an air umbrella in the Bay of Pigs invasion.
   C. United States troops were ordered to Thailand to take up positions along the Mekong River.
   D. The United States supported Prime Minister Diefenbaker's position on missile defense.

   4._____

The CORRECT answer is:
   A. I, II, III   B. II, III, IV   C. I, III, IV   D. I, II, IV

5. Which one of the following was NOT included in the Treaty of Versailles?
   The
   A. establishment of the League of Nations
   B. demilitarization of the Rhineland
   C. dismemberment of the Austro-Hungarian Empire
   D. trial of the German emperor for offenses against international morality

   5._____

6. In 1919, Bela Kun temporarily seized power in Hungary, while the Spartacists attempted an armed insurrection in Berlin.
   These actions were evidence that
   A. fascism was on the rise
   B. the Russian Revolution was giving impetus to communist movements in other countries
   C. the monarchist groups were trying to hold on to their power in post-war Europe
   D. there was strong opposition to the Treaty of Versailles

7. Which one of the following officially marked the end of World War I?
   The
   A. ratification of the Treaty of Versailles
   B. conclusion of a separate peace treaty with Germany
   C. ratification of the Treaty of Trianon
   D. joint resolution of Congress which declared the end of hostilities

8. The specific reason for General MacArthur's removal from command in Korea in 1951 was his action, contrary to specific orders from the President, in
   A. pursuing military operations north of the Yalu River
   B. issuing public statements on policy
   C. negotiating with Chiang Kai-shek for joint operations
   D. negotiating with the North Korean authorities

9. The *domino* theory of the Vietnamese conflict held that a(n)
   A. communist victory in Vietnam would assure communist victory throughout Asia
   B. escalation of the war will assure victory for South Vietnam
   C. extension of the program of building fortified villages is necessary for South Vietnamese success
   D. creation of a firm foundation for the government in South Vietnam is the first essential for success in the War

10. The 1963 treaty between the United States and the Union of Soviet Socialist Republics dealt with
    A. the expansion of trade
    B. cultural exchanges
    C. the testing of nuclear weapons
    D. the neutralization of Cuba

11. With which one of the following countries did the United States sign a treaty of alliance before 1940?
    A. England
    B. France
    C. Spain
    D. Russia

12. The government of Indonesia signed an agreement ending three years of hostility toward which one of the following countries?
    A. Thailand
    B. Philippines
    C. Malaysia
    D. Netherlands

13. Which one of the following pairs a war with one of its results?
    A. Opium War - Cessation of Macao to Great Britain
    B. Russo-Japanese War - Cession of Formosa to Japan
    C. Sino-Japanese War - Cession of eastern Siberia to Russia
    D. World War I - Cession of the southern half of Sakhalin Island to Japan

14. Which one of the following describes Europe in the period 1905-1914? 14.____
The
   A. middle and upper classes lost their political and cultural leadership
   B. discontent of subject nationalities declined
   C. working class became more militant in an effort to satisfy its grievances
   D. role of the state was reduced with rising living standards

15. Which one of the following was TRUE of the Paris Peace Settlements of World War I? 15.____
   A. The wishes and aspirations of Slavic nationalities were ignored.
   B. Russia and Germany were integrated into the new European political structure.
   C. France's demand for a security pact was satisfied.
   D. There was serious neglect of the long-range economic problems of Europe.

16. The relations of the United States and Latin America were adversely affected by the 16.____
   A. Clark Memorandum
   B. activities of Ambassador Dwight Morrow in Mexico
   C. abrogation of the Platt Amendment
   D. implementation of the Roosevelt Corollary

17. In his speech at Harvard setting forth the Marshall Plan, Secretary of State Marshall 17.____
offered economic aid by the United States to
   A. all European nations who would join in drafting a program for recovery
   B. all of our allies in World War II
   C. England, France, and the Benelux countries only
   D. all European nations except the Soviet Union and its satellites

18. The entry of United States armed forces into Korea in 1950 was 18.____
   A. authorized by a resolution of the United Nations Security Council
   B. authorized by a resolution of the United Nations General Assembly
   C. approved by a Joint Resolution of Congress
   D. a unilateral action of President Truman as commander-in-chief

19. The United States and the former Soviet Union took similar positions on the issue of the 19.____
   A. Berlin Wall
   B. Anglo-French attack on Egypt
   C. United Nations action in Korea
   D. Congo peace-keeping force

20. Which one of the following is a CORRECT statement about the *Bay of Pigs* invasion? 20.____
   A. It was initiated by President Kennedy and carried out according to his plan.
   B. Plans previously made were modified by President Kennedy to exclude air support.
   C. It was executed by the C.I.A. contrary to the wishes of President Kennedy.
   D. It was undertaken by Cuban exiles without the support of the United States government.

21. Which of the following was a program of American foreign policy between 1921 and 1933? 21.____
   A. Dwight Morrow urged intervention in Mexican affairs.
   B. Charles E. Hughes sought international cooperation on disarmament.
   C. Cordell Hull brought the United States into the World Court.
   D. Henry L. Stimson applied economic sanctions to Japan.

22. Austria, Hungary, Slovakia, and the Czech Republic are similar in that they all
    A. have no coastlines
    B. are contiguous to Russia
    C. were members of the Warsaw Pact
    D. have Communist governments

23. The *cordon sanitaire* refers to the
    A. belt of states from Finland to Rumania formed to prevent the westward expansion of Communism after World War I
    B. coalition of Arab states formed to encircle Israel after World War II
    C. boycott organized to weaken the Japanese economy and thus strike at Japanese aggression in China in the 1930's
    D. belt of states formed in eastern Europe to protect the Union of Soviet Socialist Republics against anti-Communist agitation after World War II

24. The Treaty of Rapallo (1922) was SIGNIFICANT because it
    A. reflected the anti-Communist orientation of the German officer corps
    B. marked a relaxation of the isolation of the Soviet Union after World War I
    C. made it more difficult for Germany to evade some of the provisions of the Treaty of Versailles
    D. completed the encirclement of the Soviet Union by hostile powers after World War I

25. The aim of Theodore Roosevelt's mediation in the Russo-Japanese War was to
    A. cement Russo-American relations
    B. support American expansion in the Far East
    C. promote Korean nationalistic aspirations
    D. preserve the balance of power

26. With reference to World War II, the United States declared war against all of the following EXCEPT
    A. Finland
    B. Rumania
    C. Hungary
    D. Bulgaria

27. Which one of the following was expelled from the League of Nations for its acts of aggression?
    A. Japan
    B. Germany
    C. Italy
    D. Russia

28. Which one of the following is associated with the administration of Herbert Hoover? The
    A. settlement of the Mexican-United States oil controversy
    B. Kellogg-Briand Pact of Paris
    C. Young Plan on war debts and reparations
    D. Washington Arms Conference

29. Which one of the following occurred the same year as the *bank holiday* of the 1930's?
    A. The Weimar Constitution was adopted.
    B. The Locarno Pacts were signed.
    C. Hitler became German Chancellor.
    D. Italy invaded Ethiopia.

30. Which one of the following events occurred FIRST in time?
    The
    A. organization of the North Atlantic Treaty Organization
    B. Marshall Plan for European economic recovery
    C. Communist coup in Czechoslovakia
    D. enactment of the Point-Four Program

31. Which one of the following contributed to Hitler's accession to power?
    A. Support given by Ebert and Noske to the Spartacists
    B. Lack of presidential power under the Weimar Constitution
    C. Election of the Reichstag on the basis of proportional representation
    D. Failure of the Weimar Constitution to guarantee private property

32. United States troops were sent to South Korea in June 1950 to fight North Korean aggression as a result of a decision of the
    A. United Nations Security Council
    B. United Nations General Assembly
    C. United States Congress
    D. President of the United States

33. Which one of the following was stipulated in the Marshall Plan?
    A. Aid was to be limited to technical assistance.
    B. Aid was to be conditional upon the nations working out a program for economic rehabilitation.
    C. Russia and her satellite countries were to be excluded.
    D. Aid was to be limited to a stipulated amount and for a fixed period.

34. One result of the Suez Canal Crisis of 1956 was
    A. a decision by the United Nations to use a police force to restore order
    B. rejection by the United States of Nasser's request for funds to construct the Aswan Dam
    C. a Paris summit conference to improve East-West relations
    D. increased solidarity among members of the North Atlantic Treaty Organization

35. Which one of the following is TRUE concerning the terms of the peace treaties concluding World War II?
    A. Limitations on the size of armed forces were placed on all defeated nations.
    B. All defeated nations were reduced in territorial size.
    C. Mandated islands of Japan, in the Pacific, were transferred to Great Britain.
    D. The coal deposits of the Saar Basin were retained by France.

36. Which one of the following is the CORRECT chronological sequence of events associated with Japan?
    A. *Twenty-One Demands*
    B. Treaty of Portsmouth
    C. Withdrawal of Japan from the League of Nations
    D. Nine Power Treaty

The CORRECT answer is:
    A. I, II, IV, III
    B. II, III, I, IV
    C. II, I, IV, III
    D. II, IV, III, I

37. With regard to the People's Republic of China, which of the following acts was the President of the United States able to take without any action on the part of Congress?
    A. Make a declaration of war and send armed units against her.
    B. Begin negotiations on a treaty of mutual friendship and establish trade relations.
    C. Officially recognize the Communist government by receiving its ambassador.
    D. Send a fully accredited ambassador to China, charged with implementing the President's policy.

37._____

38. In which one of the following do both countries border on Vietnam?
    A. Burma and Cambodia
    B. Thailand and Burma
    C. Cambodia and Laos
    D. China and Malaya

38._____

39. All of the following contributed to the isolationist spirit in the United States before our entry into World War II EXCEPT the
    A. revisionist historical interpretation of the causes of World War I
    B. Senate investigation of the influence of the munitions industry in world politics
    C. pacifist movement among high school and college youth
    D. Republican Party platform of 1940

39._____

40. Which one of the following events connected with World War II occurred FIRST?
    Surrender of France to Germany
    Passage of the Lend-Lease Act
    Repeal of the arms embargo provision of the Neutrality Act
    Evacuation of the British army at Dunkirk

40._____

41. *Never in the field of human conflict was so much owed by so many to so* few is a quotation from a wartime speech by
    A. Franklin D. Roosevelt
    B. Winston Churchill
    C. Douglas MacArthur
    D. Charles de Gaulle

41._____

42. In which one of the following pairs dealing with the Cold War was the FIRST item a cause of the SECOND?
    A. Attack on South Korea - Formation of NATO
    B. Guerrilla war in Greece - Truman Doctrine
    C. Hungarian revolt - Geneva Conference of 1954
    D. U-2 Incident - Agency of International Development

42._____

43. In which one of the following incidents did President Eisenhower resort to military aid to gain his objectives?
    A. The bombardment of Quemoy and Matsu by the Chinese Communists in 1958
    B. The Anglo-French-Israeli invasion of the Sinai Peninsula
    C. The Hungarian revolt of 1956
    D. Castro's expropriation of American-owned property in Cuba

43._____

44. Which one of the following crises is NOT matched correctly with the two countries it affected?
    A. Fashoda Crises (1898) - Britain and France
    B. Moroccan Crises (1905-6) - France and Spain
    C. Moroccan Crises (1911) - France and Germany
    D. Serbian Crisis (1914) - Austria - Hungary and Russia

44._____

45. Which one of the following European countries did NOT attempt to expand to other continents between 1870-1914?   45._____
   A. Austria-Hungary
   B. Belgium
   C. Portugal
   D. Russia

46. In which one of the following pairs does the cause PRECEDE the effect?   46._____
   A. Twenty-One Demands - Overthrow of the Manchu Dynasty
   B. Interference in the affairs of Korea - Sino-Japanese War of 1895
   C. Stimson Doctrine - Invasion of Manchuria
   D. Boxer Rebellion - Open Door Policy

47. Which one of the following items consists of states that were independent in 1914?   47._____
   A. Liberia - Korea
   B. Thailand - Ethiopia
   C. ndo-China - Libya
   D. Malaya - Nigeria

48. Which one of the following suffered the GREATEST territorial loss in Europe after World War I?   48._____
   A. Austria-Hungary
   B. Turkey
   C. Russia
   D. Germany

49. The Treaty of Rapallo (1922)   49._____
   A. reflected the anti-Communist orientation of the German officer corps
   B. marked a relaxation of the isolation of the Soviet Union after World War I
   C. made it difficult for Germany to evade some of the provisions of the Treaty of Versailles
   D. completed the encirclement of the Soviet Union by

50. Which one of the following is NOT true of the Washington Arms Conference of 1921-22?   50._____
   A. The five major naval powers agreed to reduce the tonnage of capital ships.
   B. The Four Power Pact superseded the Anglo-Japanese Alliance of 1902.
   C. Nine powers officially gave support to the Open Door Policy.
   D. The Escalator Clause which was adopted allowed signatories to evade some of the treaty provisions.

KEY (CORRECT ANSWERS)

1. C
2. B
3. C
4. A
5. C

6. B
7. D
8. B
9. A
10. C

11. B
12. C
13. C
14. C

15. D

16. D
17. A
18. A
19. B
20. B

21. B
22. A
23. A
24. B
25. D

26. A
27. D
28. C
29. C
30. B

31. C
32. D
33. B
34. A
35. A

36. C
37. B
38. C
39. D
40. C

41. B
42. B
43. A
44. B
45. A

46. B
47. B
48. C
49. B
50. D

EXAMINATION SECTION
TEST 1

DIRECTIONS: Each question or incomplete statement is followed by several suggested answers or completions. Select the one the BEST answers the question or completes the statement. *PRINT THE LETTER OF THE CORRECT ANSWER IN THE SPACE AT THE RIGHT.*

1. Most of the people who were detained by the U.S. federal government in the months following the 9/11 attacks were detained for   1.____

    A. immigration violations
    B. suspected terrorist activities
    C. no charges at all
    D. income tax evasion

2. Rules for the U.S. special military tribunals for trying suspected terrorists, as revised by the Defense Department in March of 2002, included   2.____
    I. a unanimous vote required for conviction
    II. a unanimous vote required for the death penalty
    III. "chain of custody" proof requirement for prosecutors presenting evidence
    IV. no appeals of decisions for defendants in federal courts, but instead a petition for the appointment of a review panel

    A. I and II
    B. I, III and IV
    C. II and IV
    D. I, II, III and IV

3. Al-Jazeera, the twenty-four hour news/editorial television channel broadcast to much of the Muslim world, is based in   3.____

    A. Yemen
    B. Qatar
    C. Jordan
    D. Bahrain

4. Which of the following is the ethnic Tajik who succeeded the slain Ahmad Shah Massoud as the Military Commander of United Front-the ally of the United States in its war against the Taliban?   4.____

    A. Mohammed Fahim
    B. Ayman al-Zawahiri
    C. Abdul Haq
    D. Abdul Rashid Dostum

5. The George W. Bush administration's special peacemaking envoy for the Palestinians and Israelis was   5.____

    A. George Mitchell
    B. Anthony Zinni
    C. Ralph Peters
    D. Wesley Clark

6. As early as October 8, 2001, a left-wing activist from _____ published his theory that the Pentagon was not hit by American Airlines Flight 77, but was instead a truck bombing or missile strike that was made by the U.S. government to look like a plane crash.

   A. France
   B. Kuwait
   C. Albania
   D. Pakistan

6._____

7. Who was the first sitting head of state to be indicted for war crimes?

   A. Slobodan Milosevic
   B. Saddam Hussein
   C. Adolf Hitler
   D. Sani Abacha

7._____

8. The group that was charged in 2002 with overseeing the elimination of weapons of mass destruction in Iraq was the

   A. Iraqi National Congress (INC)
   B. United Nations Special Commission (UNSCOM)
   C. International Atomic Energy Agency (IAEA)
   D. United Nations Monitoring, Verification and Inspection Commission (UNMOVIC)

8._____

9. By 2002, the government of _____ had still not agreed to hand over three Egyptian fugitives who were linked to the 1995 assassination attempt on President Hosni Mubarak.

   A. Sudan
   B. Iraq
   C. Afghanistan
   D. Libya

9._____

10. In 2002, Afghanistan's former prime minister, _____, was reported to be actively seeking the reinstallment of the Taliban after the planned overthrow of the Karzai government.

    A. Gulbuddin Hekmatyar
    B. Rashid Dostum
    C. Mohammed Omar
    D. Ahmad Bahkter

10._____

11. In November of 2002, polls indicated that about _____% of Americans supported military action against terror in Afghanistan.

    A. 30
    B. 50
    C. 70
    D. 90

11._____

12. The largest and best-organized terrorist organization in the Philippines is

    A. Abu Sayyaf
    B. Mujahedin-e-Khalq
    C. Jemaah Islamiyah
    D. Moro Islamic Liberation Front

12._____

13. _____, the elite fighting unit that was composed of the Taliban's most devoted and skilled soldiers, dispersed into the Afghanistan mountains in November of 2001.

    A. Brigade 055
    B. The Big Red One
    C. The Republican Guard
    D. The United Front

14. Officially "atheistic" countries today include

    A. India
    B. South Africa
    C. Vietnam
    D. Republic of Tonga

15. The Pakistani Intelligence Agency charged with assisting the U.S. in finding Osama bin Laden in Afghanistan is the

    A. ISI
    B. OPGU
    C. KGB
    D. RAW

16. In late May of 2002, Lt. Gen. _____ assumed command of the Combined Joint Task Force headquarters in Afghanistan.

    A. Tommy Franks
    B. Ralph Eberhart
    C. Martin P. Schweitzer
    D. Dan McNeil

17. One of the obstacles to tracking down the sources of terrorist funding worldwide has been the informal international funds-transfer system prevalent in many Muslim societies. Built on trust among dealers, the system consists of financial transactions outside the banking system that leave no paper trail. The term for this system is

    A. hawala
    B. pankisi
    C. harakat
    D. sana'a jihad

18. Which of the following Middle Eastern countries is identified as a "parliamentary republic?"

    A. Iran
    B. Israel
    C. Egypt
    D. Lebanon

19. The event which sparked the campaign of Palestinian attacks known as the Al-Aqsa Intifadeh was

    A. Ariel Sharon's visit to the Temple Mount in September of 2000
    B. the raid on the Jenin refugee camp by Israeli soldiers in April of 2002
    C. President Bush's "Axis of Evil" speech
    D. the virtual house arrest of Yassir Arafat in Ramallah in January of 2002

20. Which of the following is NOT generally regarded as a state-sponsored terrorist group?

    A. Al-Qaeda
    B. Abu Nidal Organization
    C. Hezbollah
    D. Japanese Red Army

21. The Harakat ul-Mujahedin (HUM) is an Islamic terrorist group that operates mostly in

    A. Afghanistan
    B. the Israeli occupied territories
    C. the former Soviet Republic of Georgia
    D. the Kashmir

22. Which of the following is a chemical agent that has been used in an attack by a terrorist group?

    A. Sarin gas
    B. VX
    C. Cyanide
    D. Mustard gas

23. In 1991, Osama Bin Laden was expelled from _____ because of his anti-government activities there.

    A. Saudi Arabia
    B. Yemen
    C. Sudan
    D. the United States

24. By far, the largest number of suicide terrorist attacks in the last decades of the twentieth century were carried out by

    A. Hamas-sponsored Palestinians
    B. the Liberation Tigers of Tamil Elaam (Tamil Tigers)
    C. the Irish Republican Army
    D. Basque Fatherland and Liberty (ETA)

25. It is rare for a war to be fought between two democratic states today because

    A. most democracies are characterized by norms of peaceful dispute resolution
    B. the separation of powers in democratic states insures a rational decision-making process
    C. democratic states such as the United States and Great Britain tend to be the most powerful states in the world, and their power deters others from considering war
    D. most states have been through many debilitating wars by the time they have achieved democracy

26. The United Nations envoy to Afghanistan, appointed in October of 2001, was   26._____

    A. Mohammed Zahir Shah
    B. John Negroponte
    C. Charlotte Beers
    D. Lakhdar Brahimi

27. In March of 2002, U. S. General Tommy Franks announced that al-Qaeda terrorists were operating in   27._____

    A. Somalia
    B. Georgia
    C. Malaysia
    D. Sudan

28. In January of 2002, the University of South Florida fired a Kuwaiti-born computer science professor named Sami al-Arian on the grounds that he   28._____

    A. had met informally on several occasions with two of the 9/11 hijackers
    B. had helped raised money to support Islamic Jihad
    C. presented a physical and security risk to the university because of the hate mail and death threats he received
    D. made inflammatory statements about the U.S. government in his classroom

29. Before their defeat, the political stronghold of Afghanistan's Taliban regime was in the city of   29._____

    A. Kabul
    B. Kunduz
    C. Mazar-e Sharif
    D. Kandahar

30. The anthrax-contaminated letters that were sent out in 2001 resulted in _____ of the disease; _____ cases were fatal.   30._____

    A. 11; 2
    B. 23; 5
    C. 56; 12
    D. 122; 47

KEY (CORRECT ANSWERS)

1.	A	16.	D
2.	C	17.	A
3.	B	18.	D
4.	A	19.	A
5.	B	20.	A
6.	A	21.	D
7.	A	22.	A
8.	D	23.	A
9.	A	24.	B
10.	A	25.	A
11.	D	26.	D
12.	D	27.	A
13.	A	28.	C
14.	C	29.	D
15.	A	30.	B

TEST 2

DIRECTIONS: Each question or incomplete statement is followed by several suggested answers or completions. Select the one the BEST answers the question or completes the statement. *PRINT THE LETTER OF THE CORRECT ANSWER IN THE SPACE AT THE RIGHT.*

1. Forewarnings of the September 11 attacks included
    I. the CIA learning in May 2001 that Osama bin Laden and his associates were planning to infiltrate the United States and attack the country with explosives.
    II. CIA briefers warning President Bush in August 2001 that bin Laden might hijack U.S. airplanes
    III. the arrest of the alleged "20th hijacker," Zacarias Moussaoui, in mid-August on visa violations after he raised suspicions at a Minneapolis flight school
    IV. a videotape, broadcast in August on Al-Jazeera, of Osama bin Laden promising to cause "unimaginable" harm to the United States

    A. I and II
    B. I, II, and III
    C. II and III
    D. I, II, III and IV

2. The controversial leader of Afghanistan's Uzbek community, _____ directed the Northern Alliance campaign to recapture the town of Mazar-i-Sharif in November of 2001.

    A. Ashraf Nadim
    B. Abdul Haq
    C. Mustapha Mohammed
    D. Abdul Rashid Dostum

3. Al-Qaeda's worldwide reach is reinforced by its ties to other Sunni extremist groups. These groups include each of the following, EXCEPT

    A. Gama'a al-Islamiyya
    B. Islamic Movement of Uzbekistan
    C. Harakat ul-Mujahedin
    D. Hezbollah

4. In the spring of 2002, _____ made public his proposal that Arab countries recognize and make peace with Israel if Israel relinquished the territories it conquered in the 1967 war.

    A. Crown Prince Abdullah of Saudi Arabia
    B. Egyptian President Hosni Mubarak
    C. King Abdullah II of Jordan
    D. British Prime Minister Tony Blair

5. Abdul Rahman, the tourism and aviation minister of Hamid Karzai's transitional government in Afghanistan, was

    A. killed by U.S. bodyguards during an assassination attempt on Karzai
    B. revealed to be a high-level al-Qaeda operative

C. assassinated by high-ranking members in the Northern Alliance
D. a confirmed grower and trafficker in the opium trade

6. In December of 2002, an Israeli-owned hotel and plane in the resort city of _____ were targeted by terrorists with likely al-Qaeda connections.

    A. Petra, Jordan
    B. Antalyah, Turkey
    C. Jaffa, Israel
    D. Mombasa, Kenya

7. Al-Qaeda operative _____, who helped assemble the inner workings of the terror network, was captured in Pakistan in April of 2002

    A. Ramzi Binalshibh
    B. Abu Zubaydah
    C. Abdul Haq
    D. Ayman al-Zawahiri

8. Several weeks after the onset of fighting in Afghanistan, the U.S. began to ship some al-Qaeda combatants to a military base in

    A. Bahrain
    B. Guam
    C. Kuwait
    D. Cuba

9. From 2001-2003, a key person in the U.S. plans to oust Iraq's Saddam Hussein was _____, leader of the Iraqi National Congress.

    A. Sharif Ali Bin al- Hussein
    B. Masoud Barzani
    C. Ahmad Chalabi
    D. Barham Salih

10. Within a month of the September 11 attacks, Algerian national and al-Qaeda operative Djamel Beghal gave information to authorities that allowed them to head off a plot to

    A. explode an Air Paris jet with an explosive hidden in an operative's shoe
    B. destroy the U.S. embassy in Paris
    C. attack U.S. soldiers stationed in Kuwait
    D. destroy the Washington Monument

11. In 2000, the American warship U.S.S. *Cole* was bombed by al-Qaeda in the port city of _____, resulting in the deaths of 17 sailors.

    A. Djibouti
    B. Aden, Yemen
    C. Jiddah, Saudi Arabia
    D. Doha, Qatar

12. Which of the following is a secular country?

    A. Lebanon
    B. Israel
    C. Cuba
    D. India

13. The Bush administration's reasons for using military tribunals, rather than court trials, to try suspected terrorists included
    I. less risk to public safety
    II. protection of classified information yielded by suspects
    III. protection of American jurors, judges and witnesses from the potential dangers of trying accused terrorists
    IV. unwillingness for trials and appeals to drag on for years and become public spectacles

    A. I and II
    B. I, II and III
    C. III and IV
    D. I, II, III and IV

14. By 2002, each of the following governments was known or suspected by the U.S. to have engaged in state-sponsored terrorism, EXCEPT

    A. Sudan
    B. Lebanon
    C. North Korea
    D. Syria

15. While in the United States, the financial means for most of the 9/11 hijackers to pay rent and bills and make purchases was supplied by

    A. wire transfers from Saudi Arabia and Yemen to Western Union offices around the country
    B. burglary, robbery, and other crimes
    C. working under the terms of their U.S. visas
    D. credit cards and ATM withdrawals from U.S. bank accounts

16. Egypt's largest Islamic group, organized in 1970, has as its primary goal the replacement of its own government with an Islamic state. In 1997, the group killed 58 foreign tourists at Luxor. The group is known as

    A. Armed Islamic Group (GIA)
    B. Mujahedin-e Khalq
    C. Gama'a al-Islamiyya
    D. al-Jihad

17. The word "terrorism" was originally coined during

    A. the first century in Palestine, when Jewish zealots would kill Romans and their collaborators
    B. the eleventh century, when the Assassins, a Shi'ite sect, would murder civilian enemies

C. the eighteenth century, in post-revolutionary France
D. 1968, when the Popular Front for the Liberation of Palestine undertook the first terrorist hijacking of a commercial airplane

18. In August of 2002, Abu Musab Zarqawi, one of al-Qaeda's top two dozen leaders, left the city of _____ after spending some time there engaged in unknown activities.

    A. Mecca B. Karachi C. Aden D. Baghdad

19. Under the U.N. Charter, peace enforcement actions are sometimes referred to as Chapter _____ actions.

    A. V B. VI C. VII D. VIII

20. The U.S. Under Secretary of State for Public Diplomacy and Public Affairs, appointed in October of 2001, was

    A. Charlotte Beers
    B. Paul Wolfowitz
    C. Richard Holbrooke
    D. John Negroponte

21. A year after the 9/11 attacks, Amr Moussa, secretary-general of the Arab League, stated publicly that a U.S. attack on Iraq would

    A. destabilize the coalition that had been built up since the Gulf War
    B. open the gates of hell
    C. distract world leaders from the Israeli-Palestinian peace process
    D. lead to increased stability in the Middle East

22. Intergovernmental organizations (IGOs) such as the United Nations are intended to be

    A. regional, rather than global
    B. private
    C. organizations set up by states to operate in their behalf for their common good
    D. unrelated to military/defense issues

23. Which of the following is NOT a religious terror group?

    A. Palestinian Liberation Organization
    B. Aum Shinrikyo
    C. Al-Qaeda
    D. Hamas

24. Both of Osama bin Laden's parents were Arabs of _____ descent.

    A. Saudi Arabian B. Jordanian C. Yemeni D. Iranian

25. The first mujahedin government in Afghanistan was installed in

   A. 1974
   B. 1980
   C. 1989
   D. 1992

26. The Taliban intelligence chief who was killed in a U.S. bombing attack in December of 2001 was

   A. Qari Ahmadullah
   B. Abu Zubaydah
   C. Ayman al-Zawahiri
   D. Omar Bachri Mohammed

27. Historically, the mortality rate of smallpox was about _____ of those infected.

   A. 15
   B. 30
   C. 65
   D. 80

28. The main weakness of the Northern Alliance, the main body of rebels in Afghanistan against the ruling Taliban prior to 9/11, was that it

   A. was banished to the barren mountainous regions of northern Afghanistan
   B. did not contain significant numbers of moderate Pashtuns
   C. was controlled by the governments of neighboring central Asian countries
   D. had its leader assassinated several months earlier by al-Qaeda operatives

29. Approximately how many Muslims live in the United States today?

   A. 1 to 2 million
   B. 6 to 8 million
   C. 14 to 15 million
   D. 21 to 22 million

30. During its rule of Afghanistan, the Taliban earned an estimated $ _____ annually from taxes related to opium.

   A. 1-2 million
   B. 7-8 million
   C. 12-18 million
   D. 40-50 million

KEY (CORRECT ANSWERS)

1.	B	16.	C
2.	D	17.	C
3.	D	18.	D
4.	A	19.	B
5.	C	20.	A
6.	D	21.	B
7.	B	22.	C
8.	D	23.	A
9.	C	24.	C
10.	B	25.	D
11.	B	26.	A
12.	D	27.	B
13.	D	28.	B
14.	B	29.	B
15.	D	30.	D

TEST 3

DIRECTIONS: Each question or incomplete statement is followed by several suggested answers or completions. Select the one the BEST answers the question or completes the statement. *PRINT THE LETTER OF THE CORRECT ANSWER IN THE SPACE AT THE RIGHT.*

1. By 2002, the global reach of al-Qaeda extended to
   I. North America
   II. Africa
   III. Europe
   IV. Australia

   A. I and II
   B. I, II and III
   C. I and III
   D. I, II, III and IV

   1.____

2. People close to Osama bin Laden have said on several occasions that he imagines himself to be a modern-day _____, the Muslim commander who liberated Jerusalem from the Crusaders.

   A. Ibn Batutta
   B. Mohammed
   C. Avicenna
   D. Saladin

   2.____

3. In the spring of 2002, more than 1000 British troops, accompanied by U.S. and Afghan forces, entered the mountains southeast of Kabul in Operation _____.

   A. Anaconda
   B. Enduring Freedom
   C. Snipe
   D. Infinite Justice

   3.____

4. After the U.S. defeat of the Taliban government in Afghanistan, most intelligence experts agreed that al-Qaeda's presence was strongest in the countries of

   A. Yemen and Qatar
   B. Pakistan and Iran
   C. Yemen and Pakistan
   D. Egypt and Saudi Arabia

   4.____

5. Which of the following leaders launched a 1988 chemical attack on his own people?

   A. Sani Abacha
   B. Sadiq al Mahdi
   C. Saddam Hussein
   D. Ali Akbar Hashemi Rafsanjani

   5.____

6. In late 2002, reports began to circulate that about 5,000 Taliban and al-Qaeda fighters had been airlifted from the Afghan town of Kunduz by   6._____

   A. Pakistan
   B. Libya
   C. Iraq
   D. the United States

7. In early December of 2001, Taliban prisoners staged a revolt in the 19th-century prison fortress of _____, where the first American fatality of the war occurred.   7._____

   A. Mazar-i-Sharif
   B. Kunduz
   C. Qala-i-Jangi
   D. Tora Bora

8. The country to which John Walker Lindh first went to study Islam was   8._____

   A. Sudan
   B. Afghanistan
   C. Yemen
   D. Saudi Arabia

9. In January of 2002, Israel seized a ship carrying 50 tons of arms which Israel claimed were intended for the militant group Hamas. The weapons were reportedly purchased from   9._____

   A. Libya
   B. Iraq
   C. al-Qaeda
   D. Iran

10. Russia's support of the U.S. war in Afghanistan was given in part because Russia hoped to gain   10._____

    A. NATO membership
    B. fewer U.S. complaints about Russia's handling of the Chechen revolt
    C. a broader sphere of influence in northern Afghanistan after the Taliban were gone
    D. access to a warm-water port for oil shipments

11. In 2003, the U. S. State Department named the primary state sponsor of terrorism in the world to be   11._____

    A. Iraq
    B. Sudan
    C. Iran
    D. North Korea

12. Which of the following is a secular country?   12._____

    A. Lebanon
    B. Israel
    C. Cuba
    D. India

13. In January of 2002, the government of _____ handed over to the U.S. government an al-Qaeda operative who was ordered to carry out an attack on the U.S. "Eagle Base." 13.____

    A. Saudi Arabia
    B. Bosnia and Herzegovina
    C. Jordan
    D. Yemen

14. The kidnappers of *Wall Street Journal* reporter Daniel Pearl stated in January 2002 that they would release Pearl 14.____

    A. when the last U.S. soldier departed from Saudi Arabia's Muslim holy sites
    B. after Pakistani terrorist suspects had been released from Guantanamo Bay
    C. upon the release of convicted kidnapper Ahmed Omar Saeed Sheikh
    D. after his body had been dismembered

15. In 1996, Osama Bin Laden was expelled from _____ under pressure from the U.S. government. 15.____

    A. Sudan
    B. Saudi Arabia
    C. Afghanistan
    D. Yemen

16. What term is generally applied to groups that use the drug trade to fund terrorism? 16.____

    A. Drug laundering
    B. Narcoterrorism
    C. Prescriptive terrorism
    D. Mercantile terrorism

17. In October of 2001, mail containing anthrax spores was discovered at the offices of 17.____

    A. Edward Kennedy
    B. Tom Daschle
    C. Trent Lott
    D. Tom DeLay

18. Terrorism that seeks to form a separate state for a group is known as _____ terrorism. 18.____

    A. state-sponsored
    B. nationalist
    C. civic
    D. religious

19. At the time of the September 11 attacks, the de facto ruler of Saudi Arabia was 19.____

    A. Abdullah Ibn Abdul Aziz
    B. Saud al Faisal
    C. Fahd bin Abdelaziz al Saud
    D. Alwaleed bin Talal al Saud

20. In October of 2001, the president of _____ granted permission for U.S. forces to use an air base in his country, and for the stationing of 1,000 infantry soldiers who would support Operation Enduring Freedom.   20.___

   A. Turkey   B. Pakistan   C. Armenia   D. Uzbekistan

21. The ultimate aim of Hamas is to   21.___

   A. negotiate a land-for-peace settlement in order to create an secular Palestinian state that will exist alongside Israel
   B. create an Iranian-style Islamic republic in Lebanon and removal of all non-Islamic influences from the area.
   C. expel Israel from the occupied territories and established an Islamic Palestinian state alongside Israel
   D. establish an Islamic Palestinian state in place of Israel.

22. The Pankisi Gorge is a region in the nation of _____ that had been known, for some time prior to the 9/11 attacks, as the hideout of rebels, some with al-Qaeda links.   22.___

   A. Georgia
   B. Pakistan
   C. the Philippines
   D. Afghanistan

23. In addition to Osama bin Laden's personal fortune, al-Qaeda is funded by   23.___
   I. money extorted from wealthy Saudis and other Muslims
   II. illegal al-Qaeda activities such as smuggling, drug trafficking, and diamond and precious metal trading
   III. diverted revenues from otherwise legitimate businesses, such as the Yemeni honey trade
   IV. wealthy, sympathetic Muslims throughout the world

   A. I and IV   B. II and IV   C. I, III and IV   D. I, II, III and IV

24. In January of 2001, warships from _____, in the country's first military move since World War II, went on duty in the Indian Ocean to support U.S. troops in Afghanistan.   24.___

   A. Germany   B. Japan   C. France   D. Australia

25. In recent years, the drug trade has become a significant part of the economy of   25.___
   I. Libya
   II. North Korea
   III. Syria
   IV. Lebanon

   A. I only   B. I and III   C. III and IV   D. I, II, III and IV

26. Terrorist violence 26.____

    A. includes all forms of revolutionary violence
    B. is always opposed by governments
    C. if it is political in nature, is a problem relating only to internal political conflicts
    D. is carried out by governments and non-state actors

27. In March of 2002, the U.S. committed $64 million and between 100 and 200 troops to 27.____
    train local forces in terrorist counterinsurgency in the country of

    A. Uzbekistan
    B. Georgia
    C. Kuwait
    D. Kazakhstan

28. The country with the largest Muslim population today is 28.____

    A. Pakistan
    B. India
    C. Indonesia
    D. Nigeria

29. States in the world who have admitted to having VX or a closely related agent include 29.____
    I.   Russia
    II. United States
    III. North Korea
    IV. Iran

    A. I only
    B. I and II
    C. III only
    D. III and IV

30. In July of 2002, Spanish police arrested three al-Qaeda suspects, one of whom was in 30.____
    possession of home videos showing

    A. a dog being killed by chemical gas
    B. footage of al-Qaeda training camps in Sudan
    C. various American landmarks
    D. the murder of *Wall Street Journal* reporter Daniel Pearl

KEY (CORRECT ANSWERS)

1.	B	16.	B
2.	D	17.	B
3.	C	18.	B
4.	C	19.	A
5.	C	20.	D
6.	A	21.	D
7.	C	22.	A
8.	C	23.	D
9.	D	24.	B
10.	B	25.	C
11.	C	26.	D
12.	D	27.	B
13.	B	28.	C
14.	B	29.	B
15.	A	30.	C

EXAMINATION SECTION
TEST 1

DIRECTIONS: Each question or incomplete statement is followed by several suggested answers or completions. Select the one the BEST answers the question or completes the statement. *PRINT THE LETTER OF THE CORRECT ANSWER IN THE SPACE AT THE RIGHT.*

1. Which of the following was convicted in July 2002 of the kidnapping and murder of *Wall Street Journal* reporter Daniel Pearl?

    A. Ayman al-Zawahiri
    B. Mohammed Atef
    C. Ahmed Omar Saeed Sheikh
    D. Abu Zubaydah

    1.____

2. The al-Qaeda organization's 1998 statement, under the banner of the "World Islamic Front for Jihad Against the Jews and Crusaders," proclaimed the duty of all Muslims to be

    A. killing any non-Muslim that was found within the borders of an Islamic state
    B. expelling Westerners and non-Muslims from Muslim countries
    C. killing U.S. citizens, civilian or military, and their allies anywhere in the world
    D. killing U.S. combatants and their military allies anywhere in the world

    2.____

3. The Commander-in-Chief of the U.S. Central Command, which led the U.S. military assault on the Taliban, was General

    A. Henry Stratman
    B. Ralph Eberhart
    C. Tommy Franks
    D. Wesley Clark

    3.____

4. This former roommate of Mohammed Atta, who was to have been the "20th hijacker" of the 9/11 terrorists, was captured in Pakistan in September of 2002.

    A. Ramzi Binalshibh
    B. Richard Reid
    C. Zacarias Moussaoui
    D. Abu Zubaydah

    4.____

5. In 2002, parliamentary democracies in the Middle East included
    I. Lebanon
    II. Israel
    III. Egypt
    IV. Afghanistan
    V. Jordan

    A. I and II
    B. II only
    C. I, II and III
    D. II and IV

    5.____

Questions 6-7.

Questions 6 and 7 are based on the following information: The treatise explaining a Muslim's obligation to jihad, written by the Egyptian Abd al-Salam Faraj (one of President Anwar Sadat's assassins) served as the guidebook for the 1979 Iranian Revolution. Later, Osama bin Laden adopted it as al-Qaeda's own spiritual manifesto.

6. What is the title of this work?

   A. *The Eightfold Path*
   B. *The Neglected Duty*
   C. *The Four Agreements*
   D. *The Hadith*

7. Bin Laden seized upon the idea espoused in the work that holy war was necessary to defend not just Muslims, but

   A. Muslim holy sites
   B. the economic interests of Muslim states
   C. Muslim dignity
   D. all of humankind

8. The president of Pakistan who angered Islamists in his own country by offering assistance to the United States in its war on terror was

   A. Pervez Musharraf
   B. Mohammed Omar
   C. Nawaz Sharif
   D. Hamid Karzai

9. Approximately how many tons of the nerve agent VX remained unaccounted for in Iraq by 2002?

   A. 500 pounds
   B. 900 pounds
   C. 1.5 tons
   D. 14 tons

10. Patterns of industrialization, unrest, and social reform at the turn of the twenty-first century lent support to the opinion that the new century would become dominated by the

   A. Pacific region
   B. Middle East
   C. Atlantic alliance
   D. Latin Americans

11. A United Nations report, made public not long after the 9/11 attacks, claimed that about _____ percent of Afghan girls were enrolled in school.

   A. 7
   B. 15
   C. 33
   D. 55

12. In the summer of 2002, longtime Palestinian terrorist Abu Nidal, whose group was blamed for attacks in more than 20 countries that have killed hundreds, was found dead- either by suicide or assassinationin the city of

    A. Gaza
    B. Mecca
    C. Baghdad
    D. Ramallah

    12._____

13. The deposed king of Afghanistan, _____, was one of the main actors in the selection of its new democratic government after the defeat of the Taliban.

    A. Malik Jalani Khan Ashazai
    B. Mohamrned Zahir Shah
    C. Ramzi Binalshibh
    D. Ahmad Shah Massoud

    13._____

14. The chief moderate of the George W. Bush administration, who pushed the president to establish a serious peace initiative in Israel in 2001, was

    A. Colin Powell
    B. Donald Rumsfeld
    C. Karl Rove
    D. Condoleezza Rice

    14._____

15. The second-largest ethnic group in Afghanistan are the _____, who are the closest rivals to the dominant Pashtuns for power and prestige.

    A. Uzbeks
    B. Balochis
    C. Turkmen
    D. Tajiks

    15._____

16. According to the definition of "terrorism" agreed upon by most U.S. intelligence sources, terrorism is always
    I. premeditated—planned in advance, rather than impulsive
    II. political—not criminal, like mafia violence, but designed to change an existing political order
    III. aimed at civilians—not at military targets or combat-ready troops
    IV. carried out by subnational groups—not by the army of a country

    A. I and III
    B. I and IV
    C. II, III and IV
    D. I, II, III and IV

    16._____

17. The nominal ruler of Saudi Arabia in 2002 was

    A. Saud al Faisal
    B. Fahd bin Abdelaziz al Saud
    C. Malik Jalani Khan Ashazai
    D. Abdullah Ibn Abdul Aziz

    17._____

18. The terror group in the Philippines with ties to al-Qaeda is

    A. Jemaah Islamiyah
    B. ELA
    C. Tamil Eelam
    D. Abu Sayyaf

19. One of the characteristics that makes religious terrorism so frightening to the rest of the world is its

    A. lack of constraint on the scope of attacks
    B. world-encompassing vision of a religious state
    C. emphasis on causing painful, prolonged deaths for victims
    D. extreme rhetoric

20. Osama bin Laden's $300 million inheritance, which he used to finance al-Qaeda operations, was made by his father, Muhammad bin Laden, in the _____ industry.

    A. oil
    B. arms
    C. construction
    D. textiles

Questions 21 and 22 refer to the following information: In January of 2000, Ahmad-Hikmat Shakir, a top al-Qaeda operative and a native Iraqi, was in Kuala Lumpur, Malaysia, at the same time as two 9/11 hijackers were there to meet with another senior al-Qaeda leader. In September of 2002, Shakir was detained by Jordanian authorities.

21. After Jordan detained him, Shakir

    A. committed suicide in his cell
    B. was sent to the U.S. detainment camp at Guantanamo Bay
    C. was released and disappeared
    D. helped to plan the bombing of Kenya's Paradise Hotel in 2002

22. After he was detained, a search of Shakir's apartment in Qatar yielded

    A. explosive-making equipment
    B. flight training manuals for commercial airliners
    C. al-Qaeda training videotapes
    D. telephone records linking him to the 1993 World Trade Center bombing

23. Which of the following was a legendary mujahedin guerilla who was executed in October of 2001 by the Taliban, on charges that he was spying for the United States?

    A. Abdul Haq
    B. Mohammed Fahim
    C. Ahmad Shah Massoud
    D. Lakhdar Brahimi

24. The first American president to publicly call for a Palestinian state was

    A. John F. Kennedy   B. Jimmy Carter
    C. Bill Clinton   D. George W. Bush

25. The Nunn-Lugar Act of 1991, which gathered momentum after the September 11 attacks, launched a program designed to

    A. destroy the global biological and chemical arsenal
    B. enable local governments to respond to a biological or chemical attack
    C. reduce U.S. dependence on foreign oil
    D. prevent nuclear proliferation

26. The September 11 attacks differed from previous terrorist incidents in
    I. where they took place
    II. the magnitude of destruction and loss of life
    III. the profiles of the attackers in terms of economic and educational status
    IV. the motivation behind them

    A. I and II
    B. II and III
    C. III only
    D. I, II, III and IV

27. Which of the following Middle Eastern nations has NOT used chemical weapons against either an external enemy or its own people?

    A. Syria
    B. Iran
    C. Libya
    D. Egypt

28. Ultimately, the amount needed to finance the 9/11 terrorist operation, supplied mainly through al-Qaeda supporters and Osama bin Laden's personal fortune, was about

    A. $80,000
    B. $500,000
    C. $1.6 million
    D. $3.4 million

29. In October of 2001, the United States reached an agreement with the country of _____ allowing the long-term stationing of American troops and aircraft.

    A. Kazakhstan
    B. Pakistan
    C. Uzbekistan
    D. Yemen

30. Operation Anaconda, the U.S. military operation in March of 2002, was a battle plan aimed at Taliban and al-Qaeda fighters

    A. south of Kabul
    B. in Kunduz
    C. at the Qala-i-Jangi fortress
    D. in the Tora Bora cave region

KEY (CORRECT ANSWERS)

1.	C	16.	D
2.	C	17.	B
3.	C	18.	C
4.	A	19.	A
5.	B	20.	C
6.	B	21.	C
7.	C	22.	D
8.	A	23.	A
9.	C	24.	D
10.	A	25.	D
11.	A	26.	B
12.	C	27.	A
13.	B	28.	B
14.	A	29.	C
15.	D	30.	A

TEST 2

DIRECTIONS: Each question or incomplete statement is followed by several suggested answers or completions. Select the one the BEST answers the question or completes the statement. *PRINT THE LETTER OF THE CORRECT ANSWER IN THE SPACE AT THE RIGHT.*

1. The al-Qaeda organization was originally established by Osama bin Laden   1._____

   A. in the late 1970s to unite Arabs against the existence of the Israeli state
   B. in the late 1980s to bring together Arabs who fought in Afghanistan against the Soviet invasion
   C. after the Persian Gulf War, to expel U.S. forces from Islamic holy sites
   D. in the mid-1990s to establish a pan-Islamic Caliphate throughout the world

2. In May 2002, FBI director Robert S. Mueller III said future suicide attacks on American soil were   2._____

   A. impossible
   B. unlikely
   C. inevitable
   D. avoidable

3. In September of 2002, five suspected Yemeni-born al-Qaeda operatives were arrested in   3._____

   A. Aden
   B. Lahore, Pakistan
   C. Lackawanna, New York
   D. Hamburg, Germany

4. Before the September 11 attacks, which of the following statesmen had been scheduled to give a speech at the United Nations in support of the creation of a Palestinian state?   4._____

   A. Colin Powell
   B. Hosni Mubarak
   C. Nelson Mandela
   D. Gerhard Schroeder

5. What is the name of the extremist Islamic group active in Great Britain which calls for the murder of Jews and the institution of a worldwide Islamic regime through violent jihad?   5._____

   A. Jemaah Islamiyah
   B. Takfir wal Hijra
   C. al-Muhajiroun
   D. Mujahedin-e-Khalq

6. In 2002, approximately _____ of the 56 known, active international terrorist groups were religiously motivated.   6._____

   A. one-fifth
   B. one-third
   C. half
   D. two-thirds

7. By most accounts, the Muslim country whose women are the most liberated today is   7.____

    A. Turkey
    B. Pakistan
    C. Kuwait
    D. Jordan

8. The group that was responsible for the October 2002 bombing of a nightclub in Bali, which killed more than 200 people, was an organization sympathetic to al-Qaeda known as   8.____

    A. Al-Muhajiroun
    B. Jemaah Islamiyah
    C. the ELA
    D. the Moro Islamic Liberation Front

9. For many established countries, the process of globalization has often created a sense of _____ or "aggressive unilateralism" in reaction to the competitive international economy.   9.____

    A. economic hegemony
    B. legitimate protectionism
    C. economic Darwinism
    D. economic nationalism

10. In the twenty-first century, a rise in anarchist violence appears to have arisen in out of a wave of protests against   10.____

    A. globalization
    B. the United Nations
    C. environmental pollution
    D. war

11. Worldwide, the rallying cry of al-Qaeda is   11.____

    A. a pan-Islamic Caliphate throughout the world
    B. the liberation of Islam's three holiest places: Mecca, Medina and Jerusalem
    C. an end to economic oppression and civil rights abuses
    D. the creation of a Palestinian state

12. The first raids by U.S. ground troops during the war in Afghanistan were targeted at   12.____

    A. Kandahar
    B. Kabul
    C. Mazar-e Sharif
    D. Tora Bora

13. In October of 2001, the United States offered a _____ reward for information leading to the location or capture of Osama bin Laden.   13.____

    A. $250,000
    B. $5 million
    C. $25 million
    D. $100 million

14. In January of 2003, to anchor counterterrorism efforts in East Africa, U.S. forces established a base of operations in 14._____

    A. Ethiopia
    B. Kenya
    C. Somalia
    D. Djibouti

15. As of 2002, the only drug approved by the Federal government to protect against biological attacks specifically for inhaled anthrax was 15._____

    A. Glutase
    B. Erythromycin
    C. Cipro
    D. Doxycycline

16. The Taliban's last remaining stronghold in northern Afghanistan was the town of _____, where they were dislodged in November of 2001. 16._____

    A. Bagram
    B. Kunduz
    C. Herat
    D. Shah-i-Kot

17. "Coalition states" in the war on terror after September 11 included 17._____
    I. Pakistan
    II. Russia
    III. Jordan
    IV. China

    A. I and II
    B. II only
    C. II and III
    D. I, II, III and IV

18. In February 2003, the director of a Chicago-based Muslim charity, the Benevolence International Organization, accepted a plea bargain in which he admitted illegally passing charity funds along to militants in Bosnia and Chechnya. Federal prosecutors insisted that the defendant, Enaam Arnaout, had also sent "substantial" funds to al-Qaeda. The amount reportedly sent abroad by the organization from its 1992 founding to its 2001 forced closure was 18._____

    A. $1.6 million
    B. $11 million
    C. $20 million
    D. $56 million

19. After the Taliban had been defeated, the government of Afghanistan was chosen by a supreme council of tribal elders and respected citizens, known as the 19._____

    A. United Front
    B. Northern Alliance
    C. rabbani
    D. loyajirga

20. The final casualty toll in the 1998 bombings of the U.S. embassies in Nairobi, Kenya, and Dar es Salaam, Tanzania-bombings plotted and carried out by al-Qaeda operatives-was at least _____ dead and more than _____ injured.

    A. 16; 480
    B. 47; 1,200
    C. 301; 5,000
    D. 740; 11,000

21. In 2002, which of the following countries was host to the high-tech U.S. Combined Air Operations Center?

    A. Kuwait
    B. Turkey
    C. Saudi Arabia
    D. Bahrain

22. Among the ethnic groups in Afghanistan, the _____ are mostly Sunni Muslims, speak Persian, and live mostly in the northeast and west.

    A. Uzbeks
    B. Hazaras
    C. Tajiks
    D. Pashtuns

23. *Wall Street Journal* reporter Daniel Pearl was lured by his kidnappers and eventual murderers by the promise of information regarding

    A. Saddam Hussein
    B. John Walker Lindh
    C. Mullah Mohammed Omar
    D. Osama bin Laden

24. In 2002, nations with the highest rates of population growth included each of the following, EXCEPT

    A. Pakistan
    B. the Philippines
    C. Nigeria
    D. China

25. The total cost of security for the 2002 Winter Olympic games in Salt Lake city was about $_____ million.

    A. 3.4   B. 88   C. 145   D. 310

26. In the first week of trading after the 9/11 attacks, the Dow Jones Industrial average

    A. fell 5 percent   B. rose 9 percent
    C. fell 14 percent   D. rose 26 percent

27. By 2002, military assistance in fighting al-Qaeda had been extended by the U.S. and accepted by
    I. Uzbekistan
    II. the Philippines
    III. Yemen
    IV. Georgia

    A. I and II
    B. II only
    C. II, III and IV
    D. I, II, III and IV

27.____

28. When one state strikes at another before the target closes the gap in power separating the combatants, the ensuing war has been said to be caused by a(n)

    A. act of aggression
    B. window of opportunity
    C. cumulative resource
    D. preemptive defense maneuver

28.____

29. Reasons for the reemergence of suicide terrorism as a tactic of certain groups over the last two decades include
    I. the ability to execute accurate, large-scale attacks without sophisticated technology
    II. the fear it generates
    III. a growing pool of angry and disaffected young operatives willing to give up their lives
    IV. increasing political unrest in ethnically diverse regions

    A. I only
    B. I, II and III
    C. II only
    D. I, II, III and IV

29.____

30. Hezb-i-Islami is a group within Afghanistan that supports

    A. splitting the country up into autonomous ethnic regions
    B. the actions of the U.S. in ousting the Taliban and establishing a provisional government
    C. al-Qaeda terror activities
    D. the formation of a pan-Islamic caliphate

30.____

KEY (CORRECT ANSWERS)

1.	B	16.	B
2.	C	17.	D
3.	C	18.	C
4.	A	19.	D
5.	C	20.	C
6.	C	21.	C
7.	C	22.	C
8.	B	23.	D
9.	D	24.	C
10.	A	25.	D
11.	B	26.	C
12.	B	27.	C
13.	C	28.	B
14.	D	29.	B
15.	C	30.	B

TEST 3

DIRECTIONS: Each question or incomplete statement is followed by several suggested answers or completions. Select the one the BEST answers the question or completes the statement. *PRINT THE LETTER OF THE CORRECT ANSWER IN THE SPACE AT THE RIGHT.*

1. When the U.S. invaded Afghanistan in 2001, the strongest group in central Afghanistan were

    A. Arabs
    B. Tajiks
    C. Pashtuns
    D. Uzbeks

1.____

2. Although al-Qaeda was long suspected of having been involved in the opium trafficking operations in Afghanistan during the Taliban rule, this had not been definitively proven by 2003. The terrorist groups known to be/have been directly involved in the drug trade include
    I. Revolutionary Armed Forces of Colombia (FARC)
    II. Hezbollah
    III. Kurdistan Workers' Party
    IV. Shining Path (Sendero Luminoso)

    A. I only
    B. I and IV
    C. II and III
    D. I, II, III and IV

2.____

3. Al-Qaeda's plan to carry out terrorist operations against U.S. and Israeli tourists during millennial celebrations was thwarted by _____ authorities, who arrested and put 28 suspects on trial.

    A. Jordanian
    B. Saudi Arabian
    C. Egyptian
    D. Israeli

3.____

4. In March of 2002, British Foreign Secretary Jack Straw reported that Saddam Hussein had refused to implement _____ of the 27 obligations that were contained in nine separate U.N. Security Council resolutions imposed since 1991.

    A. 9
    B. 14
    C. 23
    D. 27

4.____

5. The United States ended routine immunizations for smallpox in

    A. 1927
    B. 1955
    C. 1971
    D. 1989

5.____

6. Other then the 9/11 attacks, events that have been linked to Osama bin Laden include the
    I. 1993 World Trade Center bomb
    II. 1996 Killing of 19 U.S. soldiers in Saudi Arabia
    III. 1998 embassy bombings in Kenya and Tanzania
    IV. 2000 Attack on U.S.S. Cole in Yemen

    A. I and III
    B. II, III and IV
    C. II and IV
    D. I, II, III and IV

    6.____

7. When President George W. Bush used the term "axis of evil" in his 2002 State of the Union address, it was known that the three nations that made up this "axis of evil" had been cooperating in the proliferation of
    I. missiles
    II. chemical weapons
    III. biological weapons
    IV. nuclear material

    A. I only
    B. I and II
    C. II and III
    D. I, II, III and IV

    7.____

8. Which of the following was NOT typically identified as a newly industrialized country (NIC) at the turn of the twenty-first century?

    A. Taiwan
    B. The Philippines
    C. Singapore
    D. Republic of Korea

    8.____

9. Which of the following is NOT a nongovernmental organization (NGO)?

    A. American Civil Liberties Union (ACLU)
    B. Oxfam
    C. International Council on Human Rights Policy (ICHRP)
    D. World Health Organization (WHO)

    9.____

10. At the time of the U.S. invasion of Afghanistan, the supreme leader of the Taliban movement was

    A. Mohammed Fahim
    B. Mohammed Omar
    C. Ahmed Rashid
    D. Osama bin Laden

    10.____

11. Which of the following is NOT a nationalist terror group?

    A. Irish Republican Army
    B. Hamas
    C. Kurdistan Workers' Party
    D. Basque Fatherland and Liberty

    11.____

12. External aid to the HAMAS organization is known to come from the government of   12._____

    A. Jordan
    B. Saudi Arabia
    C. Iran
    D. Iraq

13. Osama bin Laden's primary goal in his campaign of terror is to   13._____

    A. establish a free Palestinian state
    B. overthrow the Saudi government
    C. force all Westerners to leave the Middle East
    D. expel U.S. military forces from Saudi Arabia

14. In October of 2001, the Pakistani government arrested Sultan Bashiruddin Mahmood, who had been in extended meetings with the Taliban and Osama bin Laden the previous summer. Mahmood was a(n)   14._____

    A. Muslim cleric
    B. nuclear scientist
    C. global financier
    D. commercial airline pilot

15. In June of 2002, al-Qaeda's senior operative in Southeast Asia, Omar el-Faruq, was captured in   15._____

    A. Thailand
    B. Indonesia
    C. Australia
    D. the Philippines

16. The first large-scale germ warfare attack on U.S. soil occurred in 1984, in   16._____

    A. Couer d'Alene, Idaho
    B. New York City
    C. Rancho Santa Fe, California
    D. The Dalles, Oregon

17. In December of 2001, the chief of police in _____ refused to cooperate with federal requests to interview Arab-Americans and those with ties to the Islamic community.   17._____

    A. Portland, Oregon
    B. Dearborn, Michigan
    C. Lackawanna, New York
    D. San Francisco, California

18. In February of 2002, dozens of foreign Islamic scholars were expelled from _____ as part of a crackdown on suspected al-Qaeda members.   18._____

    A. Saudi Arabia
    B. Qatar
    C. Pakistan
    D. Yemen

19. In October of 2001, the Bush administration announced that the government's projected budget surplus had shrunk by _____ percent.

    A. 10
    B. 25
    C. 50
    D. 100

20. Money from donors finds its way to terrorist groups such as al-Qaeda by means of
    I. electronic fund transfers
    II. smuggling precious metals, gems, and cash across borders
    III. burglaries and thefts in the location where the operatives have been stationed
    IV. setting up shell corporations and putting in different locations and putting "employees" on the payroll

    A. I only
    B. I and II
    C. II, II and IV
    D. I, II, III and IV

21. Under the leadership of the Taliban, a significant symbol of the oppression of women was the head-to-toe garment known as the

    A. khimar
    B. burqa
    C. tarhah
    D. sari

22. The "epicenter" of the Al-Aqsa intifadeh in Palestine was the Gaza border crossing known as

    A. Ramallah
    B. Rafah
    C. Khan Yunis
    D. Farah

23. In the spring of 2002, Arab leaders met in _____ to endorse a new peace initiative with Israel.

    A. Beirut
    B. London
    C. Cairo
    D. Riyadh

24. By 2020, the most populous country in the world will be

    A. Pakistan
    B. China
    C. Indonesia
    D. India

25. After the Iraqi invasion of Kuwait in 1990, which Arab leader stated his willingness to fight personally against Iraq in the Gulf War?   25._____

   A. Hosni Mubarak
   B. King Hussein
   C. Yasser Arafat
   D. Ali Akbar Hashemi Rafsanjani

26. In February of 2002, Secretary of Defense Donald Rumsfeld stated that the key to lasting stability in Afghanistan would be helping Afghans to   26._____

   A. formulate a Central Asian alliance with its neighbors
   B. maintain a strong army
   C. write a new constitution
   D. establish functioning local governments

27. Each of the following is a factor that has increased the importance of nongovernmental organizations (NGOs) in world affairs, EXCEPT   27._____

   A. the end of the Cold War as the chief organizer of world affairs
   B. failures of states to provide particular rights, privileges, or services
   C. declining concerns over human rights and ecological issues
   D. increased demands on international organizations such as the United Nations, accompanied by decreased funding

28. Of the following, the type of terrorists LEAST likely to undertake murder as a tactic would be   28._____

   A. state-sponsored
   B. left-wing
   C. anarchist
   D. religious

29. In November of 2001, President Bush issued an executive order establishing _____ to deal with suspected terrorists.   29._____

   A. an international criminal court
   B. a pan-Arabian anti-terror alliance
   C. more restrictive immigration laws
   D. special military tribunals

30. The reemergence of religious terror groups has, in the opinion of many experts, shifted the goal of most terrorist attacks. The primary aim of these attacks appears to be   30._____

   A. inflicting mass casualties
   B. extortion or financial gain
   C. weakening enemy infrastructures
   D. generating maximum publicity

KEY (CORRECT ANSWERS)

1.	C	16.	D
2.	D	17.	A
3.	A	18.	D
4.	C	19.	D
5.	C	20.	B
6.	D	21.	B
7.	A	22.	B
8.	B	23.	A
9.	D	24.	D
10.	B	25.	A
11.	B	26.	B
12.	C	27.	C
13.	D	28.	B
14.	B	29.	D
15.	B	30.	A

EXAMINATION SECTION
TEST 1

DIRECTIONS: Each question or incomplete statement is followed by several suggested answers or completions. Select the one that BEST answers the question or completes the statement. *PRINT THE LETTER OF THE CORRECT ANSWER IN THE SPACE AT THE RIGHT.*

1. Which of the following was NOT a cause of postwar international conflict? The

     A. revival of Russian imperialism
     B. failure of American leaders to cooperate with the Russians
     C. emergence of new revolutionary forces
     D. power vacuum created by the fall of Germany and Japan

2. One significant difference between the United Nations and the League of Nations is that the U.N.

     A. was divorced from the post-war treaties
     B. was a grouping of sovereign states
     C. was a product of compromise
     D. had no affiliated court

3. The Yalta Conference was a failure because

     A. Roosevelt surrendered to all of the Russian demands
     B. Russian help was not needed against Japan
     C. the veto power was granted to members of the Security Council
     D. Russia failed to carry out her part of the commitments

4. The Truman Doctrine was *intended* to

     A. aid in the holding of free elections in eastern Europe
     B. keep China from going Communist
     C. aid Greece and Turkey in their fight against Communism
     D. assist Poland in her clash with Russia

5. In his efforts to contain Communism, President Truman was LEAST successful in

     A. Japan   B. China   C. Berlin   D. Greece

6. A vigorous critic of Truman's foreign policy was

     A. George Marshall   B. Dean Acheson
     C. Douglas MacArthur   D. Arthur Vandenberg

7. The long-range significance of Truman's intervention in Korea was that

     A. Communism was dealt a severe defeat
     B. American troops defeated the Chinese Communists
     C. an effort had been made to halt overt aggression in the name of the UN
     D. the Russians failed to veto the intervention

8. After 1945, American armed forces were

   A. demobilized with unusual slowness
   B. denied special educational opportunities
   C. retained in Europe in large numbers to contain Russia
   D. disbanded with indecent haste

8._____

9. The MOST controversial issue growing out of the Yalta Conference related to

   A. holding the San Francisco Conference
   B. inducing Stalin to enter the Far Eastern War
   C. dropping the atomic bomb
   D. liberating western Europe

9._____

10. Russia's aggressiveness after 1945 resulted in all of the following EXCEPT:

    A. Russia's violation of her Yalta pledges
    B. A psychological Pearl Harbor
    C. Rearmament in America
    D. A strengthening of our no-alliance tradition

10._____

11. Post-war Soviet aggressions led to all of the following EXCEPT the

    A. Berlin airlift
    B. Communist West German Republic at Bonn
    C. North Atlantic Pact
    D. Truman Doctrine

11._____

12. At the Yalta Conference

    A. Stalin promised to enter the war against Japan
    B. the decision was reached to atom-bomb Japan
    C. China was clearly betrayed
    D. Stalin successfully held out against free elections for Poland

12._____

13. Chiang Kai-shek's regime in China collapsed *primarily* because:

    A. he had lost the support of his people
    B. Truman secretly supported his Communist rivals
    C. Washington had refused to send him any aid
    D. Chiang fled to Formosa

13._____

Questions 14-20.

DIRECTIONS: Questions 14-20 contain quotes made by one of the following statesmen. Insert the letter corresponding to the statesman in your answer space. You may use a name more than once and not every name need be used.

   A. George Marshall   B. Harry Truman
   C. Henry Wallace   D. George Kennan
   E. John Foster Dulles

14. "....we should recognize that we have no more business in the political affairs of Eastern Europe than Russia has in the political affairs of Latin America, Western Europe and the United States."

14.____

15. "I believe that it must be the policy of the United States to support free people who are resisting attempted subjugation by armed minorities or by outside pressures. I believe that we must assist free peoples to work out their own destinies in their own way."

15.____

16. "But we have seen that the Kremlin is under no ideological compulsion to accomplish its purposes in a hurry. Like the Church, it is dealing in ideological concepts which are of long-term validity, and it can afford to be patient. It has no right to risk the existing achievements of the revolution for the sake of vain baubles of the future."

16.____

17. "Consider the twenty-odd non-Western nations which are next door to the Soviet world. They are expected to live precariously, permanently barred from areas with which they normally should have trade, commerce and cultural relations. Today they live close to despair because the United States, the historic leader of the forces of freedom, seems dedicated to the negative policy of 'containment' and 'stalemate'."

17.____

18. "It is logical that the United States should do whatever it is able to do to assist in the return of normal economic health in the world, without which there can be no political stability and no assured peace. Our policy is directed not against any country or doctrine but against hunger, poverty, desperation, and chaos."

18.____

19. "Obviously, we cannot build a 20,000 mile Maginot Line or natch the Red armies, man for man, gun for gun and tank for tank... There is one solution and only one; that is for the free world to develop the will and organize the means to retaliate instantly against open aggression by Red armies, so that if it occurs anywhere, we could and would strike back where it hurts, by means of our own choosing."

19.____

20. "... the main element of any United States policy toward the Soviet must be that of a long-term, patient but firm and vigilant containment of Russian expansive tendencies."

20.____

21. United States governmental relief abroad after World War II was prompted *mainly* by

    A. Christian principles
    B. sympathy for those who had suffered much more
    C. a desire to halt Communism
    D. a feeling of kinship with Britain

21.____

22. At the time of Yalta most Americans

    A. opposed Russian intervention in the war with Japan
    B. favored Russian participation
    C. were indifferent
    D. expected Japan's speedy collapse

22.____

23. Truman's Korean intervention was

    A. at first applauded and later condemned
    B. clearly unconstitutional
    C. plainly anticipated by the North Koreans
    D. first condemned and later applauded

23.____

24. After American troops approached the Korean-Manchurian border in 1950

    A. they fought the Chinese to a standstill
    B. they suffered a humiliating defeat
    C. genuine volunteers from China entered the conflict
    D. MacArthur was unwilling to bomb Chinese bases

25. The Korean War resulted in all of the following EXCEPT:

    A. A strong demand in America for a go-it-alone policy
    B. Heavy criticism in America of the UN
    C. A popular denunciation in the United States of "Truman's war"
    D. A sharp drop in the price level

26. In the Suez crisis, Eisenhower did all of the following EXCEPT:

    A. Provide needed oil
    B. Back our NATO allies
    C. Endorse the UN stand
    D. Strengthen Nasser's position

27. The Hungarian revolt of 1956

    A. helped Communism world-wide
    B. earned Hungary's gratitude for America
    C. forced Russia to grant home rule
    D. intensified the Suez crisis

28. Nasser nationalized the Suez Canal *primarily* to

    A. avert an Israeli seizure
    B. avenge a United States affront
    C. defy the UN
    D. forestall Communist infiltration

29. The Berlin airlift ended when

    A. Russia recognized defeat
    B. the West agreed to reduce garrisons there
    C. Korea diverted Western attention
    D. communists won Berlin elections

30. By ratifying the Atlantic Pact, the United States pledged itself to

    A. pay much of the cost of European armament
    B. support the policy of allied states all over the world
    C. support friendly South American regimes
    D. resist aggression in Europe

31. Early in 1954, as the Indochinese war reached a climax, the American government considered supporting the French with

    A. air power
    B. marines
    C. a greatly increased economic program
    D. paratroops

32. American support of the Aswan dam project was *withdrawn* when

    A. Nasser purchased Czech arms
    B. Dulles declared the original offer abandoned
    C. Egypt invaded Israel
    D. Nasser nationalized the Suez Canal

33. The Paris conference in 1960 collapsed when

    A. Khrushchev demanded an American apology for the U-2 incident
    B. Eisenhower demanded a Russian apology for shooting down the unarmed U-2
    C. the Russians commenced a new blockade of Berlin
    D. Secretary Herter refused to admit Administration responsibility for U-2 flights

34. "... that if we lose the war to Communism in Asia the fall of Europe is inevitable, win it and Europe most probably would avoid war and yet preserve freedom.... We must win. There is no substitute for victory."
    The above statement BEST sums up the thinking of

    A. Harry Truman   B. Douglas MacArthur
    C. John Foster Dulles   D. Dwight Eisenhower

35. The BASIC issue between the United States and Communist China grew out of

    A. the status of Formosa
    B. American assistance to Nationalist China
    C. Communist atrocities in Tibet
    D. the blockade activities of the American Seventh Fleet

36. "We supposed that our revolutionary message to the world was 'democracy' but in reality it is 'abundance'."
    The above statement comes CLOSEST to the thinking of

    A. Karl Marx   B. John Spanier
    C. David Potter   D. Hans Morgenthau

37. The United States and Russia collaborated in

    A. suppressing the revolt in Hungary
    B. backing Israel's invasion of Egypt
    C. opposing English-French seizure of Suez
    D. the invasion of Lebanon in 1958

38. The Eisenhower Doctrine

    A. led to the unleashing of Chiang Kai-shek
    B. committed the United States to the defense of Quemoy and Matsu
    C. bolstered NATO
    D. was a pledge of aid to the Middle East to check Communist penetration

39. The conclusion that the Cold War could *largely* be attributed to Stalin's defective judgment comes CLOSEST to the thinking or

    A. George Kennan   B. Arthur Schlesinger, Jr.
    C. Robin Winks   D. Louis Halle

40. One IMPORTANT obstacle to the Marshall Plan's success *disappeared* when,

    A. Stalin died
    B. Bevin engineered the ousting of Russia
    C. French communists declared their support
    D. Molotov withdrew from the European planning conference

41. NOT among Russian grievances toward America during World War II was

    A. the end of lend lease
    B. the loan to Britain
    C. United States domination of the Japanese occupation
    D. United States successful support of a UN resolution calling for Russian evacuation of Poland

42. The LAST point at issue in Korean peace negotiations was

    A. Formosa
    B. the location of the armistice line
    C. Chinese admission to the UN
    D. the repatriation of prisoners

43. The Geneva agreement to partition Vietnam was disapproved by the

    A. French
    B. rebel Vietminh
    C. Soviet Union
    D. United States

44. SEATO was

    A. supported by India
    B. more effective than NATO
    C. a graphic illustration of American commitments in the Orient
    D. a formal military alliance created to protect Asia from Communism

45. "The Soviets appeared from the end of the war to accept the melancholy assumption that we were really out to create an anti-Soviet block for the purpose of destroying them; ... and that was one of the greatest diplomatic blunders of our time."
    Which one of the following people would be LEAST likely to believe that statement?

    A. George Kennan
    B. Staughton Lynd
    C. Arthur Schlesinger Jr.
    D. Dean Acheson

46. In which area of the globe does Spanier consider American policy to have been *particularly* inept and clumsy?

    A. Berlin   B. China   C. Near East   D. Far East

47. Spanier's MAJOR complaint against Eisenhower was that

    A. his administration lost Cuba to the Communists
    B. he personally failed to liberate Eastern Europe as he promised
    C. during his term of office vital public projects were sacrificed in order to balance the budget
    D. he failed to strengthen the NATO pact

48. The United States policy of containment of China differed MOST markedly from our containment of Russia in that

    A. it had been entirely peaceful
    B. we had been unable to enlist any significant aid from the major powers
    C. it had enjoyed far less support among the American people
    D. Congress had often balked at implementing programs

49. What one of the following could be considered to be Eisenhower's MOST successful venture in foreign affairs? The

    A. defense of Quemoy and Matsu
    B. aerial surveillance of the Soviet Union
    C. refusal to budge on the Berlin question
    D. strengthening of our traditional friendship with England and France

50. During the decade of the 1950's, the United States and the Soviet Union clashed MOST often over

    A. nuclear testing in the atmosphere
    B. unification of Germany
    C. disarmament
    D. the status of Berlin

KEY (CORRECT ANSWERS)

1. B	11. B	21. C	31. A	41. D
2. A	12. A	22. B	32. A	42. D
3. D	13. A	23. A	33. A	43. D
4. C	14. C	24. B	34. B	44. C
5. B	15. B	25. D	35. B	45. B
6. C	16. D	26. B	36. C	46. C
7. C	17. E	27. D	37. C	47. C
8. D	18. A	28. B	38. D	48. B
9. B	19. E	29. A	39. B	49. A
10. D	20. D	30. D	40. D	50. D

www.ingramcontent.com/pod-product-compliance
Lightning Source LLC
Chambersburg PA
CBHW082035300426
44117CB00015B/2498